Handbook of Upper Canadian Chronology

revised edition

Frederick H. Armstrong

Dundurn Press
Toronto and London
1985

Acknowledgements

The publication of this book was made possible by support from several sources. The author and publisher wish to acknowledge the generous assistance and ongoing support of the Canada Council and the Ontario Arts Council. We wish to acknowledge as well the assistance from the Smallman Foundation, The University of Western Ontario, and the Ontario Heritage Foundation, an agency of the Ontario Ministry of Citizenship and Culture.

J. Kirk Howard, Publisher

© Frederick H. Armstrong, 1967, 1985

All rights reserved. No part of this publication may be produced, stored in a retrieval system, or transmitted in any form or by any means, electronic, mechanical, photocopying, recording, or otherwise (except brief passages for purposes of review) without the prior permission of Dundurn Press Limited.

Design and Production: Ron and Ron Design Photography
Printing and Binding: Marquis Printing Limited, Canada

Dundurn Press Limited
P.O. Box 245, Station F
Toronto, Canada
M4Y 2L5

Canadian Cataloguing in Publication Data

Armstrong, F. H. (Frederick Henry), 1926-
  Handbook of Upper Canada chronology

(Dundurn Canadian historical document series ; publication no. 3)
First published: Handbook of Upper Canadian chronology and territorial legislation. London, Ont. : Lawson Memorial Library, The University of Western Ontario, 1967.
ISBN 1-55002-543-0

1. Ontario - History - Chronology. 2. Ontario - Politics and government - Registers. I. Title. II. Title: Handbook of Upper Canadian chronology and territorial legislation. III. Series.

FC440.A75 1985   917.3'02   C85-098840-3
F1032.A75 1985

Handbook of Upper Canadian Chronology

revised edition

Frederick H. Armstrong

First Great Seal of Upper Canada Royal Warrant, 28 March 1792

Obverse (back cover): Anchor or Sword within cornucopiae Inscription from Horace

Inner Band
IMPERII· PORRECTA • MAJESTAS • RERUM • CAESARE
"The greatness of the Empire is advanced by the guardianship of the Caesar/Sovereign"

Outer Band
SIGIL [LUM] • PROV [INCIAE] • NOS [TRAE] • CAN [ADAE] • SUP [ERIORIS]
"The Seal of Our Province of Upper Canada"

Reverse (front cover): Royal Arms as used 1714–1801
GEORGIUS • III • D[EI] • G [RATIA] •
MAG [NAE] • BRI [TANNIAE] • FR [ANCIAE] • ET •
HIB [ERNIAE]• REX • F [IDEI] • D [EFENSOR] •
BRUN [SVICENSIS] • ET • LUN [EBURGENSIS] •
DUX • S[ACRI] • R[OMANI] •
I [MPERII] • AR[CHI] • THES [AURARIUS] • ET •
EL [ECTOR]
"George III by the Grace of God, King of Great Britain, France and Ireland, Defender of the Faith, Duke of Brunswick and Luneburg, Arch-Treasurer of the Holy Roman Empire, and Elector"

To
Fred Landon
(1880-1969)

Table of Contents

Foreword 20
Preface to First Edition 21
Preface to Second Edition 23
Introduction 25
Key to Symbols 28

Part I. British Sovereigns, Ministers, Officials, and Major Events 29
A. Monarchs 29
B. Officials in England 29
    a. Prime Ministers and Parties in Power .. 29
    b. Secretaries of State for the Colonies ... 29
        1. Secretaries of State for the Home Department 30
        2. Secretaries of State for War and the Colonies 30
    c. Under-Secretaries of State for the Colonies 30
        1. Under-Secretaries 31
        2. Parliamentary Under-Secretaries . 31
        3. Permanent Under-Secretaries 31
C. Governors 32
    a. Governors-in-Chief, 1791–1841 32
    b. Lieutenant-Governors of Upper Canada, 1791–1841 33
D. Other Officials 33
    a. Civil Establishment 33
        1. Civil and Private Secretaries to the Lieutenant-Governors 33
        2. Chief Clerks 34
        3. Second Clerks 34
        4. Third Clerks 34

E. Constitutional Development and International Events and Treaties 35

Part II.   Provincial Officials, 1791–1841 . . 37
A. The Capital 37
B. The Executive Council 38
    a. Alphabetical List 38
    b. Chronological List 39
    c. Staff of the Executive Council 41
        1. Clerks 41
        2. First Clerks 41
        3. Second Clerks 41
        4. Doorkeepers 41
C. Officers of the Crown and Senior Civil Servants 42
    a. Adjutants General of the Militia Department 42
    b. Attorneys General 42
    c. Auditors General of Land Patents 42
    d. Auditors General of Public Accounts 43
    e. Crown Lands Office 43
        1. Commissioners of Crown Lands . . 43
        2. Chief Clerks 43
    f. Indian Office 43
        1. Superintendents General of Indian Affairs in Canada 43
        2. Deputy Superintendents in Upper Canada 44
        3. Chief Superintendents for Upper Canada 44
    g. Inspector General's Office 44
        1. Inspectors General 44
        2. First Clerks 44
        3. Second Clerks 44
    h. King's Printers and Editors of the *Upper Canada Gazette* 44

i. Provincial Secretaries and Registrar's
     Office 45
     1. Provincial Secretaries and
        Registrars 45
     2. Clerks 45
     3. Second Clerks 45
     4. Third Clerks 46
  j. Receiver General's Office 46
     1. Receivers General of Public
        Accounts 46
     2. First Clerks 46
     3. Second Clerks 46
     4. Third Clerks 46
  k. Solicitors General 46
  l. Surveyor General's Office 47
     1. Surveyors General of the Province
        of Quebec 47
     2. Surveyors General of Upper
        Canada 47
     3. Deputy Surveyors General of
        Upper Canada 47
     4. First (Senior) Clerks 47
     5. Second Clerks 47

Part III. The Parliaments, 1792-1840 48
A. Statistics 48
   a. Duration of Parliaments and Sessions .. 48
   b. Statistics on Statutes Passed 50
B. The Legislative Council 53
   a. Alphabetical List 53
   b. Chronological List 55
   c. Speakers 57
   d. Staff of the Legislative Council 58
      1. Clerks 58
      2. Chaplains 58
      3. Doorkeepers 58
      4. Messengers 58
C. The House of Assembly 59
   a. Alphabetical List 59

b. Members by Parliament 74
c. Members by Riding 93
    1. Addington 93
    2. Brockville 93
    3. Carleton 93
    4. Cornwall 94
    5. Dundas 94
    6. Durham 94
    7. Essex 95
    8. Frontenac 96
    9. Glengarry 96
    10. Grenville 97
    11. Haldimand 98
    12. Halton 98
    13. Hamilton 98
    14. Hastings 98
    15. Huron 99
    16. Kent 99
    17. Kingston 100
    18. Lanark 100
    19. Leeds 101
    20. Lennox 101
    21. Lincoln 102
    22. London 105
    23. Middlesex 105
    24. Niagara 105
    25. Norfolk 106
    26. Northumberland 106
    27. Ontario 107
    28. Oxford 107
    29. Prescott 108
    30. Prince Edward 108
    31. Russell 109
    32. Simcoe 109
    33. Stormont 109
    34. Suffolk 110
    35. Wentworth 110
    36. York County 111
    37. York Town - Toronto 112
d. Speakers 113

e. Staff of the House of Assembly 113
    1. Clerks 113
    2. Clerks of the Crown in Chancery . 113
    3. Chaplains 113
    4. Sergeants-at-Arms 114
    5. Librarians 114
    6. Doorkeepers 114

Part IV. The Judiciary and the Legal Profession 115
A. The Judiciary 115
  a. Introduction 115
  b. The Courts of Common Pleas 116
    1. Lunenburgh (Eastern) District . . . 116
    2. Mecklenburg (Midland) District . . 117
    3. Nassau (Home) District 117
    4. Hesse (Western) District 117
  c. The Court of the King's Bench 117
    1. Chief Justices 118
    2. Puisné Judges 118
    3. Clerks of the Crown and Common Pleas. 118
    4. Reporters 118
  d. The Court of Chancery 119
    1. Vice-Chancellors 119
    2. Masters in Chancery 119
    3. Registrars 119
    4. Sergeants at Arms 119
  e. The Court of Probate 119
    1. Official Principals 120
    2. Registrars 120
B. The Legal Profession 120
  a. Introduction 120
  b. Treasurers of the Law Society of Upper Canada 121
  c. Attorneys 122

    d. Barristers 127
        1. On Barristers Roll of the Law
           Society of Upper Canada 128
        2. Barristers Whose Names are not
           upon the Rolls of the Court 132
    e. Notaries Public 132
        1. Notaries Public granted
           Commissions 132
        2. Notaries Public appointed prior to
           1842 132
    f. Solicitors 136
    g. Queen's Counsels 136

**Part V. Local and Municipal Government,
          1788-1849** 137
A. Townships 137
    a. Introduction 137
    b. List of Townships 141
B. Counties 149
    a. Introduction 149
    b. Legislation Establishing Counties
       and Ridings 150
    c. List of Counties with Dates of Creation 150
    d. Lieutenants of Counties 152
    e. Registrars of Counties 154
C. Districts 158
    a. Introduction 158
    b. General Legislation Relating to Districts 160
    c. Key List of Districts 161
    d. Districts with Legislation and Officials . 162
        1. Bathurst 162
        2. Brock 164
        3. Colborne 165
        4. Dalhousie 166
        5. Eastern (Lunenburgh) 167
        6. Gore 170
        7. Home (Nassau) 172
        8. Huron 175
        9. Johnstown 176

        10. Kent (provisional) 178
        11. London 179
        12. Midland (Mecklenburg) 181
        13. Newcastle 184
        14. Niagara 186
        15. Ottawa 188
        16. Prince Edward 190
        17. Simcoe 191
        18. Talbot 193
        19. Victoria 194
        20. Wellington 195
        21. Western (Hesse) 196
D. Towns and Cities 199
  a. Introduction 199
  b. General Legislation Relating to Towns
     and Cities 200
  c. Towns and Cities with Legislation
     and Officials 202
        1. Amherstburgh 202
        2. Belleville 202
        3. Brantford 202
        4. Brockville 203
        5. Bytown (Ottawa) 204
        6. Cobourg 205
        7. Cornwall 205
        8. Dundas 207
        9. Hamilton 207
        10. Kingston 208
        11. London 209
        12. Merrickville 210
        13. Napanee 210
        14. Niagara-on-the-Lake 210
        15. Perth 211
        16. Picton 211
        17. Port Hope 212
        18. Prescott 212
        19. Sandwich (Windsor) 214
        20. St. Catharines 214
        21. Woodstock 215
        22. York/Toronto 215

Part VI. Special Government Departments and Commissions 217
A. The Customs Department 217
    a. Introduction 217
    b. Ports of Entry and Collectors of Customs 217
B. The Emigrant Office 226
        a. Superintendents 226
        b. Clerks 226
        c. Agents at Toronto 226
        d. Agents at Quebec 226
C. The Post Office 227
    a. Introduction 227
    b. Post Office Officials in Britain 227
        1. Postmasters General 227
        2. Secretaries 229
    c. Post Office Officials for British North America 229
        1. Deputy Postmasters General for British North America 229
        2. Deputy Postmasters General for Canada 229
    d. Post Offices in Upper Canada 229
    e. Postmasters in the Major Centres 237
D. Special Commissions 240
    a. Introduction 240
    b. Commissions Arising from the War of 1812 240
        1. Special Commissions for the Trial of High Treason in Upper Canada . 240
        2. Commissioners to Receive Claims for War Losses 240
        3. Commissioners for Investigating Claims for War Losses 241
    c. Commissions Arising from the Rebellion of 1837 241
        1. Special Commission to Examine Persons Arrested for High Treason 241
        2. Board to Distribute Money to the Wounded 241
    d. Civil Commissions 241
        1. Commission re Union Bill, 1822... 241
        2. Arbitrators of Customs. 241

   3. Provincial Board of Education.... 242
   4. Commission to Revise the
     Statutes...................... 242
E. Surveyors............................ 242
  a. Introduction 242
  b. Provincial Land Surveyors 242
  c. Dates of Township Surveys, 1784-1859 . 247
F. Agents for the Affairs of Upper Canada
  in England............................ 247

Part VII. Supplementary Information 248
A. Corporate Legislation 248
  a. Introduction 248
  b. Banks and Financial Institutions 248
  c. Canals 249
  d. Educational and Institutional 249
  e. Harbours and Bridges 250
  f. Manufacturing 251
  g. Navigation 252
  h. Railroads....................... 252
  i. British Statutes and Charters 253
B. Corporate Officers 253
  a. Introduction 253
   1. The "Pretended" Bank of Upper
    Canada 253
   2. Bank of Upper Canada 253
   3. Bank of British North America .. 254
   4. British America Fire and Life
    Assurance Company 254
   5. Canada Company............. 254
   6. Commercial Bank of the Midland
    District 255
   7. Farmer's Joint Stock Banking
    Company 255
   8. Gore Bank 255
   9. Home District Savings Bank 256
   10. People's Bank 256
   11. Toronto Board of Trade 256
   12. Welland Canal Company 256

C. Disasters 257
D. Ecclesiastical 258
    a. Anglican Church (Church of England) . 258
        1. Archbishops of Canterbury 258
        2. Bishops presiding over Upper
           Canada 258
        3. Archdeacons 258
    b. Baptists 259
        Major Events 259
    c. Roman Catholic Church 259
        Bishops 259
    d. Methodist Church 260
        1. Major Events 260
        2. Conferences in Canada 260
        3. Editors of *Christian Guardian* .. 262
        4. Stewards of the Book Room 263
    e. Presbyterian Church 263
        Major Events 263
    f. Quakers 264
        Major Events 264
E. Imperial Honours 264
F. Population Statistics 265
    a. Introduction 265
G. War and Revolution 265
    a. Battles of the War of 1812 265
    b. The Mackenzie Rebellion at Toronto,
       1837 269
    c. The Duncombe Rebellion in Western
       Upper Canada, 1837 269
    d. The Aftermath of 1837 and the Patriot
       Raids, 1838 271

Part VIII.   Select Bibliography   273
A. Introduction 273
B. Bibliographic Sources 273
C. Special Sources 273

Tables and Diagrams
1. Development of the District System 198
2. The Union of Methodism................. 261
3. Population of Upper Canada and its Major Urban Centres...... 272

Maps
1. Original Counties...................... 138
2. Districts in 1788 and 1802............... 138
3. Districts in 1836...................... 139
4. District System-1841................... 140
5. County System-1851................... 140

Subject Index 276

Foreword

In 1967, on behalf of The University Library system which sponsored the first edition of this work as a centennial publication, I wrote:

"We in the University of Western Ontario Library system are happy to have had a small part in bringing out Dr. Fred Armstrong's work on Upper Canadian Chronology and Territorial Legislation. This publication should prove to be an invaluable time saver for all students working in Upper Canadian history. The undersigned has used and knows well the value of such references as N.O. Coté *Political Appointments and Elections in Canada 1841-60*, Quebec, 1860, and similar works by the same compiler. Unfortunately, until now, there have been no comparable volumes dealing with Upper Canada. Now the need has been filled thanks to the indefatigable exertions of Dr. Armstrong.

"One cannot believe that a work as large as this covering such a diversity of topics should not have gaps. Readers will undoubtedly think of additional facts to be included. This work therefore may be considered as a preliminary document. After a few years in the hands of scholars it will probably bear reprinting. We thank Dr. Armstrong for all that he has done in the service of scholarship."

The work, long out of print, has saved scholars incalculable hours. Dr. Armstrong's meticulous research was evidenced by the small number of errors which came to light. Those students who used the first edition will welcome this second edition with its revised, amplified and additional tables. Deeply in debt to Dr. Armstrong, as we already are, we are now in greater debt than ever.

James J. Talman

Preface to The First Edition

The following tables are intended to be useful rather than definitive; hopefully they will stimulate still further research and bring in additional data. An extended illness has prevented the writer from examining certain documents in other cities as he would have wished, but he believes that the major sources have been consulted. All suggestions for amplifications, further tables, additional sources of information and corrections of fact will be most welcome.

Miss Julia Jarvis has been good enough to let me use the material she and Miss Alison Ewart prepared on the Family Compact which appeared in the *Canadian Historical Review* for 1926. The Royal Society of Canada, Ottawa, have given kind permission for me to use W.W. Campbell's work on the Legislative Assembly which appeared in their 1911 *Transactions*, and the Royal Historical Society and Dr. Edmund Fryde have allowed me to copy sections of some tables in the new edition *The Handbook of British Chronology*.

The Centennial Commission provided a research grant to enable me to free time for this work, and Dean Robert N. Shervill of Middlesex College and Dean John G. Rowe of Talbot College made additional funds available for research assistance and other needs. Professor James J. Talman, Librarian of the University of Western Ontario, not only arranged publication by the Library as their 1967 Centennial project; but also he has always given me the benefit of his advice based on so many years of writing and teaching Ontario history.

Many other individuals were of great assistance; the late Dr. Fred Landon, Miss Edith G. Firth, Keeper for the Manuscripts at the Toronto Public Libraries, Professor J.M.S. Careless, former Chairman of the Department of History at the University of Toronto, Professor Graeme Patterson, and my colleagues, Professors F.A. Dreyer, A.M.J. Hyatt and P.F. Neary, all read parts of the manuscript and made many useful emendations. Helpful suggestions have also been made by Professor C.F.J. Whebell of the UWO Department of Geography, the late Rev. John L.H. Henderson of Huron College, Professor J. Donald Wilson, The University of British Columbia, Professor M. Zaslow, and Mr. Edward C.H. Phelps of this University, Dr. W.I. Smith of the Public Archives of Ottawa, Mr. Daniel J. Brock, of London and my research assistants, Mr. Gary J. Phillips and Mr. John L. Henderson Jr.

Municipal officials were most considerate with their time and assistance, including the clerks of Belleville, Brockville, Cobourg, Dundas, Kingston, Niagara-on-the-Lake, Ottawa, Picton, Port Hope, Prescott, and St. Catharines. The city clerk of Hamilton went to particular trouble to obtain information from the early manuscript records. Assistance was also obtained from the Hamilton Public Library and the editor of the *Picton Gazette*.

I would especially like to record my thanks to the late Miss Anne Sexton, who was both editor of the publications of the Lawson Library and keeper of the Canadiana Collections. Her early death in July, 1967 was a great loss to the study of history in this province.

I, of course, take full responsibility for the work.

Frederick H. Armstrong.

Talbot College,
The University of Western Ontario,
London, Ontario,
November, 1967.

Preface to The Second Edition

In preparing a new edition of the *Handbook of Upper Canadian Chronology* after 17 years it is a pleasure to be able to again thank so many of the individuals who assisted in the preparation of the first edition and have continued to give me the benefit of their advice. James J. Talman, my colleague at the Department of History at The University of Western Ontario, who as University Librarian arranged for the publication of the first edition, has continued to give me the benefit of his vast knowledge and is again writing the foreword. Peter F. Neary and A.M.J. Hyatt, successive Chairmen of the Department of History of the University have been helpful in expediting my work in innumerable ways.

Chuck F.J. Whebell and Robert W. Wightman of the Department of Geography have not only advised on many points, but the former also has allowed me to reprint some of his maps of Upper Canada and the latter has kindly let me make use of his data on the Upper Canadian/Ontario townships. Colin F. Read of Huron College, University of Western Ontario, and Ronald J. Stagg of Ryerson Polytechnical Institute have allowed the use of their research notes on the 1837 Rebellions. Judson D. Purdy of the Faculty of Education at Western has been most helpful. J.M.S. Careless and Graeme Patterson of the Department of History at the University of Toronto have made valuable suggestions, as did the late George Spragge, whose family have been good enough to allow me to reproduce some of his maps showing the evolution of the districts which originally appeared in *Ontario History*. Daniel J. Brock of London, J. Donald Wilson of the University of British Columbia, John Clarke of Carleton University and Donald Swainson of Queen's University have continued to provide me with a great deal of information.

Again I have drawn upon the advice of many librarians and archivists and would especially like to thank the staff of the Baldwin Room at the Metro Toronto Library, especially Edith G. Firth, former Keeper of the Manuscripts, John Crosthwait, Christine Mosser, and Sandra Alston. As well, Michael Pearson, Head of the History Division of the Library, has always been ready to assist with sometimes obscure questions. At our Regional Room at the University of Western Ontario Edward C.H. Phelps the Regional History Librarian and John H. Lutman have solved countless problems. At the United Church Archives the Archivist, The Reverend G. Glenn Lucas and Neil Semple provided me with information on the evolution of the Methodist and Presbyterian Churches. Others who have provided information include Shirley C. Spragge, Queen's University Archives; Henri Pilon, Trinity College Archives; Patricia Kennedy, Public Archives of Canada; John J. Mezaks, Supervisor of the Government Records Section, his associates, Barbara L. Craig, Terrence M. Campbell, Catherine J.

Shepard and Larry E. Weiler, and David Russell, the former Supervisor and Allan J. McDonald, the present Supervisor of Private Manuscripts, Ontario Archives and Kathleen R. Mathews of the Hamilton Public Library Board. Victor Russell of the City of Toronto Archives and his associates also have been most helpful, as has Eric J. Spicer, The Parliamentary Librarian at Ottawa, and his staff. As well I have been assisted on various points by individuals such as Miss Elida Clench, Niagara-on-the-Lake and Guy St. Denis, London.

Colin E. Friesen, the bursar, and Desmond Neill, the librarian, at Massey College have gone out of their way during many summers' research to provide me with a pleasant base for my work.

Charles Addington, Archivist of Huron College, and Ian Mason of Sarnia have assisted in checking and in sorting out many detailed points in organizing the text, and my secretary Chris Speed has been extraordinarily patient with typing a rather difficult manuscript.

Olga B. Bishop has been kind enough to assist with her vast knowledge and fine eye for detail in the organization and preparation of the manuscript.

Over the years the Canada Council and the Social Sciences and Humanities Research Council of Canada have been most supportive of my work, and most recently the latter has provided a Sabbatical leave grant for the completion of this and other manuscripts. The University of Western Ontario has provided many small grants in aid of travel and research. Publication of this edition has been made possible by grants from the Ontario Heritage Foundation and the J.B. Smallman fund of The University of Western Ontario.

Naturally, I take full responsibility for the results.

Frederick H. Armstrong.

Department of History,
The University of Western Ontario,
London, Ontario,
June, 1984

Introduction

The first edition of this book, written in 1967, was prepared because of the difficulties that inevitably seemed to arise in finding answers to even the simplest questions regarding the tenure of officials or the organization of both provincial and local government. An attempt to find out who was the receiver general in 1825, or which district included the County of Haldimand in 1830, could easily take considerable time, frequently without producing results. Much fine basic work had been done in some fields, such as that of William R. Riddell on legal history, Julia Jarvis and Alison Ewart on the Executive and Legislative Councils, W.W. Campbell on the early Legislative Assemblies, and George Spragge on the districts; but the results of their labours are scattered through a variety of old and often hard to obtain publications. In addition, there were many types of officials, including both the provincial executive, the civil service and most of the local office holders, who had received little attention from the historians, except for often inaccurate lists in local histories. Municipal government, too, remained an uninvestigated field. Yet, until we had more information on these questions, the internal workings of the Family Compact, its control of appointments, and methods of local administration, would of necessity remain areas of uncertainty. For instance, investigation of the problem of the extent of pluralism, or any examination of the early careers of many important officials, required accurate tables of the men who administered the province.

The original tables thus represented an attempt to collate existing information and, at the same time, to add further data that might be of use to the historian. All these tables have now been checked for corrections and amplifications. Where necessary, a certain amount of reorganization has been done. Parts VI and VII contain largely new material or complete revisions of the tables that formed the last part of the first edition. Here sections have been added on appointees and offices, such as the Post Office Department and its officials and the provincial surveyors.

In addition the events of the War of 1812 have been revised, and lists added on the major events of the Rebellions of 1837 and the Patriot Raids that followed. There are also now tables covering the provincial and British statutes relating to the incorporation of Upper Canadian companies, as well as lists of the officers of the major Upper Canadian corporations and British companies chartered to do business in Upper Canada. Other new tables include basic population statistics for the province and its major centres and a very preliminary list of the disasters that took place in the colony and on its adjacent waters.

Part VIII provides a brief guide to major bibliographical sources relating to Upper Canada, as well as a listing of some basic works of valuable material in researching Upper Canadian chronology. Charts have been added covering the organization of the local government and some church denominations. Maps have been provided to show the evolution of the districts and counties.

Unfortunately, for reasons discussed below, some of the tables are almost impossible to complete and the accuracy of some of the facts cannot be guaranteed. All aside, from what has been lost, the fact is that Upper Canadians were simply not very consistent record keepers. Nevertheless, the revised and amplified tables should provide a broader data base for researchers on the subject.

The period covered begins with the establishment of the four original local administrative districts in 1788 in what was soon to become Upper Canada. For provincial affairs the tables include office holders and members of the Legislature up to the Union of 1841, when the Cotés' *Tables of Political Appointments* begin. For local officials and data on local territorial organization, the tables continue up to the abolition of the old system of local government on 31 December, 1849, as the Cotés' work does not touch on these matters.

A few comments should be made on the major sources used and the problems they pose. There is no complete list of appointments made during the Upper Canadian period. The two-volume "General Index to Commissions" in the Public Archives of Canada (RG68) is one of the most comprehensive sources. The first volume includes commissions dating from the French Regime, and the two Canadas 1791-1841. The second volume covers the United Province of Canada period after 1841. The commissions are fairly complete for many of the offices during the early years after 1791; but the government apparently became very lax in issuing commissions for many posts after 1800. Legal authorities were still regularly commissioned, but many other officials, such as collectors of customs, were not. District treasurers appointed by the local officials were never commissioned. Even when commissions were issued regularly there is some evidence that a few may have been lost before the "General Index" was prepared. Very occasionally the commission was only issued after the individual had held office for several months.

Another source of confusion arises from the fact that there was a general reissuing of commissions after the local government territorial redistribution of 1800 and again after the 1841 union with Lower Canada. Thus many of the men commissioned in 1841-42 were not new appointments, but rather long-term office holders. Further, an individual was sometimes recommissioned for the same office. The commissions for the District (after 1850 County) Court judges are particularly confusing in this regard as there was often more than one district judge in a district, and joint commissions, which usually recommissioned a sitting judge and added a new one, are quite frequent.

A further valuable source of appointments is the *Upper Canada Gazette*, although it was never complete, or completely accurate in its listings. Moreover, the notices often appeared several months late. Prior to the War of 1812 the *Gazette* provides little information. After 1814, however, the numbers of appointments noted in that journal gradually become more frequent until, by the 1830's, they are virtually complete. Often the name of the appointee's predecessor is included—thus providing otherwise unobtainable data on continuity for many posts.

Establishing the date on which an official relinquished office is even more difficult than finding when he assumed it. The *Gazette* never gives an exact date of retirement, but sometimes a commission of an individual to a new post provides a date by which former duties must have been relinquished. A very few office holders were dismissed by commission.

The *Proclamations* published by the Ontario Archives in 1906 fill in a few facts not obtainable elsewhere; however, many of the *Proclamations* have been lost. The *Appendices* to the *Journals of the Legislative Assembly*, particularly the "Public Accounts" which appear after 1828, form another source of information. Unfortunately, the compilers were often erratic in choosing the facts that appeared in the *Appendices*, so continuous information of any type is rarely guaranteed. Volume III of *The Arthur Papers*, (published by the Toronto Public Library in 1959) contains a partial list of his appointments. The *Blue Books* contain a great deal of information, and the papers of the Receiver General, particularly The Public Accounts, may well provide more data after they have been organized by The Public Archives at Ottawa.

Aside from the above, much valuable information was obtained from old almanacs and directories. County histories, and atlases, which sometimes provide lists of officials, are useful but rarely reliable. For provincial legislation a most comprehensive reference has been G.W. Wicksteed, *Table of the Provincial Statutes in force or which have been in force in Upper Canada in their chronological order* (Toronto, 1856). He also prepared an index volume which must be used with caution because of the system of indexing used at the time. Many of the original statutes have been difficult to locate, but there are several helpful consolidations, such as those of 1795, 1812, 1831 and 1843. The Legislative Library of the Province of Ontario has just published a valuable, three volume work entitled *Legislation and Legislatures of Ontario*, which presents much information on the provincial parliaments of Upper Canada.

The spelling of proper names has presented a constant problem. The Upper Canadians themselves were little concerned with spelling; members of the same family sometimes spelled their names differently: Sir Allan MacNab's father used Macnab, and the Macdonell clan sometimes used McDonell. Some individuals, such as William Lyon Mackenzie, even spelt their names in more than one way in the same letter. In as far as is reasonable the spellings have been regularized.

Because of this problem, the repetition and similarity of many names, and the fact that alphabetical tables have been provided in many cases, such as that of the legislators, where they will most likely be needed, following such precedents as the *Handbook of British Chronology* a nominal index has not been included with this edition. It could well prove to be more confusing than helpful. A subject index has been added.

Two types of tables had to be omitted because of their excessive length: the officers of the militia and the commissions of the peace. Some 1700 magistrates were commissioned between 1788 and 1841, aside from those commissioned for special purposes. The officers of the militia, with their many changes in rank, would provide an even longer list. Both groups merit a separate monograph on their own and this writer is planning a study on the magistrates.

Key to Symbols

Symbols have been kept to a minimum, but the following are used throughout the text:
Where date is that of commission no symbol appears.

A = appointment date before a commission.
B = date bonded.
D = dismissed.
G = date appointment *Gazetted* —(usually later than date of commission).
R = resigned.
S = date sworn.
+ = died in office.
Bracket around date = known to be in office in that year, but may either have been appointed earlier, or continued in office later, as the case may be.

Abbreviations

CE = Church of England (Anglican)
P = Presbyterian

Part I
British Sovereigns, Ministers, Officials and Major Events

A. Monarchs

George III	25 Oct., 1760 - 29 Jan., 1820
Regency	5 Feb., 1811 - 29 Jan., 1820
George IV	29 Jan., 1820 - 26 June, 1830
William IV	26 June, 1830 - 20 June, 1837
Victoria	20 June, 1837 - 22 Jan., 1901

B. Officials in England
a. Prime Ministers and Parties in Power

William Pitt	Tory	19 Dec., 1783 -
Henry Addington	Tory	17 Mar., 1801 -
William Pitt (2nd ministry)	Tory	10 May, 1804 - 23 Jan., 1806[+]
William, Baron Grenville	All-the-Talents	11 Feb., 1806 -
William Henry, 3rd Duke of Portland	Tory	31 Mar., 1807 -
Spencer Perceval	Tory	4 Oct., 1809 - 11 May, 1812[+]
Robert, 2nd Earl of Liverpool	Tory	8 June, 1812 -
George Canning	Liberal Tory	10 Apr., 1827 - 8 Aug., 1827[+]
Frederick, Viscount Goderich	Liberal Tory	31 Aug., 1827 -
Arthur, 1st Duke of Wellington	Tory	22 Jan., 1828 -
Charles, 2nd Earl Grey	Whig	22 Nov., 1830 -
William, 2nd Viscount Melbourne	Whig	16 July, 1834 -
Wellington, (2nd ministry)	Tory	17 Nov., 1834 -
Sir Robert Peel	Tory	10 Dec., 1834 -
Melbourne (2nd ministry)	Whig	18 Apr., 1835 -
Peel (2nd ministry)	Tory	30 Aug., 1841 -

b. Secretaries of State For the Colonies

From the abolition of the American Department in 1782 the colonies were under the jurisdiction of the Home Secretary until 1794 when the office was divided and a new secretaryship created for war and the colonies. Transfer of the colonies, however, did not take place until August 12, 1801, although the Secretary of State for War did have a certain interest in colonial matters because of the military situation. After 1801 the War Office and Colonial Office remained under a single secretary until 1854.

For political affiliations see list of prime ministers.

1. Secretaries of State for the Home Department

William Wyndham Grenville (1st Lord Grenville 1790)	5 June, 1789
Henry Dundas (1st Viscount Melville 1802)	8 June, 1791
William Henry, 3rd Duke of Portland	11 July, 1794
Thomas, 1st Lord Pelham (2nd Earl of Chichester 1805)	30 July, 1801

2. Secretaries of State for War and the Colonies

Henry Dundas	11 July, 1794
Robert Hobart, 4th Lord Hobart (4th Earl of Buckinghamshire 1804)	17 Mar., 1801
John, 2nd Earl Camden (1st Marquis Camden 1812)	12 May, 1804
Robert, Viscount Castlereagh (2nd Marquis of Londonderry 1821) (1st term)	10 June, 1805
William Windham	14 Feb., 1806
Castlereagh (2nd term)	25 Mar., 1807
Robert, 2nd Earl of Liverpool	31 Oct., 1809
Henry Bathurst, 3rd Earl Bathurst	11 June, 1812
Frederick John Robinson, 1st Viscount Goderich 1827 (1st Earl of Ripon 1833) (1st term)	30 Apr., 1827
William Huskisson	30 Sept., 1827
Sir George Murray	30 May, 1828
Goderich (2nd term)	22 Nov., 1830
Edward G. Stanley (Lord Stanley 1834, 14th Earl of Derby 1851) (1st term)	3 Apr., 1833
Thomas Spring Rice (1st Lord Monteagle of Brandon 1839)	5 June, 1834
George, 4th Earl of Aberdeen	Nov., 1834
Charles Grant, 1st Lord Glenelg 1835	18 Apr., 1835
Constantine, 1st Marquis of Normanby	20 Feb., 1839
Lord John Russell (1st Earl Russell 1861)	30 Aug., 1839
Stanley (2nd term)	3 Sept., 1841

c. Under-Secretaries of State for the Colonies

The original order for the establishment of the new War and Colonial Office dated February 27, 1794, provided for an under-secretary, and arrangements were made for a second under-secretary on November 26, 1806, because of the increased duties owing to the Napoleonic Wars. After 1816 there was again only one secretary. The early under-secretaries were normally political appointees who changed with the secretary. Some of them were only concerned with military matters, and their influence varied greatly from individual to individual. In 1825 a permanent under-secretary was appointed to head up the department, and from 1830 there was also a parliamentary under-secretary; the two having coordinate authority and the duties being divided on a geographical basis.

1. Under-Secretaries. (excluding those concerned only with military affairs). (M.P. marked with an X)

X John Sullivan	– 14 May, 1804

(Sullivan an M.P. part of term only)

Edward Cooke (1st term)	14 May, 1804 – 16 Feb., 1806
Sir George Shee	16 Feb., 1806 – 25 Mar., 1807
Edward Cooke (2nd term)	25 Mar., 1807 – 31 Oct., 1809
Charles Cecil Jenkinson (3rd Earl of Liverpool 1828)	31 Oct., 1809 – 10 June, 1810
X Robert Peel (2nd bart. 1830)	10 June, 1810 – 4 Aug., 1812
X Henry Goulburn	4 Aug., 1812 – 11 Dec., 1821
X Robert John Wilmot-Horton (3rd bart. 1834)	11 Dec., 1821 – 5 Jan., 1828
X Hon. E. G. Stanley (14th Earl of Derby 1851)	15 Oct., 1827 – 5 Feb., 1828
X Lord Francis Leveson-Gower (1st Earl of Ellesmere 1846)	5 Feb., 1828 – 30 May, 1828
X Horace Twiss	30 May, 1828 – 22 Nov., 1830

2. Parliamentary Under-Secretaries

Henry George, Viscount Howick, (3rd Earl Grey 1845)	1830 –	1833
Sir John Shaw-Lefevre	1833 –	1834
William Ewart Gladstone	1834 –	1835
Sir George Grey, Bart.	1835 –	1839
Henry Labouchere (1st Baron Taunton 1859)	1839 –	1839
Herbert Vernon Smith (1st Baron Lyvden 1859)	1839 –	1841
George William Hope	1841 –	1845

3. Permanent Under-Secretaries

Robert William Hay	5 July, 1825	– Jan., 1836
Sir James Stephen (Assistant 1834)	1836 –	1847

C. Governors
a. Governors-in-Chief, 1791-1841

Administrators are indented and preceded by Lt.-Gov. if they were the Lieutenant-Governors of Lower Canada. The first date after a governor is the date that he was commissioned, the second, the date he took office, and the third, the date he relinquished office.

Sir Guy Carleton, Baron Dorchester	22 Apr., 1786 - 23 Oct., 1786 - 9 July, 1796
Lt.-Gov. Sir Alured Clarke	25 Aug., 1791 - 1 Oct., 1793
Lt.-Gov. Robert Prescott	12 July, 1796 - 26 Apr., 1797
Robert Prescott[1]	15 Dec., 1796 - 27 Apr., 1797 - 24 Oct., 1807
Lt.-Gov. Sir Robert Shore Milnes	30 July, 1799 - 5 Aug., 1805
Thomas Dunn	12 Aug., 1805 - 24 Oct., 1807
Sir James Henry Craig	29 Aug., 1807 - 24 Oct., 1807 - 19 June, 1811
Thomas Dunn	19 June, 1811 - 14 Sept. 1811
Sir George Prevost	14 Sept., 1811 - 15 July, 1812
Sir George Prevost	21 Oct., 1811 - 15 July, 1812 - 3 Apr., 1815
Baron Francis de Rottenburg[2]	20 Feb., 1813 - 16 Mar., 1813
Baron Francis de Rottenburg[2]	12 May, 1813 - 14 June, 1813
George Glasgow[2]	14 June, 1813 - 25 Sept., 1813
Baron Francis de Rottenburg[2]	11 Oct., 1814 - 20 Nov., 1814
Sir Gordon Drummond	4 Apr., 1815 - 21 May, 1816
John Wilson	21 May, 1816 - 12 July, 1816
Sir John Coape Sherbrooke	25 Mar., 1816 - 12 July, 1816 - 30 July, 1818
Charles, 4th Duke of Richmond	8 May, 1818 - 30 July, 1818 - 28 Aug., 1819+
James Monk	20 Sept., 1819 - 17 Mar., 1820
Sir Peregrine Maitland	17 Mar., 1820 - 19 June, 1820
George, 9th Earl of Dalhousie	12 Apr., 1820 - 19 June, 1820 - 8 Sept, 1828
Lt.-Gov. Sir Francis Burton	7 June, 1824 - 16 Sept., 1825
Sir James Kempt	8 Sept., 1828 - 20 Oct., 1830
Matthew, 5th Baron Aylmer	20 Oct., 1830 - 4 Feb., 1831
Matthew, 5th Baron Aylmer	24 Nov., 1830 - 4 Feb., 1831 - 24 Aug., 1835
Archibald, 2nd Earl of Gosford (Gov. & Commissioner)	11 July, 1835 - 24 Aug., 1835 - 27 Feb., 1838
Sir John Colborne	27 Feb., 1838 - 29 May, 1838

---

[1] In England from 1799.
[2] Administrators while Prevost was in Upper Canada during War of 1812

John, 1st Earl of Durham (Gov. & Commissioner)	30 Mar., 1838 - 29 May, 1838 -	1 Nov., 1838
Sir John Colborne	1 Nov., 1838 -	17 Jan., 1839
Sir John Colborne (Baron Seaton 1839)	14 Dec., 1838 - 17 Jan., 1839 -	19 Oct., 1839
Charles Poulett Thomson (Baron Sydenham and Toronto 1840)	6 Sept.,1839 - 19 Oct., 1839 -	19 Sept.1841+

b. Lieutenant-Governors of Upper Canada, 1791 - 1841

In the absence of the Lieutenant-Governor the chief of state in the province bore the title Administrator or President (of the Executive Council). Usually this official was a senior Executive Councillor, but during the absence of Lieutenant-Governor Gore, from 1811 to 1815, the office was held by the commanders of the troops in the province. The last two of these "war-time" administrators, Murray and Robinson, bore the title of "Provisional Lieutenant-Governor".

In the following table the Administrators are indented.

John Graves Simcoe	24 Aug., 1791 - May, 1799
Peter Russell	20 July, 1796 - 17 Aug.,1799
Peter Hunter	10 Apr., 1799 - 21 Aug.,1805+
Alexander Grant	11 Sept.,1805 - 25 Aug.,1806
Francis Gore	22 Jan., 1806 - 11 June,1817
Sir Isaac Brock	9 Oct., 1811 - 13 Oct.,1812+
Sir Roger Hale Sheaffe	20 Oct., 1812 - 19 June,1813
Baron Francis de Rottenburg	19 June, 1813 - 13 Dec.,1813
Sir Gordon Drummond	13 Dec., 1813 - 25 Apr.,1815
Sir George Murray	25 Apr., 1815 - 30 June,1815
Sir Frederick Philipse Robinson	1 July, 1815 - 21 Sept,1815
Samuel Smith	11 June, 1817 - 13 Aug.,1818
Sir Peregrine Maitland	13 Aug., 1818 - 4 Nov.,1828
Samuel Smith	8 Mar., 1820 - 30 June,1820
Sir John Colborne (later Baron Seaton)	4 Nov., 1828 - 25 Jan.,1836
Sir Francis Bond Head	25 Jan., 1836 - 23 Mar.,1838
Sir George Arthur	23 Mar., 1838 - 10 Feb.,1841

D. Other Officials
a. Civil Establishment
1. Civil and Private Secretaries to the Lieutenant-Governors

Edward B. Littlehales	1792 -	1796
Alexander Burns	1797 -	1799

James Green	1799 -	1806
William Halton	1806 -	1811
James Brock	9 Oct., 1811^G-	1812
Edward MacMahon (acting)	14 Nov., 1812^G-	1813
Colley Foster	1813 -	1814
Robert Loring	(Mar.),1814 -	1815
Edward MacMahon (acting)	(Oct.),1814 -	(Nov.),1814
Edward MacMahon	3 June, 1815^G-	
William Halton	1815 -	1817
Edward McMahon (acting)	1816 -	1817
Col. Duncan Cameron	1 Jan., 1817^G-	1 Oct., 1817
Samuel Peters Jarvis	1817 -	1818
George Hillier	1818 -	1828
Edward MacMahon (acting)	1 Dec., 1828 -	31 Dec.,1828
Lieut. Zachariah Mudge	1 Dec., 1828 -	1831
Edward MacMahon (acting)	1831 -	1832
Lt. Col. William Rowan	June, 1832 -	1836
John Joseph	25 Jan.,1836^G-	1838
John Macaulay	16 June,1838^G-	1839
Samuel Bealey Harrison	18 June,1839^G-10 Feb.,	1841

2. Chief Clerks

William Stanton	(1806)	
Thomas Bingle	-	1808
Allan McLean	1 Oct.,1808^G-	
Edward MacMahon	Oct.,1812 -10 Feb.,1841	

3. Second Clerks

Benjamin Geale		
Thomas FitzGerald	Jan.,1819 -	(1825)
Saltern Givens	-	1828
Arthur Gifford	July, 1828 - 10 Feb.,1841	

4. Third Clerks

John Lyons	June, 1819 -	(1825)
James Macdonell	Nov.,1831 - 10 Feb.,1841	

E. Constitutional Development and International Events and Treaties

1760 - 8 September fall of Montreal completes British Conquest of Canada.

1763 - 10 February, Peace of Paris, ends Seven Years' War, France cedes Canada to Great Britain.

1763 - 7 October, Royal Proclamation greatly reduces size of Quebec, transferring all of the future Upper Canada, except a strip on the east, to a newly created Indian Territory. Provides for new government structure.

1766 - 24 July, Oswego Treaty ends Pontiac Rebellion of May, 1763 - August, 1765.

1774 - 22 June, The Quebec Act, (G.B., 14 Geo III, c.83), in effect 1 May, 1775, establishes government for Province of Quebec and returns the Indian Territory to its jurisdiction.

1774 - 22 June, the Quebec Revenue Act, (G.B., 14 Geo. III, c.88), in effect 4 April, 1775, establishes customs duties, tavern licenses, and other sources of revenue for Quebec, and later Upper Canada.

1783 - 3 September, Treaty of Paris (Versailles), ends American Revolutionary War. Old Northwest to be ceded to the United States at a later date.

1784 - Major Loyalist settlement in western areas of Quebec, along St. Laurence River, the eastern end of Lake Ontario up to Prince Edward County and in The Niagara Peninsula.

1787 - Great Britain approves governor and council of Quebec regulating trade and inland navigation between the Province of Quebec and the United States.

1788 - 24 July, Proclamation, local government established in future Upper Canada with the creation of four new administrative districts cut out of the district of Montreal.

1791 - 19 June, The Constitutional (Canada) Act, (G.B., 31 Geo. III, c.31), in effect December, provides for separation of Quebec into Upper and Lower Canada and establishes the form of government of the two colonies.

1791 - 24 August, Order-in-Council of Sir Alured Clarke, Administrator of Canada, separates Upper and Lower Canada.

1792 - 15 October, English Civil Law established (U.C., 32 Geo. III, c.1).

1792 - 15 October, Trial by Jury established in civil cases (U.C., 32 Geo. III, c.2).

1792 - 15 October, English Weights and Measures adopted (U.C., 32 Geo. III, C.3).

1793 - 9 July, Slavery Act, (U.C., 33 Geo. III, c.7), abolishes slavery in Upper Canada on a gradual basis and prohibits the importation of slaves.

1794 - 19 November, Jay's Treaty between Great Britain and the United States (signed in London), provided for the transfer of the Old Northwest, administrated from Upper Canada, by 1 June, 1796.

1795 - 3 August, Treaty of Greenville. Western Indians abandon claim to most of Ohio (in Old Northwest) and recognize themselve as being under the Protection of the United States.

1796 - July, Cession of the Old Northwest to the United States.

1801 - 9 July, Comprehensive Act regulating customs duties with the United States. (41 Geo. III, c.5). Remained the basis of later Upper Canadian legislation.
- (for collectors of customs see section VI. A.b.).

1802 - 7 July, Ports of Entry Act empowering Lieutenant-Governor to open and close ports of entry. (UC., 42 Geo. III, c.4), Amplified by later acts.
- (for Ports of Entry see Section VI. A.b.).

1807 - 22 December, Embargo Act, President Thomas Jefferson of the U.S. stops departure of vessels from foreign ports. Canada-U.S. trade suspended.

1809 - 15 March, Embargo Act repeal into force. Trade resumed.

1812 - 18 June, United States declares war on Great Britain.
- (for events of the War of 1812 see Section VII. G.a.).

1814 - 24 December, Treaty of Ghent (Belgium), ends War of 1812 with status quo ante bellum governing the retention of 1812 boundaries. (i.e. no change in territory).

1815 - 9 March, Treaty of Ghent proclaimed at Quebec.

1817 - 29 April, Rush-Bagot Convention regulating naval forces on Great Lakes (proclaimed in Washington 28 April, 1818).

1818 - 20 October, British-American Convention on commerce, boundaries and fisheries.

1822 - Proposed Act of Union. Attempt by Montreal business interests to have Upper canada and Lower Canada reunited by British Statute. Defeated by widespread opposition in both colonies.

1831 - 22 September, Canada Revenue Control Act(G.B.,1 & 2 Wm.IV,c.23), Amended Quebec Revenue Act to turn control of revenues under that act over to the legislatures of Upper and Lower Canada for use in setting up funds to defer charges of the administration of justice and the operation of the civil government.

1837 - 4-7 December, Mackenzie Rebellion at Toronto
- (for events see Section VII G.b.).

1837 - 6-16 Duncombe Rebellion in Southwestern Upper Canada.
- (for events see section VII. G.c.).

1838 - Patriot Raids lasting for a year after December, 1837.
- (for events see Section VIII, G.d.).

1840 - 23 July, The Union Act, (G.B., 3 & 4 Vic., c.35). Provides for the reunification of Upper and Lower Canada: the United Province of Canada.

1841 - 10 February, Act of Union comes into force and Upper canada ceases to exist as a separate entity.

Part II
Provincial Officials, 1791-1841

A. The Capital

Locating of the capital of Upper Canada was long the subject of controversy. When the province was first established Newark, soon renamed Niagara and now generally called Niagara-on-the-Lake, was chosen as the temporary capital because it was the major settlement in the central part of the province. Since the town could not be defended, and would fall immediately in case of a war with the United States, it was obvious that another centre had to be chosen for the permanent seat of government. Simcoe would have preferred the Forks of the Thames, the present site of London, because it was well located on the route to Detroit and its inland location was both central and easily defended. The area, however, was still a wilderness. Dorchester wanted Kingston as it was the largest town in the province and well situated for communications with Lower Canada. In the end Toronto was chosen as a compromise, again on a temporary basis.

Moving the capital from Newark took some time. Simcoe established the first British settlement at Toronto in 1793. At the same time he renamed the nascent village York in honour of the Duke of York who was then achieving some success in fighting the French. It retained that name until 1834 when it was incorporated as a city and the designation Toronto restored. Many of the government officials were far from eager to move from the comforts of Newark to a virtual wilderness so the transfer of the government did not really take place until 1797. For example the office of the Provincial Secretary and Registrar placed an announcement in the *Gazette* that it would cease to do business at Niagara on 15 Oct., 1797.

The question of the capital then remained in abeyance until the War of 1812, when York was twice captured in 1813 and Kingston not even threatened. As a result the Colonial Secretary, Lord Bathurst, announced the intention of the English government to move the capital to Kingston. He immediately ran into opposition from the provincial officials who were supported by Governor Gore. After some discussion the decision was reversed, the *Gazette* of 12 June, 1816, carrying the notice that York was confirmed as the seat of government.

Even this did not stop later controversy on the matter. Governor Maitland, like Simcoe, had the idea of an inland capital, though he preferred the Lake Simcoe region. The issue was also debated by the Legislature in 1830, when York was becoming too radical for the liking of many Tories, but again no action was taken. Toronto remained the capital until 1841 when Kingston finally supplanted it—for a brief span—at the union of the provinces.

B. The Executive Council

The Executive Council in Upper Canada was roughly equivalent to the English Cabinet. It was mentioned but not described in the Constitutional Act, it being understood that there would be such a body as a normal part of the English governmental system which was being established in the colony. Appointment was at the pleasure of the government, but this soon came to mean virtually for life. Indeed, inexperienced governors often were dominated by their Councils. Unlike the English Cabinet the Council was in no way responsible to the House of Assembly. Most of the members were also members of the Legislative Council, but they were not of necessity members of Parliament. Also, they were not necessarily heads of departments, though many department heads were members. In the absence of the Lieutenant-Governor the Administrator of the province was chosen from among the senior members of the Council.

The most useful study on the body is Alison Ewart and Julia Jarvis, "The Personnel of the Family Compact, 1791-1841", *Canadian Historical Review*, March, 1926, pp. 209-221.

a. Alphabetical List of the Members of the Executive Council

L = Member of the Legislative Council
S = Date Sworn, no commission issued

William Allan	L	14 Mar., 1836
Henry Allcock	L	14 Oct., 1802^S
Jacques Duperron Baby	L	9 July, 1792^S
Augustus Baldwin	L	14 Mar., 1836
Robert Baldwin		20 Feb., 1836
Sir Isaac Brock		30 Sept.,1811^S
Sir William Campbell	L	26 Oct., 1825^S
William Claus	L	12 Feb., 1818^S
William Henry Draper		27 Dec., 1836^S
Sir Gordon Drummond		4 Nov., 1813

John Henry Dunn	L	20 Feb., 1836
John Elmsley	L	1 Jan., 1796
John Elmsley	L	20 Sept., 1830
Alexander Grant	L	9 July, 1792
Sir James Buchanan Macaulay		5 May, 1825
John McGill	L	2 Mar., 1796
George Herkimer Markland	L	2 Oct., 1822
Jacob Mountain	L	30 June, 1794
William Osgoode	L	9 July, 1792^S
William Dummer Powell	L	8 Oct., 1808^S
William Robertson	L	9 July, 1792
Sir John Beverley Robinson	L	25 Apr., 1829
Peter Robinson	L	24 Dec., 1823^S
John Rolph		20 Feb., 1836
Baron Francis de Rottenburg		19 June, 1813^S
Peter Russell	L	9 July, 1792^S
Thomas Scott	L	8 Apr., 1805
Prideaux Selby		8 Oct., 1808^S
AEneas Shaw	L	21 June, 1794^S
Sir Roger Hale Sheaffe		20 Oct., 1812
Sir David William Smith		2 Mar., 1796
Samuel Smith		30 Nov., 1813
John Strachan	L	31 May, 1815
Robert Baldwin Sullivan	L	14 Mar., 1836
Richard Alexander Tucker		8 Dec., 1838^S
Joseph Wells	L	13 Sept., 1830

b. Chronological List of Members of the Executive Council

The first date given is that when a commission was issued, the second the date the member ceased to act.

    A - Administrator of Upper Canada during the War of 1812.

    N - Never sworn or attended a meeting.

    S - Date sworn, no commission was issued.

1. Jacques Duperron Baby   9 July, 1792^S - 19 Feb., 1833$^+$
2. Alexander Grant   9 July, 1792 - May, 1813$^+$
3. William Osgoode   9 July, 1792^S - July, 1794

4. William Robertson[N]	9 July, 1792	4 Nov., 1792[R]
5. Peter Russell	9 July, 1792[S] -	30 Sept.,1808[+]
6. AEneas Shaw (regular)	21 June, 1794[S] -	1803
(honorary)	1803 -	1807[R]
7. Bishop Jacob Mountain of Quebec[N]	30 June, 1794	
8. John Elmsley Sr.	1 Jan., 1796 -	July, 1802
9. John McGill (extraordinary)	2 Mar., 1796 -	8 Oct., 1808
(regular)	8 Oct., 1808 -	13 Aug., 1818
10. David William Smith	2 Mar., 1796 -	July, 1802
11. Henry Allcock	14 Oct., 1802[S] -	Sept.,1804
12. Thomas Scott	8 Apr., 1805 -	Aug., 1816
13. William Dummer Powell	8 Oct., 1808[S] -	Sept.,1825
14. Prideaux Selby	8 Oct., 1808[S] -	9 May, 1813[+]
15. Sir Isaac Brock[A]	30 Sept.,1811 -	13 Oct., 1812[+]
16. Sir Roger Hale Sheaffe[A]	20 Oct., 1812[S] -	4 June, 1813
17. Baron Francis de Rottenburg[A N]	19 June, 1813[S]	
18. Sir Gordon Drummond [A]	4 Nov., 1813 -	Mar., 1814
19. Samuel Smith [A]	30 Nov., 1813 -	Oct., 1825
20. Rev. John Strachan (honorary)	31 May, 1815 -	25 July, 1817
(regular)	25 July, 1817 -	Nov., 1835
21. William Claus	12 Feb., 1818[S] -	Sept.,1824
22. George Herkimer Markland		
(honorary)	22 Oct., 1822 -	6 July, 1827
(regular)	6 July, 1827 -	12 Mar., 1836[R]
23. Peter Robinson	24 Dec., 1823[S] -	12 Mar., 1836[R]
24. James Buchanan Macaulay	5 May, 1825 -	July, 1829
25. William Campbell	26 Oct., 1825[S] -	Mar., 1828
26. John Beverley Robinson	25 Apr., 1829 -	25 Jan., 1831[R]
27. Joseph Wells	13 Sept.,1830 -	12 Mar., 1836[R]
28. John Elmsley Jr. (first term)	20 Sept.,1830 -	3 Dec., 1833
29. Robert Baldwin	20 Feb., 1836 -	12 Mar., 1836[R]
30. John Henry Dunn	20 Feb., 1836 -	12 Mar., 1836[R]
31. John Rolph	20 Feb., 1836 -	12 Mar., 1836[R]

----------Entire Executive Council Resigned 12 Mar., 1836--------------

32. William Allan	14 Mar., 1836	- 10 Feb., 1841
33. Augustus Baldwin	14 Mar., 1836	- 10 Feb., 1841
34. John Elmsley Jr. (second term)	14 Mar., 1836	- 8 Jan., 1839
35. Robert Baldwin Sullivan	14 Mar., 1836	- 10 Feb., 1841
36. William Henry Draper	27 Dec., 1836^S	- 10 Feb., 1841
37. Richard Alexander Tucker	8 Dec., 1838	- 10 Feb., 1841

c. Staff of the Executive Council
1. Clerks of the Executive Council

John Small	31 Dec., 1791 - 18 July, 1831$^+$
Edward B. Littlehales (pro tem)	9 July, 1792^S - 16 Apr., 1793?
Richard Barnes Tickell (confidential clerk)	4 Nov., 1794^S - June, 1795$^+$
John Beikie (acting)	1831 - 1832
John Beikie	17 Dec., 1832 - 1839$^+$
William Henry Lee (acting)	1839 - 10 Feb., 1841

2. First Clerks (later confidential clerks)

Alexander McDonell	1803
John Beikie	1 Apr., 1803 - 21 July, 1831
William Henry Lee	21 July, 1833 - 10 Feb., 1841

3. Second (or Record) Clerks

John Beikie	1 July, 1800 - 1 Apr., 1803
Andrew Mercer	1 Apr., 1803 - 21 Mar., 1820
George Savage	17 Apr., 1820 - 21 Sept., 1828
William Henry Lee	22 Sept., 1828 - 21 July, 1831
James Stanton	(1835) - 26 Oct., 1836
Thomas G. Hurd	27 Oct., 1836 - 10 Feb., 1841

4. Doorkeepers of the Executive Council

John McBride	17 July, 1798 -
Hugh McLean	22 May, 1801 -
Hugh Carfrae	Oct., 1811 - 15 July, 1839$^+$

C. Officers of the Crown and Senior Civil Servants
a. Adjutants General of the Militia Department

The Upper Canada Militia Department was established by 33 Geo. III c.1 (9 July, 1793). The militia laws were consolidated in 1808 (48 Geo. III c.1, 16 Mar.), and further amended in 1838 (1 Vic., c.8.) and 1839 (2 Vic., c.9.) In 1846 the militia of Upper and Lower Canada were united under 9 Vic. c.28 (9 June).

(Lt.-Col. Francois Baby, Adjutant General of the Militia of Lower Canada	Dec., 1780	- 26 Sept., 1811)
Lt.-Col. Hugh Macdonell	1 June, 1794	- Dec., 1807
Lt.-Col. AEneas Shaw (Col. 1808, Major Gen. 1811)	2 Dec., 1807^G	- 7 Feb., 1814
Lt. John Johnston (deputy)	30 July, 1812^G	-
Lt.-Col. C. ᵀ L. Foster	7 Feb., 1814	- 25 Mar., 1815
Lt.-Col. Nathaniel Coffin (Col. 1820)	26 Mar., 1815	- Dec., 1837
Lt.-Col. James FitzGibbon (assistant)	19 Mar., 1823	-
Col. Walter O'Hara (assistant)	14 June, 1827	- (1840)
Col. James Fitzgibbon (acting)	Dec., 1837	-
Col. Richard Bullock	19 Dec., 1837	- 30 June, 1846

b. Attorneys General

John White	31 Dec., 1791	- 3 Jan., 1800$^+$
Thomas Scott	1800	- 22 Jan., 1806
William Firth	19 Mar., 1807	- Apr., 1812
John Macdonnell (acting)	29 Sept., 1811	- 13 Oct., 1812$^+$
John Beverley Robinson (acting)	19 Nov., 1812	-
D'Arcy Boulton Sr.	31 Dec., 1814	- 12 Feb., 1818
John Beverley Robinson (acting)	19 Nov., 1817	-
John Beverley Robinson	11 Feb., 1818	- 13 July, 1829
Henry John Boulton	13 July, 1829	- 6 Mar., 1833
Robert Sympson Jameson	21 June, 1833	- 23 Mar., 1837
Christopher Alexander Hagerman	23 Mar., 1837	- 15 Feb., 1840
William Henry Draper	14 Feb., 1840	- 15 Sept., 1842

c. Auditors General of Land Patents

Peter Russell	31 Dec., 1791	- 30 Sept., 1808$^+$
William Hallan	3 Oct., 1808	-
Prideaux Selby	1 Jan., 1809	- 9 May, 1813$^+$

John McGill	10 May, 1813 -	
Stephen Heward	1 July, 1818 -	1828+
D'Arcy Boulton	30 Aug., 1828 -	

On 12 Sept., 1835, the *Gazette* announced that the office of Auditor General of Land Patents had been abolished and responsibility for the documents transferred to the Executive Council office.

d. Auditors General of Public Accounts

This office apparently never developed. Russell was the only person commissioned pre-1841, and there was no Auditor General over Canada until the appointment of John Langton in 1855 as Auditor of the United Provinces.

Peter Russell	10 Aug., 1794 -	
D'Arcy Boulton Jr.?	(1832)	-

e. Crown Lands Office
1. Commissioners of Crown Lands

The office of Commissioner of Crown Lands was created when the provincial system of land sales was reorganized in 1826. The Commissioner was also Surveyor-General of the Woods, an office that had previously existed from time to time.

Peter Robinson	30 Aug., 1827 -	1836
Robert Baldwin Sullivan	16 July, 1836^G - 30 June, 1841	

2. Chief Clerks

Richard H. Thornhill	(1837) - (1838)

f. Indian Office

Prior to 1828 Sir John Johnson was the Superintendent General of Indian Affairs, residing in Lower Canada, and there was a deputy in Upper Canada. In that year he retired, his office was abolished, and a Chief Superintendent appointed instead. In 1830 the Upper and Lower Canadian halves of the Indian department were split, the department divested of its military character, and a Chief Superintendent appointed for Upper Canada. In 1844 these two departments were reunited and the next year the office of Chief Superintendent for Upper Canada abolished.

1. Superintendents General of Indian Affairs in Canada

Sir John Johnson	14 Mar., 1782 - 25 June, 1828
Henry Charles Darling, Chief Superintendent (Montreal)	1828 - 1830

2. Deputy Superintendents in Upper Canada

Jacques Duperron Baby Sr.		1789+
Prideaux Selby (assistant Secretary)	1792 -	(1809)
John Butler (chief agent)	29 May, 1793^G -	1794+
Alexander McKee	1794	- 13 Jan., 1799+
Jacques Duperron Baby (joint)	30 Jan., 1799 -	
Alexander Grant "	30 Jan., 1799 -	
William Claus	1799	- 12 Nov., 1826+
Henry Charles Darling	1826 -	1828
James Givins	1828	- 13 Apr., 1830

3. Chief Superintendents for Upper Canada

James Givins	13 Apr., 1830 -	1837
Samuel Peters Jarvis	15 June, 1837^G	- 30 June, 1845

g. Inspector General's Office
1. Inspectors General

This title was to become Minister of Finance in 1859.

John McGill	1 July, 1801	- 10 May, 1813
John Detlor (acting)	1807 -	
Jacques Duperron Baby	11 March,1815^G	- 19 Feb., 1833+
George Herkimer Markland	18 May, 1835	- 1 Oct., 1838
James Nation (acting)	15 May, 1837	- 17 June, 1839
John Macaulay	1 Oct., 1838	- 8 June, 1842

2. First Clerks

John Scarlet	1813 -	(1825)
James Nation	1 July, 1828	- 10 Feb., 1841

3. Second Clerks

Andrew Warffe	1815 -	(1825)
Raymond Baby	10 July, 1829	- 16 June, 1839
Philip Durnford	17 June, 1839	- 10 Feb., 1841

h. King's Printers and Editors of the Upper Canada Gazette

The dates in the following table are those when the individual's name actually appeared as editor of the paper. As the name of the editor sometimes did not appear there are a few gaps; sometimes there were joint editors. The title King's Printer was first used by John Bennett on 19 October, 1805, immediately after the death of Governor Hunter. Formerly he had used "by authority".

After the union of the provinces in 1841 Stewart Derbyshire and George Desbarats from Lower Canada were appointed Queen's Printers, the announcement appearing on 30 September, 1841. On 1 July, 1843, the paper announced that it would be discontinued "as of even date"; Stanton had been ordered to stop using the official seal and title of Queen's Printer. It continued to be printed as an unofficial publication until shortly before Watson's death in 1849.

Louis Roy	18 Apr., 1793 - 10 July, 1794
Gideon Tiffany	10 Dec., 1794 - 5 July, 1797
Titus Geer Simons	20 Sept.,1797 - 18 July, 1801
William Waters	6 July, 1798 - 18 July, 1801
John Bennett	28 July, 1801 - 13 Aug., 1808
John Cameron	15 Apr., 1807 - 25 Nov., 1815
Edward McBride	9 Dec., 1815 - 3 Feb., 1816
Andrew Mercer	- 22 Feb., 1816
Dr. Robert C. Horne	2 Jan., 1817 - 26 Dec., 1821
Charles Fothergill	1 Jan., 1822^G - 12 Jan., 1826
Robert Stanton	19 Jan., 1826 - 21 Sept.,1844
Richard Watson	21 Sept.,1844 - 7 Apr., 1849^+

i. Provincial Secretaries and Registrar's Office

1. Provincial Secretaries and Registrars

William Jarvis	31 Dec., 1791 - 13 Aug., 1817^+
Thomas Talbot (acting)	Feb., 1792 -
William Birdseye Peters (ass't)	3 May, 1796 -
William Monson Jarvis (acting)	13 Aug., 1817 -
Duncan Cameron	1 Oct., 1817 - 9 Sept.,1838+?
Samuel Peters Jarvis (acting)	30 Oct., 1817 -
Samuel Peters Jarvis (deputy)	13 May, 1827^G- 1839
Richard Alexander Tucker	1 Oct., 1838^G- 10 Feb., 1841

2. Clerks (Senior Clerks)

William Botsford Jarvis	1 Jan., 1818 - (1825)
Thomas D. Harington	(1837)- 10 Feb., 1841

3. Second Clerks

Edward Kent	(1838)-

4. Third Clerks

William Kent (1838)-

j. Receiver General's Office
1. Receivers General of Public Accounts

Peter Russell   31 Dec., 1791 - 30 Sept., 1808+
Prideaux Selby   8 Oct., 1808 - 9 May, 1813+
    John McGill (acting)   10 May, 1813 -
John McGill
George Crookshank   2 Dec., 1819^G- 19 Oct., 1820
John Henry Dunn   19 Oct., 1820 - 31 Dec., 1843

2. First Clerks

Stephen Heward   (1815)-   1818?
George Hamilton   Nov., 1819 -   (1825)
Bernard Turquand   22 Oct., 1828 - 10 Feb., 1841

3. Second Clerks

Robert W. Prentice   Nov., 1819 -   (1825)
Walter Rose   25 Oct., 1828 - 31 Mar., 1837
George Roe   1 Apr., 1837 - 10 Sept., 1837+

4. Third Clerks

W. Sergeant   (1837)-
George Hamilton   (1838)-
J. F. Maddock   (1838)- 10 Feb., 1841

k. Solicitors General

Robert Isaac Dey Gray   18 July, 1796 - 7 Oct., 1804+
D'Arcy Boulton Sr.   19 Feb., 1805 - 31 Dec., 1814
John Beverley Robinson   1815 - 11 Feb., 1818
Henry John Boulton (acting)   11 Mar., 1818 -
Henry John Boulton   2 Dec., 1819^G- 13 July, 1829
Christopher Alexander Hagerman   13 July, 1829 - 23 Mar., 1837
    William Henry Draper (acting) Mar., 1833 -   Mar., 1834
William Henry Draper   23 Mar., 1837 - 14 Feb., 1840
Robert Baldwin   14 Feb., 1840 - 14 June, 1841

1. Surveyor General's Office

1. Surveyors General of the Province of Quebec (with authority over Upper Canada before a separate department established in 1792)

Samuel Holland	1764 - 27 Dec., 1801+

2. Surveyors General of Upper Canada

David William Smith (acting?)	23 Sept.,1792 - May, 1804
Charles Burton Wyatt	May, 1804 - Jan., 1807
William Chewett)) (joint acting) Thomas Ridout)	6 Jan., 1807 - 1810
Thomas Ridout	12 Sept.,1810^G - 8 Feb., 1829+
William Chewett (acting)	12 Feb., 1829 - Aug.?, 1829
Samuel P. Hurd	Sept.,1829 - 1836
John Radenhurst (acting)	1836 -
John Macaulay	11 Oct., 1836^G - 16 June, 1838^G
Robert Baldwin Sullivan	16 June, 1838^G - Oct., 1840
Kenneth Cameron (acting)	Oct., 1840 - 10 Feb., 1841

3. Deputy Surveyors General (Senior Surveyors and Draftsmen) of Upper Canada

William Chewett	1791 - 1832
James Grant Chewett	1832? - 1841

4. First (Senior) Clerks

Thomas Ridout	1793? - 1810
William Chewett	13 Jan., 1810 - (1825)
John Radenhurst	9 Feb., 1829 - 1840
William Spragge	1840 - 10 Feb.,1841

5. Second Clerks

Robert Stanton (Extra)	1 Jan., 1810 -
Samuel Ridout	(1818) -
William Morrison (Extra)	(1818) -
William Prosperous Spragge	17 Jan., 1829 -
George Charmbury Ridout	- 3 Sept.,1825+

47

Part III
The Parliaments, 1792-1840

A. Statistics
a. Duration of Parliaments and Sessions

1st Parliament - Elected   Aug. 1792

	1st Session	17 Sept. - 15 Oct. 1792	(Newark)
	2nd "	31 May - 9 July 1793	"
	3rd "	2 June - 9 July 1794	"
	4th "	6 July - 10 Aug. 1795	"
	5th "	16 May - 3 June 1796	"
	Dissolved	1 July, 1796	

2nd Parliament - Elected   Aug. 1796

	1st Session	1 June - 3 July 1797	(York)
	2nd "	5 June - 5 July 1798	"
	3rd "	12 June - 29 June 1799	(Newark)
	4th "	2 June - 4 July 1800	(York)
	Dissolved	7 July, 1800	

3rd Parliament - Elected   July 1800

	1st Session	28 May - 9 July 1801	"
	2nd "	25 " - 7 July 1802	"
	3rd "	24 Jan. - 5 Mar. 1803	"
	4th "	1 Feb. - 9 Mar. 1804	"
	Dissolved	14 May, 1804	

4th Parliament - Elected   May 1804

	1st Session	1 Feb. - 2 Mar. 1805	"
	2nd "	4 " - 3 Mar. 1806	"
	3rd "	2 " - 10 Mar. 1807	"
	4th "	20 Jan. - 16 Mar. 1808	"
	Dissolved	21 May, 1808	

5th Parliament - Elected   May 1808

    1st Session   2 Feb. - 9 Mar. 1809   (York)

    2nd   "   1 Feb. - 12 Mar. 1810   "

    3rd   "   1 "   - 13 Mar. 1811   "

    4th   "   3 "   - 6 Mar. 1812   "

    Dissolved   1 May, 1812

6th Parliament - Elected   June 1812

    1st Session   27 July - 5 Aug. 1812   "

    2nd   "   25 Feb. - 13 Mar. 1813   "

    3rd   "   15 Feb. - 14 "   1814   "

    4th   "   1 "   - 14 "   1815   "

    5th   "   6 "   - 1 Apr. 1816   "

    Dissolved   18 Apr., 1816

7th Parliament - Elected   Apr. 1816

    1st Session   4 Feb. - 7 Apr. 1817   "

    2nd   "   5 "   - 1 Apr. 1818   "

    3rd   "   12 Oct. - 27 Nov. 1818   "

    4th   "   7 June - 12 July 1819   "

    5th   "   21 Feb. - 7 Mar. 1820   "

    Dissolved   By death of George III which was
                          proclaimed in Upper Canada 3 May

8th Parliament - Elected   July 1820

    1st Session   31 Jan.   - 14 Apr. 1821   "

    2nd   "   21 Nov. 1821 - 17 Jan. 1822   "

    3rd   "   15 Jan.   - 19 Mar. 1823   "

    4th   "   11 Nov. 1823 - 19 Jan. 1824   "

    Dissolved   22 June, 1824

9th Parliament - Elected   July 1824

    1st Session   11 Jan.   - 13 Apr. 1825   "

    2nd   "   7 Nov. 1825 - 30 Jan. 1826   "

    3rd   "   5 Dec. 1826 - 17 Feb. 1827   "

    4th   "   15 Jan.   - 25 Mar. 1828   "

    Dissolved   24 June, 1828

```
10th Parliament - Elected                    July 1828
    1st Session         8 Jan.    - 20 Mar. 1829         "
    2nd    "            8  "      -  6   "  1830         "
    Dissolved          By death of George IV which was
                       proclaimed in Upper Canada 8 Sept.

11th Parliament - Elected                    Oct. 1830
    1st Session         7 Jan.    - 16 Mar. 1831         "
    2nd    "           13 Nov. 1831 - 28 Jan. 1832       "
    3rd    "           31 Oct. 1832 - 13 Feb. 1833       "
    4th    "           19 Nov. 1833 -  6 Mar. 1834       "
    Dissolved           1 Sept., 1834

12th Parliament - Elected                    Oct. 1834
    1st Session        15 Jan.    - 16 Apr. 1835    (Toronto)
    2nd    "           14 Jan     - 20 Apr. 1836         "
    Dissolved          28 May, 1836

13th Parliament - Elected                    July 1836
    1st Session         8 Nov. 1836 -  4 Mar. 1837       "
    2nd    "           19 June    - 11 July 1837        "
    3rd    "           28 Dec. 1837 -  6 Mar. 1838       "
    4th    "           27 Feb.    - 11 May  1839         "
    5th    "            3 Dec. 1839 - 10 Feb. 1840       "
    Dissolved          10 Feb., 1840$^G$
```

b. Statistics on Statutes Passed

Reserved and approved statutes can cause confusion as the same statute could be numbered twice: in year it was passed and in year approved. Here totals include them in year passed.

Parliament	Session	Year	Regnal Year	Passed	Reserved & Approved	Total
			George III			
1	1	1792	32	8	------------	8
	2	1793	33	13	------------	13
	3	1794	34	12	------------	12
	4	1795	35	5	------------	5
	5	1796	36	7	------------	7

2	1	1797	37	16	2	18
	2	1798	38	4	3	7
	3	1799	39	5	------------	5
	4	1800	40	6	------------	6
3	1	1801	41	12	------------	12
	2	1802	42	5	------------	5
	3	1803	43	12	------------	12
	4	1804	44	11	------------	11
4	1	1805	45	10	------------	10
	2	1806	46	7	------------	7
	3	1807	47	12	------------	12
	4	1808	48	16	------------	16
5	1	1809	49	9	------------	9
	2	1810	50	13	------------	13
	3	1811	51	9	------------	9
	4	1812	52	11	------------	11
6	1	1812	52	5	------------	5
	2	1813	53	11	------------	11
	3	1814	54	19	------------	19
	4	1815	55	18	------------	18
	5	1816	56	39	------------	39
7	1	1817	57	9	------------	9
	2	1818	58	13	------------	13
	3	1818	59	19	------------	19
	4	1819	59	23	2	25
	5	1820	60	7	------------	7

The Seventh Parliament was automatically dissolved by the death of George III, 29 Jan., 1820, but news of that event did not reach Upper Canada until after the statutes passed in the fifth session received Royal Assent on 7 Mar. These statutes are sometimes cited as 60 George III, and sometimes as I George IV.

Parliament	Session	Year	Regnal Year	Passed	Reserved & Approved	Total
			George IV			
(7	5	1820	1	7	--------	7)
8	1	1821	2	31	1	32
	2	1822	2	27	--------	27
	3	1823	4	38	--------	38
	4	1824	4	37	--------	37
9	1	1825	6	6	1	7
	2	1826	7	31	--------	31
	3	1827	8	25	--------	25
	4	1828	9	20	1	21
10	1	1829	10	22	1	23
	2	1830	11	35	1	36
			William IV			
11	1	1831	1	26	--------	26
	2	1831-2	2	34	1	35
	3	1833	3	59	1	60
	4	1834	4	53	3	56
12	1	1835	5	46	--------	46
	2	1836	6	36	16	52
13	1	1837	7	113	5	118
			Victoria			
	2	1838	7 Wm. IV & 1 Vic.	4	--------	4
	3	1838	1	62	--------	62
	4	1839	2	71	1	72
	5	1840	3	71	5	76

B. The Legislative Council

The Legislative Council was established by the Constitutional Act as the provincial equivalent of the House of Lords and had all the functions of an Upper House. The Speaker of the Council was normally the Chief Justice of the Court of King's Bench. The Constitutional Act specified that the council would consist of at least seven members, supplemented by the addition of any citizen of the colony who was ennobled — an event that never took place in the history of the colony. In the early years the membership was small, and in practice made smaller by poor attendance; but after the early 1830's there were large numbers of members appointed at periodic intervals. There was usually an attempt to appoint representatives of all regions on the council; but inevitably it was dominated by representatives from York/Toronto.

a. Alphabetical List of Members of the Legislative Council

```
E - Member of the Executive Council
G - Gazetted as appointed, but never became a member
S - Date sworn, no commission issued
```

Name	Location		Date
Peter Adamson	Esquesing	-	2 Feb., 1831
William Allan	York	E	12 Oct., 1825
Henry Allcock	York	E	4 Jan., 1803
Jacques Duperron Baby	Sandwich/York	E	12 July, 1792
Augustus Baldwin	York	E	26 Jan., 1831
Walter Boswell	Cobourg	-	29 Jan., 1831
Zaccheus Burnham	Cobourg	-	26 Jan., 1831
Duncan Cameron	York	-	13 July, 1820
Sir William Campbell	York	E	10 Oct., 1826
Richard Cartwright, Jr.	Kingston	-	12 July, 1792
Thomas Clark	Chippawa	-	16 Nov., 1815
William Claus	-	E	3 Feb., 1812^S
James Crooks	Flamboro West	-	16 Mar., 1831
George Crookshank	York	-	1 Jan., 1821
Hon. Peter Boyle De Blaquiere	Woodstock	-	3 Dec., 1839^S
William Dickson	Niagara	-	14 Nov., 1815
Richard Duncan	Williamsburgh	-	12 July, 1792
John Henry Dunn	York	E	1 Mar., 1822
John Elmsley Sr.	York	E	12 June, 1799
John Elmsley, Jr.	York	E	26 Jan., 1831
Adam Fergusson	Gore District	-	27 Feb., 1839
Alexander Fraser	Eastern District	-	3 Dec., 1839

Isaac Fraser	Ernestown	- 16 July, 1839
Thomas Fraser	-	- 16 Nov., 1815
Henry Graham	Bathurst District	- 19 Apr., 1839
Alexander Grant, Sr.	York/Lake St. Clair	E 12 July, 1792
Alexander Grant, Jr.	Brockville	- 19 Nov., 1831
James Gordon	Amherstburg	- 8 Jan., 1829
George Hamilton	Hamilton	- 23 Jan., 1836
John Hamilton	Queenston	- 29 Jan., 1831
Robert Hamilton	Niagara	- 12 July, 1792
Charles Jones	Brockville	- 7 Jan., 1829
Jonas Jones	Toronto	- 27 Feb., 1839[S]
James Kerby	Fort Erie	- 27 Feb., 1831
John Kirby	Kingston	- 2 Mar., 1831
Arthur Lloyd	March	- 6 Dec., 1831
John Macaulay	Kingston/Toronto	E 23 Jan., 1836
John Simcoe Macaulay	Toronto	- 9 Feb., 1839
John McDonald	Gananoque	- 20 Mar., 1839
Alexander Macdonell	Kingston	- 12 Oct., 1831
Alexander Macdonell	Eastern District	- 27 Jan., 1831
John McGill	York	E 10 June, 1797
John McGillivray	Williamstown	- 3 Dec., 1839
Angus McIntosh	Sandwich Township	- 11 July, 1820
Archibald McLean	Cornwall/Toronto	- 23 Jan., 1836
Neil McLean	Cornwall	- 16 Nov., 1815
George Herkimer Markland	York	E 14 July, 1820
William Morris	Perth	- 22 Jan., 1836
Jacob Mountain	Quebec City	E 3 July, 1794
John Munro	Eastern District	- 12 July, 1792
Abraham Nelles	Grimsby	- 5 Jan., 1832
Robert Neilson	Gore District	- 14 Feb., 1839[G]
William Osgoode	York	E 12 July, 1792
William Dummer Powell	York	E 21 Mar., 1816
Thomas Radcliffe	Adelaide	- 27 Feb., 1839
Thomas Ridout	York	- 11 Oct., 1825
William Robertson	Sandwich	E 12 July, 1792

Sir John Beverley Robinson	York	E	1 Jan., 1830
Peter Robinson	York	E	6 Jan., 1829
Peter Russell	York	E	12 July, 1792
Thomas Scott	York	E	7 Aug., 1806
AEneas Shaw	York	E	19 June, 1794^S
Thomas Alexander Stewart	Peterborough	-	20 Nov., 1833
John Strachan	York	E	10 July, 1820
Robert Baldwin Sullivan	Toronto	E	27 Feb., 1839
Thomas Talbot	Pt. Talbot	-	Sept., 1809
Philip Vankoughnet	Cornwall		23 Jan., 1836
Joseph Wells	York	E	12 July, 1820
Robert Charles Wilkins	Prince Edward	-	14 Mar., 1839
John Willson	Gore District	-	11 Dec., 1839

b. Chronological List of Members of the Legislative Council

Dates given are those of commission where commissions were issued. Members were usually not sworn until later, sometimes several years later, and attendance at meetings was often erratic. Appointment was for life, but a few members were dropped for non-attendance.

D - Dropped for non-attendance
N - Never sworn or attended a meeting
S - Date sworn, or commission was issued
U - Reappointed to the Legislative Council of the United Province

1.	Jacques Duperron Baby	12 July, 1792 - 19 Feb., 1833$^+$
2.	Richard Cartwright Jr.	12 July, 1792 - 27 July, 1815$^+$
3.	Richard Duncan	12 July, 1792 - 1805^D
4.	Alexander Grant Sr.	12 July, 1792 - May, 1813$^+$
5.	Robert Hamilton	12 July, 1792 - 8 Mar., 1811$^+$
6.	John Munro	12 July, 1792 - Oct., 1800$^+$
7.	William Osgoode	12 July, 1792 - 24 Feb., 1794
8.	William Robertson^N	12 July, 1792 - **4 Nov., 1792**
9.	Peter Russell	12 July, 1792 - 30 Sept., 1808$^+$
10.	AEneas Shaw	19 June, 1794^S - 15 Feb., 1815$^+$
11.	Jacob Mountain, Bishop of Quebec^N	3 July, 1794 - 25 June, 1825$^+$
12.	John Elmsley Sr.	10 Dec., 1796 - 13 Oct., 1802
13.	John McGill	10 June, 1797 - 31 Dec., 1834$^+$
14.	Henry Allcock	4 Jan., 1803 - 1 July, 1805
15.	Thomas Scott	7 Aug., 1806 - 28 July, 1824$^+$

16. Thomas Talbot[N 1]	Sept.,1809 - 10 Feb., 1841	
17. William Claus	3 Feb., 1812[S] - 12 Nov., 1826[+]	
18. Thomas Clark	16 Nov., 1815 - 13 Oct., 1835[+]	
19. William Dickson	16 Nov., 1815 - 10 Feb., 1841	
20. Thomas Fraser	16 Nov., 1815 - 1819	
21. Neil McLean[N]	16 Nov., 1815 -	
22. William Dummer Powell	21 Mar., 1816 - 6 Sept.,1834[+]	
23. Rev. John Strachan	10 July, 1820 - 10 Feb., 1841	
24. Angus McIntosh[N 2]	11 July, 1820 - 24 Jan., 1833[+]	
25. Joseph Wells	12 July, 1820 - 10 Feb., 1841	
26. Duncan Cameron	13 July, 1820 - 9 Sept.,1838[+]	
27. George Herkimer Markland[3]	14 July, 1820 - 1838	
28. George Crookshank	1 Jan., 1821 - 10 Feb., 1841	
29. John Henry Dunn	1 Mar., 1822 - 10 Feb., 1841	
30. Thomas Ridout	11 Oct., 1825 - 8 Feb., 1829[+]	
31. William Allan	12 Oct., 1825 - 10 Feb., 1841	
32. Sir William Campbell	10 Oct., 1826 - 18 Jan., 1834[+]	
33. Peter Robinson	6 Jan., 1829 - 8 July, 1838[+]	
34. Charles Jones	7 Jan., 1829 - 21 Aug., 1840[+]	
35. James Gordon[4]	8 Jan., 1829 - 10 Feb., 1841 [U]	
36. John Beverley Robinson	1 Jan., 1830 - 10 Feb., 1841	
37. Augustus Baldwin	26 Jan., 1831 - 10 Feb., 1841[U]	
38. Zaccheus Burnham	26 Jan., 1831 - 10 Feb., 1841	
39. John Elmsley Jr.	26 Jan., 1831 - 10 Feb., 1841	
40. Alexander Macdonell	27 Jan., 1831 - 10 Feb., 1841	
41. Walter Boswell	29 Jan., 1831 - 10 Feb., 1841	
42. John Hamilton	29 Jan., 1831 - 10 Feb., 1841[U]	
43. Peter Adamson	2 Feb., 1831 - 10 Feb., 1841	
44. James Kerby	26 Feb., 1831 - 10 Feb., 1841	

[1] Talbot was neither sworn nor commissioned, nor did he ever attend; however, he assumed the dignity of the office and used "Hon." before his name.
[2] McIntosh returned to Scotland in 1831 to take possession of his family estates.
[3] Markland resigned in 1838. There were eventually both moral and financial investigations of his conduct.
[4] Gordon was not appointed to the Legislative Council of the United Province until 4 Oct., 1845.

45. John Kerby	2 Mar., 1831 - 10 Feb., 1841
46. James Crooks	16 Mar., 1831 - 10 Feb., 1841[U]
47. Bishop Alexander Macdonell (R.C.)	12 Oct., 1831 - 14 Jan., 1840[+]
48. Alexander Grant Jr.[5]	19 Nov., 1831 - 10 Feb., 1841
49. Arthur Lloyd	6 Dec., 1831 - 10 Feb., 1841
50. Abraham Nelles[6]	5 Jan., 1832 - 10 Feb., 1841
51. Thomas Alexander Stewart	20 Nov., 1833 - 10 Feb., 1841
52. William Morris	22 Jan., 1836 - 10 Feb., 1841[U]
53. George Hamilton	23 Jan., 1836 - 27 Mar., 1836[+]
54. John Macaulay	23 Jan., 1836 - 10 Feb., 1841[U]
55. Archibald McLean	23 Jan., 1836 - 10 Feb., 1841
56. Philip Vankoughnet	23 Jan., 1836 - 10 Feb., 1841
57. John Simcoe Macaulay	9 Feb., 1839 - 10 Feb., 1841
--. Robert Neilson[7]	14 Feb., 1839[G]
58. Jonas Jones	27 Feb., 1839[S] - 10 Feb., 1841
59. Adam Fergusson	27 Feb., 1839 - 10 Feb., 1841[U]
60. Thomas Radcliffe	27 Feb., 1839 - 10 Feb., 1841
61. Robert Baldwin Sullivan	27 Feb., 1839 - 10 Feb., 1841
62. Robert Charles Wilkins	14 Mar., 1839 - 10 Feb., 1841
63. John A. McDonald	20 Mar., 1839 - 10 Feb., 1841
64. Henry Graham[N]	19 Apr., 1839
65. Isaac Fraser	16 July, 1839 - 10 Feb., 1841
66. Hon. Peter Boyle de Blaquiere	3 Dec., 1839[S] - 10 Feb., 1841[U]
67. Alexander Fraser	3 Dec., 1839 - 10 Feb., 1841[U]
68. John McGillivray	3 Dec., 1839 - 10 Feb., 1841
69. John Willson	11 Dec., 1839 - 10 Feb., 1841

c. Speakers of the Legislative Council

Normally the Speaker of the Legislative Council was the Chief Justice of the Court of the King's Bench.

William Osgoode	10 Sept., 1792
Peter Russell	6 July, 1795

---

[5]Grant is marked "excused" on the rolls after 1832.
[6]Nelles did not attend after 1832.
[7]Neilson was Gazetted as appointed, but the appointment was never made.

John Elmsley	23 Dec., 1796
Henry Allcock	4 Jan., 1803
Richard Cartwright	30 Jan., 1805
Thomas Scott	13 Jan., 1807
William Dummer Powell	21 Mar., 1816
Jamers Baby (pro tem)	17 Jan., 1825 - 20 Jan., 1825
William Campbell	17 Oct., 1825
Jacques Duperron Baby	20 Dec., 1828
John Beverley Robinson	2 Jan., 1830
Jonas Jones (pro tem)	2 Feb., 1839

d. Staff of the Legislative Council
1. Clerks

Peter Clarke	1792 - 1793+
James Clarke	27 May, 1793 -
Peter Clarke Jr.	17 July, 1798 -
John Powell	19 Feb., 1807 - 3 May, 1827+
Dr. Grant Powell	14 May, 1827 - 10 June, 1838+
John Joseph	25 June, 1838 - 10 Feb., 1841

2. Chaplains

Rev. William Macaulay	(1821) - 31 Oct., 1834
Rev. Thomas Phillips	1 Nov., 1834 - (1839)

3. Doorkeepers

John McBride	17 July, 1798 -
Hugh McLean	21 May, 1801 -
Hugh Carfrae	Oct., 1811 - 15 July, 1839+
Thomas Brooks	31 Oct., 1839 - 10 Feb., 1841

4. Messengers

Lewis Bright	1812 - 10 Feb., 1841

C. The House of Assembly

a. Alphabetical List

For details of changes during a Parliament see Riding list

NAME	PARLIAMENT	RIDING
ADAMS, Gideon	6	Grenville
AIKMAN, Michael	13	Wentworth
ALLCOCK, Henry	3	Durham, Simcoe and East York
ALWAY, Robert	12	Oxford
" "	13	Oxford
ARMSTRONG, James Rogers	13	Prince Edward
ATKINSON, James	9	Frontenac
BABY, Francis	1	Kent
" "	8	Essex
" "	9	Essex
" "	10	Essex
BABY, Jean Baptiste	5	Essex
BALDWIN, Robert	10	York (town)
BALDWIN, William Warren	8	York and Simcoe
" " "	10	Norfolk
BEARDSLEY, Bartholomew C.	9	Lincoln 2nd and 3rd
" " "	11	Lincoln 2nd and 3rd
BEASLEY, Richard	2	Durham, York, and Lincoln 1st
" "	3	West York, Lincoln 1st and Haldimand
" "	5	West York
BEASLEY, Richard	9	Halton
BEIKIE, John	6	Stormont and Russell
BERCZY, William Bent	10	Kent
" " "	11	Kent
BETHUNE, Donald	10	Kingston
BIDWELL, Barnabas	8	Lennox and Addington

BIDWELL, Marshall Spring	9	Lennox and Addington
" " "	10	Lennox and Addington
" " "	11	Lennox and Addington
" " "	12	Lennox and Addington
BLACKLOCK, Ambrose	10	Stormont
BOCKUS, (or Bochus) Charles	13	Prince Edward
BOOTH, Joshua	1	Ontario and Addington
BOSTWICK, John	8	Middlesex
BOULTON, D'Arcy	4	Stormont and Russell
BOULTON, George Strange	9	Durham
" " "	11	Durham
" " "	12	Durham
" " "	13	Durham
BOULTON, Henry John	11	Niagara (town)
BRANT, John	11	Haldimand
BROUSE, George	10	Dundas
BROWN, John	11	Durham
" "	12	Durham
BROWNELL, John	5	Stormont and Russell
BRUCE, William	12	Stormont
BUELL, William Sr.	3	Leeds
BUELL, William Jr.	10	Leeds
" "	11	Leeds
" "	12	Leeds
BURKE, George Thew	9	Carleton
BURNHAM, Zaccheus	7	Northumberland and Durham
" "	9	Northumberland
BURRITT, Henry	13	Grenville
BURRITT, Stephen	5	Grenville
BURWELL, Mahlon	6	Oxford and Middlesex
" "	7	Oxford and Middlesex
" "	8	Middlesex
" "	11	Middlesex
" "	13	London (town)

CALDWELL, Francis	12	Essex
" "	13	Essex
CAMERON, Duncan	9	Glengarry
CAMERON, John	7	Glengarry
CAMERON, Malcolm	13	Lanark
CAMPBELL, Alexander	1	Dundas
CAMPBELL, John	11	Frontenac
CARTWRIGHT, John Solomon	13	Lennox and Addington
CASEY, Samuel	8	Lennox and Addington
CASEY, Willet	5	Lennox and Addington
" "	7	Lennox and Addington
CAWTHRA, John	10	Simcoe
CHESSER, John	12	Prescott
CHISHOLM, Alexander	12	Glengarry
" "	13	Glengarry
CHISHOLM, William	8	Halton
" "	11	Halton
" "	13	Halton
CHRYSLER, John	4	Dundas
" "	6	Dundas
" "	7	Dundas
" "	9	Dundas
CLARK, John	8	Lincoln 1st
" "	9	Lincoln 1st
" "	11	Lincoln 1st
CLENCH, Ralfe	3	Lincoln 2nd and 3rd and 4th
" "	4	Lincoln 2nd and 3rd and 4th
" "	6	Lincoln 2nd
" "	7	Lincoln 2nd
COLEMAN, Thomas	9	Hastings
COOK, John	11	Dundas
" "	12	Dundas
" "	13	Dundas

Name		Riding
CORNWALL, John	2	Suffolk and Essex
CORNWALL, Joshua	7	Kent
CORNWALL, Nathan	12	Kent
" "	13	Kent
COTTER, James	7	Prince Edward except Ameliasburg Township
COWAN, David	4	Essex
CROOKS, James	8	Halton
" "	11	Halton
CROOKS, William	11	Lincoln 2nd and 3rd
CUMMING, John	9	Kingston (town)
DALTON, Thomas	10	Frontenac
DETLOR, George Hill	13	Lennox and Addington
DICKSON, Robert	10	Niagara (town)
DICKSON, Thomas	6	Lincoln 3rd
DORLAND, Philip	1	Prince Edward and Adolphus Township
DORLAND, Thomas	4	Lennox and Addington
" "	5	Lennox and Addington
DRAPER, William Henry	13	Toronto (city)
DUNCOMBE, Charles	11	Oxford
" "	12	Oxford
" "	13	Oxford
DUNCOMBE, David	12	Norfolk
" "	13	Norfolk
DUNLOP, Robert Graham	12	Huron
" "	13	Huron
DURAND, James	4	Wentworth
" "	6	West York, Saltfleet, Ancaster, etc.
" "	7	Wentworth
" "	12	Halton

ELLIOTT, George	13	Durham
ELLIOTT, Mathew	3	Essex
" "	4	Essex
" "	5	Essex
ELLIOTT, William	11	Essex
EWING, Benjamin	9	Northumberland
" "	10	Northumberland
FAIRFIELD, Benjamin	6	Lennox and Addington
FAIRFIELD, William	2	Ontario and Addington
FANNING, John	6	Lincoln, 4th
FERGUSON, John	3	Frontenac
FERRIE, Colin Campbell	13	Hamilton
FOTHERGILL, Charles	9	Durham
" "	10	Durham
FRASER, Alexander	10	Glengarry
" "	11	Glengarry
FRASER, Donald	11	Lanark
FRASER, Isaac	7	Lennox and Addington
FRASER, Richard Duncan	11	Grenville
FRASER, Thomas	2	Dundas
" "	5	Glengarry
FRENCH, Jeremiah	1	Stormont
GAMBLE, John William	13	York 1st
GAMBLE, Moses	7	Halton
GATES, Walter F.	8	Grenville
GIBSON, David	12	York 1st
" "	13	York 1st
GILCHRIST, John	12	Northumberland
GORDON, James	8	Kent
" "	9	Kent
GOUGH, Thomas Barnes	5	East York and Simcoe

Name	No.	Riding
GOWAN, Ogle Robert	12	Leeds
" " "	13	Leeds
GREY, Robert Isaac Dey	2	Stormont
" " " "	3	Stormont and Russell
" " " "	4	Stormont and Russell
HAGERMAN, Christopher Alexander	8	Kingston
" " "	11	Kingston
" " "	12	Kingston
" " "	13	Kingston
HAGERMAN, Daniel	8	Lennox and Addington
HALL, George Barker	7	Essex
HAMILTON, George	8	Wentworth
" "	9	Wentworth
" "	10	Wentworth
HAMILTON, Robert	8	Lincoln 3rd
HAMILTON, William	8	Prescott and Russell
HARDISON, Benjamin	2	Lincoln 4th and Norfolk
HATT, Richard	7	Halton
HENDERSON, Rufus E.	10	Grenville
HILL, Solomon	4	West York, Lincoln 1st, Haldimand
HOPKINS, Caleb	10	Halton
" "	12	Halton
HORNOR, Thomas	8	Oxford
" "	9	Oxford
" "	10	Oxford
" "	11	Oxford
HOTHAM, Richard Phillips	13	Prescott
HOWARD, Mathew Munsel	11	Leeds
" "	12	Leeds
HOWARD, Peter	4	Leeds
" "	5	Leeds
" "	7	Leeds
HUNTER, Roger Rollo	13	Oxford

Name				
INGERSOLL, Charles	9	Oxford
" "	11	Oxford
JAMESON, Robert Sympson	12	Leeds
JARVIS, George Stephen Benjamin	13	Cornwall (town)
JARVIS, William Botsford	11	York (town)
JESSOP, Edward	2	Grenville
" "	11	Grenville
JONES, Charles	8	Leeds
" "	9	Leeds
JONES, David	9	Leeds
" "	12	Brockville
JONES, Ephraim	1	Grenville
JONES, Henry	11	Brockville
JONES, Jonas	7	Grenville
" "	8	Grenville
" "	9	Grenville
" "	13	Leeds
JONES, Solomon	2	Leeds and Frontenac
KEARNS, John	13	Prescott
KERR, William J.	8	Lincoln 2nd
KETCHUM, Jesse	10	York
" "	11	York
KILBORN, John	10	Leeds
LEFFERTY, John Johnson	9	Lincoln 2nd and 3rd
" " "	10	Lincoln 3rd
" " "	12	Lincoln 3rd
LEWIS, John Bower	11	Carleton
" " "	12	Carleton
" " "	13	Carleton
LEWIS, Levi	5	Lincoln 1st and Haldimand
LOCKWOOD, Joseph N.	10	Hastings
LONGLEY, George	10	Grenville
LOUNT, Samuel	12	Simcoe
LYON, George	11	Carleton

LYONS, James	9	Northumberland
" "	10	Northumberland
" "	11	Northumberland
McBRIDE, Edward	9	Niagara (town)
McCARGER, Milo	13	Grenville
McCALL, Duncan (or McColl)	9	Norfolk
" "	10	Norfolk
" "	11	Norfolk
McCORMICK, William	6	Essex
" "	7	Essex
" "	8	Essex
McCRAE, Thomas	3	Kent
McCRAE, William	12	Kent
" "	13	Kent
MACDONALD, Archibald	11	Northumberland
MACDONELL, Alexander (Collachie)	3	Glengarry and Prescott
" "	4	Glengarry and Prescott
" "	5	Glengarry
" "	6	Glengarry
" "	8	Glengarry
" "	9	Glengarry
MACDONELL, Alexander (+1835)	12	Prescott
MACDONELL, Alexander	12	Northumberland
" "	13	Northumberland
MACDONELL, Angus (Collachie)	3	Durham, Simcoe, York East Riding
" "	4	Durham, Simcoe, York East Riding
MACDONELL, Angus (Sandaig)	3	Glengarry and Prescott
MACDONELL, Donald (Greenfield)	9	Prescott and Russell
" "	10	Prescott and Russell
" "	11	Prescott and Russell

MACDONELL, Donald (Greenfield)	12	Glengarry
" "	13	Glengarry
MACDONELL, Donald AEneas	12	Stormont
" " "	13	Stormont
MACDONELL, Hugh (Aberchalder)	1	Glengarry 1st
MacDONELL, John (Aberchalder)	1	Glengarry 2nd
MacDONNELL, John	2	Glengarry 2nd
MACDONELL, John (Greenfield)	6	Glengarry
MACDONELL, John	7	Prescott
McGREGOR, John	4	Kent
" "	5	Kent
" "	6	Kent
McINTOSH, John	13	York 4th
MacKAY, Thomas	12	Russell
" "	13	Russell
McKEE, Thomas	2	Kent
" "	3	Essex
MACKENZIE, William Lyon	10	York
" " "	11	York
" " "	12	York 2nd
McLEAN, Alexander	13	Stormont
McLEAN, Allan	4	Frontenac
" "	5	Frontenac
" "	6	Frontenac
" "	7	Frontenac
" "	8	Frontenac
McLEAN, Archibald	8	Stormont
" "	9	Stormont
" "	10	Stormont
" "	11	Stormont
" "	12	Cornwall (town)
" "	13	Stormont
McMARTIN, Alexander	6	Glengarry
" "	7	Glengarry
" "	8	Glengarry
" "	11	Glengarry

McMICKING, Gilbert	12	Lincoln 4th
" "	13	Lincoln 4th
MacNAB, Allan Napier	11	Wentworth
" " "	12	Hamilton (town)
" " "	13	Wentworth
McNABB, James	5	Hastings and Ameliasburg Township
" "	7	Hastings and Ameliasburg Township
McNEILLEDGE, Colin	11	Norfolk
MACOMB, William	1	Kent
MACON, Jean Baptiste	11	Essex
MALCOLM, Finlay	10	Oxford
MALLOCH, Edward	12	Carleton
" "	13	Carleton
MALLORY, Benejah	4	Norfolk, Oxford, Middlesex
" "	5	Oxford and Middlesex
MANAHAN, Anthony	13	Hastings
MARKLE, Abraham	6	West York, Saltfleet, Ancaster, etc.
MARKS, John B.	13	Frontenac
MARSH, Abraham	5	Stormont and Russell
MATHEWS, John	9	Middlesex
" "	10	Middlesex
MATHEWSON, James	13	Frontenac
MEARS, Thomas	5	Prescott
" "	6	Prescott
MERKLEY, Henry	5	Dundas
MERRITT, William Hamilton	11	Haldimand
" " "	12	Haldimand
" " "	13	Haldimand

MOORE, Elias	12	Middlesex
" "	13	Middlesex
MORRIS, James	13	Leeds
MORRIS, William	8	Carleton
" "	9	Lanark
" "	10	Lanark
" "	11	Lanark
" "	12	Lanark
MORRISON, Thomas David	12	York 3rd
" " "	13	York 3rd
MOUNT, Roswell	11	Middlesex
MURNEY, Edmund	13	Hastings
NELLES, Robert	3	West York, Lincoln 1st, Haldimand
" "	4	West York Lincoln 1st, Haldimand
" "	6	Lincoln 1st
" "	7	Lincoln 1st
NICHOL, Robert	6	Norfolk
" "	7	Norfolk
" "	8	Norfolk
NORTON, Hiram	11	Grenville
" "	12	Grenville
" "	13	Grenville
PARKE, Thomas	12	Middlesex
" "	13	Middlesex
PATTIE, David	8	Prescott and Russell
PATTINSON, Richard	6	Essex
PAWLING, Benjamin	1	Lincoln 2nd
PERRY, Peter	9	Lennox and Addington
" "	10	Lennox and Addington
" "	11	Lennox and Addington
" "	12	Lennox and Addington
PETERSON, Paul	8	Prince Edward
" "	9	Prince Edward
" "	10	Prince Edward

Name	No.	Location
PETTITT, Nathaniel	1	Durham, York, and Lincoln 1st
PINHEY, Hamnet	11	Carleton
PLAYTER, Ely	9	York County and Simcoe
POWELL, John A. H.	13	Lanark
PRINCE, John	13	Essex
RADENHURST, Thomas M.	10	Carleton
RANDALL, Robert	8	Lincoln 4th
" "	9	Lincoln 4th
" "	10	Lincoln 4th
" "	11	Lincoln 4th
RICHARDSON, Charles	12	Niagara
" "	13	Niagara (town)
RIDOUT, Thomas	6	East York and Simcoe County
ROBINSON, Christopher	2	Ontario and Addington
ROBINSON, John Beverley	8	York (town)
" " "	9	York (town)
" " "	10	York (town)
ROBINSON, Peter	7	East York
" "	8	York and Simcoe
ROBINSON, William Benjamin	11	Simcoe
" " "	12	Simcoe
" " "	13	Simcoe
ROBLIN, John Philip	5	Lennox and Addington
" "	11	Prince Edward
" "	12	Prince Edward
RODGERS, David McGregor	2	Prince Edward and Adolphus Township
" " "	3	Hastings and Northumberland
" " "	4	Hastings and Northumberland
" " "	5	Northumberland and Durham

" " "	6	Northumberland and Durham
" " "	8	Northumberland
ROLPH, George	10	Halton
ROLPH, John	9	Middlesex
" "	10	Middlesex
" "	13	Norfolk
RUTTAN, Henry	8	Northumberland
" "	13	Northumberland
RYKERT, George	12	Lincoln 2nd
" "	13	Lincoln 2nd
RYMAL, Jacob	12	Wentworth
SALMON, William	13	Norfolk
SAMSON, James Hunter	10	Hastings
" " "	11	Hastings
" " "	12	Hastings
SCOLLICK, William	9	Halton
SECORD, David	5	Lincoln 2nd
" "	7	Lincoln 3rd
SHADE, Absalom	11	Halton
" "	13	Halton
SHAVER, Peter	8	Dundas
" "	10	Dundas
" "	11	Dundas
" "	12	Dundas
" "	13	Dundas
SHERWOOD, Henry	13	Brockville (town)
SHERWOOD, Levius Peters	6	Leeds
" "	8	Leeds
SHERWOOD, Samuel	3	Grenville
" "	4	Grenville
SHIBLEY, Jacob	12	Frontenac
SMALL, James Edward	12	Toronto (city)
" "	13	York 3rd

Name	No.	Location
SMITH, David William	1	Suffolk and Essex
" " "	2	Lincoln 3rd
" " "	3	Norfolk, Oxford and Middlesex
SMITH, Harmannus	12	Wentworth
SMITH, John David	10	Durham
SMITH, Thomas	2	Kent
SOVEREIGN, Philip	5	Norfolk
SPENCER, Hazelton	1	Lennox, Hastings and Northumberland
STINSON, John	5	Prince Edward except Ameliasburg Township
" "	6	Prince Edward except Ameliasburg Township
STRANGE, John	12	Frontenac
STREET, Samuel	2	Lincoln 2nd
" "	5	Lincoln 3rd
SWAYZE, Isaac	1	Lincoln 3rd
" "	2	Lincoln 2nd, 3rd, 4th
" "	3	Lincoln 2nd, 3rd, 4th
" "	4	Lincoln 2nd, 3rd, 4th
" "	6	Lincoln 4th
" "	7	Lincoln 4th
TAYLOR, Josias	12	Lanark
TERRY, Parshall	1	Lincoln 4th and Norfolk
TERRY, William	10	Lincoln 2nd and 3rd
THOMPSON, Edward William	9	York County and Simcoe
" " "	13	York 2nd
THOMPSON, Timothy	2	Lennox, Hastings, and Northumberland
" "	3	Lennox and Addington
" "	6	Lennox and Addington
THOMSON, Hugh Christopher	9	Frontenac
" " "	10	Frontenac
" " "	11	Frontenac

THORBURN, David	12	Frontenac
" "	13	Lincoln 3rd
THORPE, Robert	4	Durham, Simcoe and East York
VAN ALSTINE, Peter	1	Prince Edward and Adolphus Township
VANKOUGHNET, Philip	7	Stormont and Russell
" "	8	Stormont
" "	9	Stormont
" "	11	Stormont
WALKER, Hamilton	9	Grenville
WALSH, Francis Leigh	8	Norfolk
" "	9	Norfolk
" "	12	Norfolk
WARREN, John	11	Haldimand
WASHBURN, Ebenezer	3	Prince Edward
" "	4	Prince Edward
WATERS, Charles	12	Prescott
WEAGER, Jacob	3	Dundas
WEEKES, William	4	Durham, Simcoe, and East York
WELLS, William B.	12	Grenville
" "	13	Grenville
WERDEN, Asa	11	Prince Edward
WHITE, John	1	Leeds and Frontenac
WHITE, Reuben	8	Hastings
" "	9	Hastings
" "	11	Hastings
WICKENS, Charles	13	Simcoe
WILKINSON, John Alexander	9	Essex
" "	10	Essex
" "	12	Essex
WILKINSON, Richard	2	Glengarry 1st
WILKINSON, Walter Butler	4	Glengarry and Prescott

WILLCOCKS, Joseph	4	West York, Lincoln 1st and Haldimand
" "	5	Lincoln 1st and Haldimand
" "	6	Lincoln 1st
WILLSON, Crowell	5	Lincoln 4th
WILMOT, Samuel Street	8	Durham
WILSON, James	5	Prince Edward except Ameliasburg Township
" "	8	Prince Edward
" "	9	Prince Edward
" "	10	Prince Edward
" "	12	Prince Edward
WILLSON, John	5	West York
" "	8	Wentworth
" "	9	Wentworth
" "	10	Wentworth
" "	11	Wentworth
WILSON, William	11	Norfolk
WOODRUFF, Richard	13	Lincoln 1st
WOODRUFF, William	10	Lincoln 2nd and 3rd
WOOLVERTON, Dennis	12	Lincoln 1st
YAGER, Henry W.	12	Hastings
YOUNG, James	6	**Hastings and Ameliasburg Township**

b. Members by Parliament

First Parliament, 1792-1796

Opened 17 Sept., 1792

Ridings	Representatives
Dundas	Alexander Campbell
Durham, York and 1st riding of Lincoln	Nathaniel Pettitt
Glengarry, 1st riding	Hugh Macdonell
Glengarry, 2nd riding	John Macdonell
Grenville	Ephraim Jones

Kent	William Macomb
	Francis Baby
Leeds and Frontenac	John White
Lennox, Hastings and Northumberland	Hazelton Spencer
Lincoln, 2nd riding	Benjamin Pawling
Lincoln, 3rd riding	Isaac Swayze
Lincoln, 4th riding, and Norfolk	Parshall Terry
Ontario and Addington	Joshua Booth
Prince Edward and Adolphus Township	Philip Dorland (refused oath as a Quaker)
	- Peter Van Alstine, (seated 1 June, 1793)
Stormont	Jeremiah French
Suffolk and Essex	David William Smith

Second Parliament, 1797
Opened 1 June, 1797

Ridings	Representatives
Dundas	Thomas Fraser
Durham, York, and 1st riding of Lincoln	Richard Beasley
Glengarry, 1st riding	Richard Wilkinson
Glengarry, 2nd riding	John Macdonell
Grenville	Edward Jessop
Kent	Thomas Smith
	Thomas McKee
Leeds and Frontenac	Solomon Jones, M.D.
Lennox, Hastings and Northumberland	Timothy Thompson
Lincoln, 2nd riding	Samuel Street
Lincoln, 3rd riding	David William Smith
Lincoln, 4th riding and Norfolk	Benjamin Hardison
Ontario and Addington	Christopher Robinson (+ 2 Nov., 1798)
	- William Fairfield (seated, 12 June, 1799)

Prince Edward and Adolphus Township	David McGregor Rogers
Stormont	Robert I.D. Gray
Suffolk and Essex	John Cornwall

Third Parliament, 1800-1804
Opened 28 May, 1801

Ridings	Representatives
Dundas	Jacob Weager
Durham, Simcoe and East Riding York	Henry Allcock (unseated)
	- Angus Macdonell (seated, 30 July, 1801)
Essex	Mathew Elliott
	Thomas McKee
Frontenac	John Ferguson
Glengarry and Prescott	Alexander Macdonell
	Angus Macdonell
Grenville	Samuel Sherwood
Hastings and Northumberland	David McGregor Rogers
Kent	Thomas McCrae Sr.
Leeds	William Buell Sr.
Lennox and Addington	Timothy Thompson
Lincoln, 2nd, 3rd, 4th Ridings	Ralfe Clench
	Isaac Swayze
Norfolk, Oxford and Middlesex	David William Smith
Prince Edward	Ebenezer Washburn
Stormont and Russell	Robert I.D. Gray
West York, 1st Riding Lincoln and Haldimand	Robert Nelles
	Richard Beasley

Fourth Parliament, 1804-1808
Opened 1 Feb., 1805

Ridings	Representatives
Dundas	John Chrysler

Durham, Simcoe, and East Riding York	Angus Macdonell (drowned, Oct., 1804)
	– William Weekes, (seated, 27 Feb., 1805. (killed in a duel, 10 Oct., 1806)
	– Robert Thorpe (seated, 26 Jan., 1807)
Essex	Mathew Elliott
	David Cowan
Frontenac	Allan McLean
Glengarry and Prescott	Alexander Macdonell
	Walter Butler Wilkinson
Grenville	Samuel Sherwood
Hastings and Northumberland	David McGregor Rogers
Kent	John McGregor
Leeds	Peter Howard
Lennox and Addington	Thomas Dorland
Lincoln, 2nd, 3rd, and 4th Ridings	Isaac Swayze
	Ralfe Clench
Norfolk, Oxford and Middlesex	Benejah Mallory
Prince Edward	Ebenezer Washburn
Stormont and Russell	Robert Isaac Dey Gray, (drowned, Oct., 1804)
	– D'Arcy Boulton, (seated, 5 Feb., 1806)
Wentworth	James Durand (declared elected, 12 May, 1807).
West York, 1st Riding Lincoln and Haldimand	Solomon Hill (died, 20 Aug., 1807)
	– Joseph Willcocks (seated, 26 Jan., 1808)
	– Robert Nelles

Fifth Parliament, 1808-1812

Opened 2 Feb., 1809

Ridings	Representatives
Dundas	Henry Merkley (absent first session)

Essex	Mathew Elliott
	Jean Baptiste Baby
Frontenac	Allan McLean
Glengarry	Alexander Macdonell
	Thomas Fraser
Grenville	Stephen Burritt
Hastings and Ameliasburg Township	James McNabb
Kent	John McGregor
Leeds	Peter Howard
Lennox and Addington	John Philip Roblin (unseated, 7 Mar., 1810)
	- Willet Casey (seated, 1 Feb., 1811)
	- Thomas Dorland
Lincoln, 1st Riding and Haldimand	Joseph Willcocks
	Levi Lewis
Lincoln 2nd Riding	David Secord
Lincoln, 3rd Riding	Samuel Street
Lincoln, 4th Riding	Crowell Willson
Norfolk	Philip Sovereign
Northumberland and Durham	David McGregor Rogers
Oxford and Middlesex	Benejah Mallor (absent first session)
Prescott	Thomas Mears
Prince Edward, except Ameliasburg Township	James Wilson (unseated, 3 Mar., 1810)
	- John Stinson, (seated, 1 Feb., 1811)
Stormont and Russell	John Brownell. (+Dec., 1809)
	- Abraham Marsh (elected, 18 Sept., 1810)
York, East Riding and Simcoe County	Thomas B. Gough

York, West Riding	Richard Beasley (unseated, 1809)
	- John Willson (seated, 1 Feb., 1810)

Sixth Parliament, 1812-1816
Opened, 27 July, 1812

Ridings	Representatives
Dundas	John Chrysler
Essex	Richard Pattinson
	William McCormick
Frontenac	Allan McLean
Glengarry	Alexander McMartin
	John Macdonell+
	- Alexander Macdonell
Grenville	Gideon Adams
Hastings and Ameliasburg Township	James Young
Kent	John McGregor
Leeds	Levius Peter Sherwood
Lennox and Addington	Benjamin Fairfield
	Timothy Thompson
Lincoln, 1st Riding	Joseph Willcocks (deserted to the enemy)
	- Robert Nelles (present, 6 Feb., 1816)
Lincoln, 2nd Riding	Ralfe Clench
Lincoln, 3rd Riding	Thomas Dickson
Lincoln, 4th Riding	John Fanning+
	- Isaac Swayze (present, 19 Feb., 1814)
Norfolk	Robert Nichol
Northumberland and Durham	David McGregor Rogers
Oxford and Middlesex	Mahlon Burwell
Prescott	Thomas Mears
Prince Edward, except Ameliasburg Township	John Stinson

Stormont and Russell	John Beikie
York, East Riding and Simcoe County	Thomas Ridout
York, West Riding Saltfleet, Ancaster, &c.	Abraham Markle (deserted to the enemy)
	- James Durand (present 7 Feb., 1816)

Seventh Parliament, 1816-1820
Opened, 4 Feb., 1817

Ridings	Representatives
Dundas	John Chrysler (seated 10 Mar., 1817)
Essex	William McCormick
	George Barker Hall
Frontenac	Allan McLean
Glengarry	Alexander McMartin
	John Cameron
Grenville	Jonas Jones
Halton	Moses Gamble (not qualified; new election, 24 Mar., 1817)
	- Richard Hatt (seated, 6 Feb., 1818) (+before 21 Feb., 1820)
Hastings and Ameliasburg Township	James McNabb
Kent	Joshua Cornwall
Leeds	Peter Howard
Lennox and Addington	Willet Casey
	Isaac Fraser
Lincoln, 1st Riding	Robert Nelles
Lincoln, 2nd Riding	Ralphe Clench
Lincoln, 3rd Riding	David Secord
Lincoln, 4th Riding	Isaac Swayze
Norfolk	Robert Nichol
Northumberland and Durham	Zaccheus Burnham
Oxford and Middlesex	Mahlon Burwell
Prescott	John Macdonell

Prince Edward, except Ameliasburg Township	James Cotter
Stormont and Russell	Philip Vankoughnet
Wentworth	James Durand (expelled, 7 Mar., 1817) (re-elected, seated 6 Feb., 1818)
York, East Riding and Simcoe	Peter Robinson

Eighth Parliament, 1820-1824

Opened, 31 January, 1821

Ridings	Representatives
Carleton	William Morris
Dundas	Peter Shaver
Durham	Samuel Street Wilmot
Essex	Francis Baby
	William McCormick
Frontenac	Allan McLean
Glengarry	Alexander Macdonell
	Alexander McMartin
Grenville	Walter F. Gates
	Jonas Jones
Halton	James Crooks
	William Chisholm
Hastings	Rueben White
Kent	James Gordon
Kingston	Christopher Alexander Hagerman
Leeds	Levius Peters Sherwood
	Charles Jones
Lennox and Addington	Samuel Casey
	Daniel Hagerman (+30 June 1821)
	- Barnabas Bidwell
	- Matthew Clark
	- George Ham (see Riding)
Lincoln, 1st Riding	John Clarke
Lincoln, 2nd Riding	William J. Kerr

Lincoln, 3rd Riding	Robert Hamilton
Lincoln, 4th Riding	Robert Randall
Middlesex	Mahlon Burwell
	– John Bostwick (seated, 17 Mar., 1821)
Norfolk	Robert Nichol
	Francis Leigh Walsh
Northumberland	David McGregor Rogers
	Henry Ruttan
Oxford	Thomas Hornor
Prescott and Russell	William Hamilton. (declared not elected 24 Mar., 1821)
	– David Pattie (seated, 24 Mar., 1821)
Prince Edward	James Wilson
	Paul Peterson
Stormont	Archibald McLean
	Philip Vankoughnet
Wentworth	George Hamilton
	John Willson
York (town)	John Beverley Robinson
York and Simcoe	Peter Robinson
	William Warren Baldwin M.D.

Ninth Parliament, 1824-1828
Opened 11 January, 1825

Ridings	Representatives
Carleton	George T. Burke
Dundas	John Chrysler
Durham	George Strange Boulton (unseated; new writ ordered, 1 Mar., 1825)
	– Charles Fothergill succeeded, present 7 Nov., 1825)
Essex	John Alexander Wilkinson
	Francis Baby

Frontenac	Hugh Christopher Thomson
	James Atkinson
Glengarry	Alexander Macdonell
	Duncan Cameron (election voided, new writ ordered, 12 Mar., 1825)
Grenville	Jonas Jones
	Hamilton Walker
Halton	Richard Beasley
	William Scollick
Hastings	Rueben White
	Thomas Coleman
Kent	James Gordon
Kingston (town)	John Cumming
Lanark	William Morris
Leeds	Charles Jones
	David Jones
Lennox and Addington	Marshall Spring Bidwell
	Peter Perry
Lincoln, 1st Riding	John Clark
Lincoln, 2nd and 3rd Ridings	Bartholomew C. Beardsley
	John J. Lefferty, M.D.
Lincoln, 4th Riding	Robert Randall
Middlesex	John Rolph
	John Mathews
Niagara (town)	Edward McBride
Norfolk	Francis Leigh Walsh
	Duncan McCall
Northumberland	Zaccheus Burnham
	- James Lyons. (seat voided, 23 Feb., 1825)
	- Benjamin Ewing (declared elected. Lyons protests

	Ewing. Lyons finally declared elected 28 Mar., 1825)
Oxford	Thomas Hornor
	Charles Ingersoll
Prescott and Russell	Donald Macdonell
Prince Edward	James Wilson
	Paul Peterson
Stormont	Archibald McLean
	Philip Vankoughnet
Wentworth	John Willson
	George Hamilton
York (town)	John Beverley Robinson
York County and Simcoe	William Thompson
	Ely Playter (withdrew from Province, seat declared not vacated, 17 Feb., 1827)

Tenth Parliament, 1828-1830
Opened, 8 January, 1829

Ridings	Representatives
Carleton	Thomas Radenhurst
Dundas	Peter Shaver
	George Brouse
Durham	John David Smith
	Charles Fothergill
Essex	John A. Wilkinson
	Francis Baby
Frontenac	**Hugh C. Thomson**
	Thomas Dalton
Glengarry	Alexander Fraser
Grenville	George Longley
	Rufus E. Henderson
Halton	George Rolph
	Caleb Hopkins

Hastings	Joseph N. Lockwood
	James H. Samson
Kent	William Berczy
Kingston	Donald Bethune
Lanark	William Morris
Leeds	John Kilborn
	William Buell, Jr.
Lennox and Addington	Marshall Spring Bidwell
	Peter Perry
Lincoln, 1st and 2nd Ridings	William Terry
	William Woodruff
Lincoln, 3rd Riding	John J. Lefferty
Lincoln, 4th Riding	Robert Randall
Middlesex	John Mathews
	John Rolph, M.D.
Niagara (town)	Robert Dickson
Norfolk	Duncan McCall
	William Warren Baldwin, M.D.
Northumberland	James Lyons
	Benjamin Ewing
Oxford	Thomas Hornor
	Finlay Malcolm
Prescott and Russell	Donald Macdonald
Prince Edward	**Paul Peterson**
	James Wilson
Simcoe	John Cawthra
Stormont	Archibald McLean
	Ambrose Blacklock
Wentworth	John Willson
	George Hamilton
York	Jesse Ketchum
	William Lyon Mackenzie
York (town)	John Beverley Robinson
	(Chief Justice 13 July 1829)
	- Robert Baldwin

Eleventh Parliament, 1830-1834

Opened, 7 January, 1831

Ridings	Representatives
Brockville	Henry Jones
Carleton	John Bower Lewis
	- Hamnet Pinhey (declared elected 31 Oct., 1832)
	- George Lyon. (declared elected 16 Jan., 1833. Pinhey unseated)
Dundas	Peter Shaver
	John Cook
Durham	George Strange Boulton
	John Brown
Essex	William Elliott
	Jean Baptiste Macon
Frontenac	**Hugh Christopher Thomson**
	John Campbell
Glengarry	Alexander McMartin
	Alexander Fraser
Grenville	Richard Duncan Fraser
	Edward Jessup (+ before 1 Nov., 1831)
	- Hiram Norton (seated 21 Dec., 1831)
Haldimand	John Brant (declared not elected, 1 Feb., 1831)
	- John Warren (declared elected, same date) (+ before, 7 Nov., 1831)
	- William Hamilton Merritt (seated 7 Nov., 1832)
Halton	William Chisholm
	James Crooks, (seat vacant Apr., 1831)

	- Absalom Shade (elected Apr., 1831)
Hastings	Reuben White
	James Hunter Samson
Kent	William Berczy
Kingston	Christopher Alexander Hagerman
Lanark	William Morris
	Donald Fraser (declared elected, 31 Oct., 1832). (unseated, 30 Nov., 1832).
Leeds	William Buell, Jr.
	Mathew Munsel Howard
Lennox and Addington	Peter Perry
	Marshall Spring Bidwell
Lincoln, 1st Riding	John Clark
Lincoln, 2nd and 3rd Ridings	William Crooks
	Bartholomew C. Beardsley
Lincoln, 4th Riding	Robert Randall
Middlesex	Mahlon Burwell
	Roswell Mount (+19 Jan., 1834)
Niagara (town)	Henry John Boulton
Norfolk	Duncan McCall (+26 Nov., 1832)
	- Colin McNeilledge (seated 14 Jan., 1833)
	William Wilson
Northumberland	Archibald Macdonald
	James Lyons
Oxford	Charles Ingersoll+
	- Thomas Hornor (seated 9 Nov., 1832)
	Charles Duncombe
Prescott and Russell	Donald Macdonald
Prince Edward	Asa Werden (unseated) (re-elected, 11 Mar., 1831)
	John Roblin

Simcoe	William Benjamin Robinson
Stormont	Archibald McLean
	Philip Vankoughnet
Wentworth	John Willson
	Allan Napier MacNab
York (town)	William Botsford Jarvis
York	William Lyon Mackenzie
	Jesse Ketchum

Twelfth Parliament, 1834-1836

Opened, 15 January, 1835

Ridings	Representatives
Brockville (town)	David Jones
Carleton	Edward Malloch
	John Bower Lewis
Cornwall (town)	Archibald McLean
Dundas	John Cook
	Peter Shaver
Durham	George S. Boulton
	John Brown
Essex	Francis Caldwell
	John Alexander Wilkinson
Frontenac	Jacob Shibley
	John Strange
Glengarry	Donald Macdonell
	Alexander Chisholm
Grenville	Hiram Norton
	William B. Wells
Haldimand	William Hamilton Merritt
Halton	Caleb Hopkins
	James Durand
Hamilton (town)	Allan Napier MacNab
Hastings	Henry W. Yager
	James Hunter Samson (+27 Mar., 1836)

Huron	Robert Graham Dunlop (elected 8 July, 1835[G])
Kent	William McCrae
	Nathan Cornwall
Kingston (town)	Christopher Alexander Hagerman
Lanark	William Morris. (made a Legislative Councillor, 27 Jan., 1836)
	- Josias Taylor
Leeds	Ogle R. Gowan (unseated, 14 Feb., 1835)
	- William Buell Jr. (seated, 12 Apr., 1836)
	Robert Sympson Jameson (unseated, 14 Feb., 1835)
	- Mathew M. Howard (declared elected, 12 Apr., 1836)
Lennox and Addington	Marshal Spring Bidwell
	Peter Perry
Lincoln, 1st Riding	Dennis Woolverton
Lincoln, 2nd Riding	George Rykert
Lincoln, 3rd Riding	John Johnson Lefferty (unseated, 2 Feb., 1835)
	- David Thorburn (declared elected, 2 Feb., 1835)
Lincoln, 4th Riding	Gilbert McMicking
Middlesex	Thomas Parke
	Elias Moore
Niagara	Charles Richardson
Norfolk	Francis L. Walsh
	David Duncombe
Northumberland	Alexander Macdonell
	John Gilchrist

Oxford	Charles Duncombe
	Robert Alway
Prescott	Alexander Macdonell (+ 16 Feb., 1835)
	- John Chesser (returned, 2 Apr., 1835)
	- Charles Waters
Prince Edward	John P. Roblin
Russell	Thomas MacKay
	James Wilson
Simcoe	William Benjamin Robinson
	Samuel Lount
Stormont	William Bruce
	Donald A. E. Macdonell
Toronto (city)	James Edward Small
Wentworth	Harmannus Smith
	Jacob Rymal
York, 1st Riding	David Gibson
York, 2nd Riding	William Lyon Mackenzie
York, 3rd Riding	Thomas David Morrison M.D.
York, 4th Riding	John Macintosh

Thirteenth Parliament, 1836-1841

Opened, 8 Nov., 1836

Ridings	Representatives
Brockville (town)	Henry Sherwood
Carleton	John Bower Lewis
	Edward Malloch
Cornwall (town)	George Stephen Benjamin Jarvis
Dundas	Peter Shaver
	John Cook
Durham	George Strange Boulton
	George Elliott

Essex	John Prince
	Francis Caldwell
Frontenac	John B. Marks
	James Mathewson
Glengarry	Donald Macdonell
	Alexander Chisholm
Grenville	Hiram Norton (resigned Oct., 1838 - went to U.S.A.)
	- Milo McCarger (succeeds, 15 Apr., 1839
	- William B. Wells (expelled 27 Feb., 1838)
	- Henry Burritt (present, 4 Dec., 1839)
Haldimand	William Hamilton Merritt
Halton	William Chisholm
	Absalom Shade
Hamilton	Colin Campbell Ferrie
Hastings	Edmund Murney
	Anthony Manahan
Huron	Robert Graham Dunlop
Kent	William McCrae
	Nathan Cornwall
Kingston (town)	Christopher Alexander Hagerman
Lanark	John A. H. Powell
	Malcolm Cameron
Leeds	Jonas Jones (appointed Registrar, Dundas County, new writ 20 June, 1837)
	- James Morris (seated, 30 Dec., 1837)
	Ogle Robert Gowan
Lennox and Addington	John Solomon Cartwright
	George Hill Detlor
Lincoln, 1st Riding	Richard Woodruff

Lincoln, 2nd Riding	George Rykert
Lincoln, 3rd Riding	David Thorburn
Lincoln, 4th Riding	Gilbert McMicking
London (town)	Mahlon Burwell
Middlesex	Thomas Parke
	Elias Moore
Niagara (town)	Charles Richardson
Norfolk	David Duncombe, M.D.
	Dr. John Rolph M.D. (expelled from House, 20 Jan., 1838)
	- William Salmon, succeeds (seated, 27 Feb., 1838)
Northumberland	Alexander Macdonell
	Henry Ruttan
Oxford	Robert Alway
	Charles Duncombe (expelled from house, 20 Jan., 1838).
	- Roger Rolle Hunter (seated, 27 Feb., 1839)
Prescott	John Kearns
	Richard Phillips Hotham
Prince Edward	James Rogers Armstrong
	Charles Bockus
Russell	Thomas MacKay
Simcoe	William Benjamin Robinson
	Charles Wickens
Stormont	Archibald McLean (appointed to the King's Bench 23 Mar., 1837)
	- Alexander McLean (seated, 20 Dec., 1837)
	Donald AEneas McDonell
Toronto (city)	William Henry Draper

Wentworth	Allan Napier MacNab
	Michael Aikman
York, 1st Riding	David Gibson (expelled as a rebel, 15 Jan., 1838)
	- John William Gamble (seated 5 Feb., 1838)
York, 2nd Riding	Edward William Thompson
York, 3rd Riding	Thomas David Morrison (left country, new writ ordered, 28 Mar., 1839)
	- James Edward Small (seated, 29 Apr., 1839)
York, 4th Riding	John McIntosh

c. Members by Riding

Details of the legislation referred to in the following tables can be found in Part V, Section B. Subsection b. In the tables the number following the date is the number of the Parliament, e.g., 1792 - 1; 1830 - 11.

1. Addington County

1792-1800 with Ontario

1800 - 1841 with Lennox

2. Town of Brockville

1830 Separate riding under 1 Geo. IV c.2 (1820)

    1830 - 11 - Henry Jones

    1834 - 12 - David Jones

    1836 - 13 - Henry Sherwood

3. Carleton County

1820 separate riding under 1 Geo. IV c.2.

    1820 - 8 - William Morris

    1824 - 9 - George T. Burke

    1828 - 10 - Thomas Radenhurst

    1830 - 11 - John Bower Lewis

1832 second member under 2 Wm. IV c.18.

    - Hamnet Pinhey (seated 2 Nov., 1832 - unseated 16 Jan., 1833)

    - George Lyon (seated 16 Jan., 1833)

    1834 - 12 - John Bower Lewis   -   Edward Malloch

    1836 - 13 - John Bower Lewis   -   Edward Malloch

4. Town of Cornwall

1792 - 1834 see Stormont

1834 separate riding under 1 Geo. IV c.2 (1820)

    1834 - 12 - Archibald McLean

    1836 - 13 - George Stephen Benjamin Jarvis

5. Dundas County

1792 created by Proclamation of 16 July

    1792 - 1 - Alexander Campbell

    1797 - 2 - Thomas Fraser

    1800 - 3 - Jacob Weager

    1804 - 4 - John Chrysler

    1808 - 5 - Henry Merkley

    1812 - 6 - John Chrysler

    1816 - 7 - "   "

    1820 - 8 - Peter Shaver

    1824 - 9 - John Chrysler

1828 2 members under 1 Geo. IV c.2 (1820)

    1828 - 10 - Peter Shaver   -   George Brouse

    1830 - 11 -   "   "   -   John Cook

    1834 - 12 -   "   "   -   "   "

    1836 - 13 -   "   "   -   "   "

6. Durham County

1792 Durham, York, and 1st Riding of Lincoln one riding under Proclamation of 16 July.

<u>Durham, York and 1st Riding of Lincoln</u>

    1792 - 1 - Nathaniel Pettitt

    1797 - 2 - Richard Beasley

1800 Durham, York East Riding and Simcoe one riding under 40 Geo. III c.3.

Durham, York East Riding and Simcoe

    1800 - 3 - Justice Henry Allcock (unseated)

           - Angus Macdonell (30 July, 1801 seated)

    1804 - 4 -   "   "   (+ Oct. 1804; drowned)

           - William Weekes (Feb. 27, 1805 seated - 10 Oct., 1806+;
              killed in a duel)

           - Robert Thorpe

1808 Northumberland combined with Durham by 48 Geo. III c.11

    Northumberland and Durham

    1808 - 5 - David McGregor Rogers

    1812 - 6 -   "   "   "

    1816 - 7 - Zaccheus Burnham

1820 separate riding under 1 Geo. IV c.2 (2 members from 1828)

    Durham

    1820 - 8 - Samuel Street Wilmot

    1824 - 9 - George Strange Boulton (unseated - new writ
              ordered 1 Mar., 1825)

           - Charles Fothergill (present 1 Nov., 1825)

    1828 -10 - John David Smith   -   Charles Fothergill

    1830 -11 - George Strange Boulton -   John Brown

    1834 -12 -   "   "   "   -   "   "

    1836 -13 -   "   "   "   -   George Elliott

7. Essex County

1792 - 1800 with Suffolk.

1800 - separate riding with two members under 40 Geo. III c.3.

    1800 - 3 - Matthew Elliott   - Thomas McKee

    1804 - 4 -   "   "   - David Cowan

    1808 - 5 -   "   "   - Jean Baptiste Baby

    1812 - 6 - Richard Pattinson   - William McCormick

    1816 - 7 - George Barker Hall   -   "   "

    1820 - 8 - Francis Baby   -   "   "

    1824 - 9 -   "   "   -   John Alexander
                                             Wilkinson

    1828 - 10 -   "   "   -   John Alexander
                                             Wilkinson

1830 - 11 - William Elliott	-	Jean Baptiste Macon
1834 - 12 - Francis Caldwell	-	John Alexander Wilkinson
1836 - 13 - " "	-	John Prince

8. Frontenac County

1792 - 1800 with Leeds

1800 separate riding under 40 Geo. III c. 3

    1800 - 3 - John Ferguson

    1804 - 4 - Allan McLean

    1808 - 5 -   "   "

    1812 - 6 -   "   "

    1816 - 7 -   "   "

    1820 - 8 -   "   "

1824 2 members under 1 Geo. IV. c.2 (1820)

    1824 - 9 - Hugh Christopher Thomson - James Atkinson

    1828 - 10 -   "   " - Thomas Dalton

    1830 - 11 -   "   " - John Campbell

    1834 - 12 - Jacob Shibley - John C. Strange

    1836 - 13 - John B. Marks - James Mathewson

9. Glengarry County

1792 Proclamation of 16 July divides county into 2 Ridings. 1st Riding: late Township of Charlottenburg. 2nd Riding: rest of county

    <u>1st Riding</u>

    1792 - 1 - Hugh Macdonell

    1797 - 2 - Richard Wilkinson

    <u>2nd Riding</u>

    1792 - 1 - John Macdonell of Aberchallader

    1797 - 2 -   "   "

1800 40 Geo. III c. 3 establishes two member Glengarry & Prescott riding.

    <u>Glengarry & Prescott</u>

    1800 - 3 - Alexander Macdonell - Angus Macdonell

    1804 - 4 -   "   " - Walter Butler Wilkinson

1808 Two members under 48 Geo. III c.11 - except 10th Parliament 1828.

Glengarry

1808	-	5 - Alexander Macdonell	-	Thomas Fraser
1812	-	6 - " "	-	John Macdonell
			-	Alexander McMartin
1816	-	7 - John Cameron		" "
1820	-	8 - Alexander Macdonell	-	" "
1824	-	9 - " "	-	Duncan Cameron
1828	-	10 - Alexander Fraser	-	_____
1830	-	11 - " "	-	Alexander McMartin
1834	-	12 - Donald Macdonell	-	Alexander Chisholm
1836	-	13 - " "	-	" "

10. Grenville County

1792 created by Proclamation of 16 July

    1792 - 1 - Ephraim Jones

    1797 - 2 - Edward Jessop

    1800 - 3 - Samuel Sherwood

    1804 - 4 - "   "

    1808 - 5 - Stephen Burritt

    1812 - 6 - Gideon Adams

    1816 - 7 - Jonas Jones

1820 two members under 1 Geo. IV c.2.

1820	-	8 - Walter F. Gates	-	Jonas Jones
1824	-	9 - Hamilton Walker	-	" "
1828	-	10 - George Longley	-	Rufus E. Henderson
1830	-	11 - Richard D. Fraser	-	Edward Jessup
				(died 1 Nov. 1831)
				Hiram Norton
				(21 Dec. 1831 seated)
1834	-	12 - William B. Wells	-	Hiram Norton
1836	-	13 - " "		" "
		(expelled - new writ)		(Oct. 1838 resigned)
		27 Feb. 1838)		
		- Henry Buritt		Milo McCarger
		(present 4 Dec. 1839)		(15 April, 1839
				succeeds)

97

11. Haldimand County

1792 - 1830 see Lincoln

1830 1 member under 1 Geo. IV c.2.

1830 - 11 - John Brant (declared not elected 1 Feb., 1831)

- John Warren (declared elected 1 Feb., 1831,

5 Sept., 1832+)

- William H. Merritt (seated 7 Nov. 1832)

1834 - 12 -   "   "

1836 - 13 -   "   "

12. Halton County

1792 - 1817 see York West Riding.

1817 one member under 57 Geo. III c.1.

1817 - 7 - Moses Gamble (not qualified 24 March, 1817)

- Richard Hatt (seated 15 May, 1817 and died before

21 Feb., 1820)

1820 two members under 1 Geo. IV c.2.

1820 - 8 - James Crooks	-	William Chisholm
1824 - 9 - Richard Beasley	-	William Scollick
1828 - 10 - George Rolph	-	Caleb Hopkins
1830 - 11 - William Chisholm	-	James Crooks (seat vacant by Apr., 1831)
		Absalom Shade (elected Apr., 1831)
1834 - 12 - Caleb Hopkins	-	James Durand
1836 - 13 - William Chisholm	-	Absalom Shade

13. Town of Hamilton

1817 - 1834 see Wentworth

1834 separate riding under 1 Geo. IV c.2. (1820)

1834 - 12 - Allan Napier MacNab

1836 - 13 - Colin Campbell Ferrie

14. Hastings County

1792 - 1800 with Lennox and Northumberland.

1800 joined with Northumberland only as one seat riding under 40 Geo. III c.3.

Hastings and Northumberland

    1800 - 3 - David McGregor Rogers

    1804 - 4 -   "   "   "

1808 separate riding but including Township Ameliasburg in Prince Edward by 48 Geo. III c.11.

Hastings and Township Ameliasburg

    1808 - 5 - James McNabb

    1812 - 6 - James Young

    1816 - 7 -   "   "

1820 separate riding under 1 Geo. IV c.2.

Hastings

    1820 - 8 - Reuben White

1824 separate riding with two members under 1 Geo. IV c.2.

1824 - 9 - Reuben White	-	Thomas Coleman
1828 - 10 - Joseph W. Lockwood	-	James Hunter Samson
1830 - 11 - Reuben White	-	" "
1834 - 12 - Henry W. Yager	-	" "
		(died 27 Mar., 1836)
1836 - 13 - Edward Marney	-	Anthony Manahan

15. Huron County

1800 - 1836 see Middlesex

1836 separate riding under 1 Geo. IV c.2. (1820) as soon as created a county in 1835.

    1835 - 12 - Robert Graham Dunlop (election in <u>Gazette</u> 8 July, 1835)

    1836 - 13 -   "   "   "

16. Kent County

1792 created by Proclamation of 16 July, originally the only county with two members.

1792 - 1 - William Macomb	-	Francis Baby
1797 - 2 - Thomas Smith	-	Thomas McKee

1800 reduced to one member under 40 Geo. III c.3

    1800 - 3 - Thomas McCrae Sr.

    1804 - 4 - John McGregor

    1808 - 5 -   "   "

    1812 - 6 -   "   "

```
        1816 -  7 - Joshua Cornwall
        1820 -  8 - James Gordon
        1824 -  9 -     "            "
        1828 - 10 - William Berczy
        1830 - 11 -     "            "
1834 two members under 1 Geo. IV c.2 (1820)
        1834 - 12 - William McCrae      -   Nathan Cornwall
        1836 - 13 -     "            "   -        "        "
```

17. Town of Kingston

1792 - 1800 see Leeds

1800 - 1820 see Frontenac

1820 separate riding under 1 Geo. IV c.2.

```
        1820 -  8 - Christopher Alexander Hagerman
        1824 -  9 - John Cumming
        1828 - 10 - Donald Bethune
        1830 - 11 - Christopher Alexander Hagerman
        1834 - 12 -     "            "          "
        1836 - 13 -     "            "          "
```

18. Lanark County

1820 - 1824 see Carleton

1824 county established by 5 Geo. IV c.5 and automatically receives a member under 1 Geo. IV c.2. (1820)

```
        1824 -  9 - William Morris
        1828 - 10 -     "       "
        1830 - 11 -     "       "      -  Donald Fraser
                                          (declared elected
                                          31 Oct., 1832)
                                          (unseated 30 Nov.,
                                          1832)
        1834 - 12 -     "       "      -  Josiah Taylor (to
                                          Legislative Council
                                          new writ 27 Jan.,
                                          1836)
        1836 - 13 - John A. H. Powell  -  Malcolm Cameron
```

19. Leeds County

1792 Joint Leeds and Frontenac riding created by Proclamation of 16 July.

Leeds and Frontenac

1792 - 1 - John White

1797 - 2 - Dr. Solomon Jones

1800 separated from Frontenac under 40 Geo. III c.3.

Leeds

1800 - 3 - William Buell Sr.

1804 - 4 - Peter Howard

1808 - 5 - "   "

1812 - 6 - Levius Peters Sherwood

1816 - 7 - Peter Howard

1820 two members under 1 Geo. IV c.2.

1820 - 8 - Levius Peters Sherwood -	Charles Jones
1824 - 9 - David Jones -	" "
1828 - 10 - John Kilborn -	William Buell Jr.
1830 - 11 - Mathew Munsel Howard -	" "
1834 - 12 - Ogle R. Gowan -	Robert Sympson Jameson
(unseated 14 Feb., 1835) -	(unseated 14 Feb. 1835)
- William Buell Jr. (12 Apr. 1836 seated) -	Mathew M. Howard (12 Apr., 1836 declared elected)
1836 - 13 - Jonas Jones (20 June, 1837, new writ) -	Ogle R. Gowan
- James Morris (Dec., 1837 seated)	

20. Lennox County

1792 Proclamation of 16 July creates riding of Lennox, Hastings and Northumberland, but Township of Adolphus in Lennox excluded.

Lennox, Hastings and Northumberland

1792 - 1 - Hazelton Spencer

1797 - 2 - Timothy Thompson

1800 Incorporated with Addington by 40 Geo. III c.3.

Lennox and Addington

1800 - 3 - Timothy Thompson

1804 - 4 - Thomas Dorland

1808 Increased to two seats by 48 Geo. III c.11.

1808 - 5 - Thomas Dorland	-	John Philip Roblin (Mar. 1810 unseated)
	-	Willet Casey (1 Feb. 1811 seated)
1812 - 6 - Benjamin Fairfield	-	Timothy Thompson
1816 - 7 - Isaac Fraser	-	Willet Casey
1820 - 8 - Samuel Casey	-	Daniel Hagerman (died 30 June, 1821)
	-	Barnabas Bidwell (21 Nov. 1821 succeeds) (petition against 24 Nov. 1821 unseated)
	-	Matthew Clark (1 Mar., 1822^G) (unseated)
	-	George Ham (9 Feb., 1824^G) (unseated)
1824 - 9 - Peter Perry	-	Marshall S. Bidwell
1828 - 10 - " "	-	" "
1830 - 11 - " "	-	" "
1834 - 12 - " "	-	" "
1836 - 13 - John S. Cartwright	-	George H. Detlor

21. Lincoln County

Lincoln has an exceptionally complex riding history. The following are the statutes relating to the riding pattern of the county.

1792 Proclamation of 16 July divides Lincoln into four ridings, Durham, York and Lincoln 1st Riding; Lincoln 2nd Riding; Lincoln 3rd Riding; Lincoln 4th Riding and Norfolk.

1800 40 Geo. III c.3. Reorganizes Lincoln into two ridings each with two members: West Riding York, 1st Riding Lincoln and Haldimand; and 2nd, 3rd and 4th Ridings of Lincoln.

1808 48 Geo. III c.11. Lincoln divided into five one member ridings: 1st Riding Lincoln and part of Haldimand 2 members 2nd, 3rd Lincoln and 4th Ridings of Lincoln one member each.

1820 1 Geo. c.2. Lincoln four 1 member ridings (including Haldimand).

1833 3 William IV c.15. Elections in Lincoln to be by riding, each riding to have one member.

i. Lincoln 1st Riding

Durham, York and 1st Riding Lincoln

1792 - 1 - Nathaniel Pettitt

1797 - 2 - Richard Beasley

West York, 1st Lincoln and Haldimand

1800 - 3 - Richard Beasley   -   Robert Nelles

1804 - 4 - Solomon Hill   -   "   "

    (died 30 Aug. 1807)

    - Joseph Willcocks

    (seated 26 Jan. 1808)

Lincoln, 1st Riding and Haldimand

1808 - 5 - Joseph Willcocks   -   Levi Lewis

1812 - 6 -   "   " (deserted)   (second member dropped)

    - Robert Nelles

    (present 6 Feb. 1816)

1816 - 7 - Robert Nelles

1820 - 8 - John Clarke

1824 - 9 -   "   "

1828 - 10 - William Torry

1830 - 11 - John Clarke

1834 - 12 - Dennis Woolverton

1836 - 13 - Richard Woodruff

ii. Lincoln 2nd Riding

    2nd Riding

1792 - 1 - Benjamin Pawling

1797 - 2 - Samuel Street

    2nd, 3rd and 4th Ridings

1800 - 3 - Ralfe Clench   -   Isaac Swayze

1804 - 4 -   "   "   -   "   "

2nd Riding

1808 - 5 - David Secord

1812 - 6 - Ralfe Clench

1816 - 7 - "   "

1820 - 8 - William J. Kerr

1824 - 9 - Bartholemew C. Beardsley

1828 - 10 - William Woodruff

1830 - 11 - William Crooks

1834 - 12 - George Rykert

1836 - 13 -   "   "

ii. Lincoln 3rd Riding

3rd Riding

1792 - 1 - Isaac Swayze

1797 - 2 - David William Smith

2nd, 3rd & 4th Ridings

1800 - 3 - Ralfe Clench   -   Isaac Swayze

1804 - 4 -   "   "   "   "

3rd Riding

1808 - 5 - Samuel Street

1812 - 6 - Thomas Dickson

1816 - 7 - David Secord

1820 - 8 - Robert Hamilton

1824 - 9 - John J. Lefferty

1828 - 10 -   "   "

1830 - 11 - Bartholomew C. Beardsley

1834 - 12 - John J. Lefferty (unseated 2 Feb., 1835)

          David Thorburn (declared elected 2 Feb., 1835)

1836 - 13 -   "   "

iv. Lincoln 4th Riding

4th Riding and Norfolk

1792 - 1 - Parshall Terry

1797 - 2 - Benjamin Hardison

2nd, 3rd & 4th Ridings

1800 - 3 - Ralfe Clench   -   Isaac Swayze

1804 - 4 -   "   "   -   "   "

4th Riding

```
1808 -  5 - Crowell Willson
1812 -  6 - John Fanning (+)
             Isaac Swayze (present 19 Feb., 1814)
1816 -  7 -    "         "
1820 -  8 - Robert Randall
1824 -  9 -    "         "
1828 - 10      "         "
1830 - 11 -    "         "
1834 - 12 - Gilbert McMicking
1836 - 13 -    "         "
```

22. Town of London

1800 - 08 see Oxford, Middlesex, and Norfolk

1808 - 20 see Oxford and Middlesex

1820 - 36 see Middlesex

1836 - separate riding under 1 Geo. IV c. 2 (1820)

    1836 - 13 - Mahlon Burwell

23. Middlesex County

1800 - 20 with Oxford

1820 separate riding under 1 Geo. IV c.2. - 2 members

```
    1820 -  8 - Mahlon Burwell   -    John Bostwick
    1824 -  9 - John Rolph       -        John Mathews
    1828 - 10 -    "     "       -           "     "
    1830 - 11 - Mahlon Burwell   -    Roswell Mount
                                      (19 Jan. 1834+)
    1834 - 12 - Thomas Parke     -    Elias Moore
    1836 - 13 -    "     "       -       "      "
```

24. Town of Niagara

1792 - 1824 see Lincoln

1824 separate riding under 1 Geo. IV c.2 (1820)

```
    1824 -  9 - Edward McBride
    1828 - 10 - Robert Dickson
    1830 - 11 - Henry John Bulton
    1834 - 12 - Charles Richardson
    1836 - 13 -    "         "
```

105

25. Norfolk County

1792 - 1800 by Proclamation of 16 July included with 4th Riding of Lincoln

1800 - 08 with Middlesex

1808 separate riding under 48 Geo. II c.11

    1808 - 5 - Philip Sovereign

    1812 - 6 - Robert Nichol

    1816 - 7 -   "   "

1820 two members under 1 Geo. IV c.2

    1820 - 8 - Robert Nichol   -   Francis Leigh Walsh

    1824 - 9 - Duncan McCall   -   "   "

    1828 - 10 -   "   "   -   Dr. William Warren Baldwin

    1830 - 11 -   "   "   -   William Wilson

        (died 26 Nov., 1832)

        - Colin McNeilledge (seated 14 Jan., 1833)

    1834 - 12 - Dr. David Duncombe   -   Francis Leigh Walsh

    1836 - 13 -   "   "   -   Dr. John Rolph

        (expelled 20 Jan., 1838)

        William Salmon (seated 27 Feb., 1838)

26. Northumberland County

1792 - 1800 with Lennox and Hastings

1800 - 1808 with Hastings

1808 - 1820 with Durham

1820 separate riding under 1 Geo. IV c.2. Two members

    1820 - 8 - David M. Rogers   -   Henry Ruttan

    1824 - 9 - Zaccheus Burnham   -   James Lyons (Lyons was ousted on 23 Feb., 1825 in favour of Benjamin Ewing, but finally declared elected on 28 Mar., 1825)

        1828 - 10 - Benjamin Ewing   -   James Lyons

        1830 - 11 - Archibald Macdonald   -   "   "

        1834 - 12 - Alexander Macdonell   -   John Gilchrist

        1836 - 13 -   "   "   -   Henry Ruttan

27. Ontario County

1792 with Addington by Proclamation of 16 July

   Ontario and Addington

        1792 - 1 - Joshua Booth

        1797 - 2 - Christopher Robinson

                  (+2 Nov., 1798)

                - William Fairfield

                  (12 June, 1799 sworn)

1800 county abolished by 40 Geo. III c.3.

      (Present Ontario county is a different area)

28. Oxford County

1800 Reorganization of province by 40 Geo. III c.3 sets up riding of new counties of Oxford and Middlesex including Norfolk.

   Oxford Middlesex and Norfolk

        1800 - 3 - David W. Smith

        1804 - 4 - Benejah Mallory

1808 Revision under 48 Geo. III c.11 separates Norfolk.

   Oxford and Middlesex

        1808 - 5 - Benejah Mallory

        1812 - 6 - Mahlon Burwell

        1816 - 7 -   "   "

1820 Middlesex separate riding under 1 Geo. IV c.2

   Oxford

        1820 - 8 - Thomas Hornor

        1824 - 9 -   "   "

                                    - Charles Ingersoll

        1828 - 10 -   "   " - Finlay Malcolm

        1830 - 11 - Charles Duncombe - Charles Ingersoll (+)

                                    - Thomas Hornor

                                      (seated 9 Nov., 1832)

107

```
1834 - 12 -    "         "                    - Robert Alway
1836 - 13 -    "         "
         (new writ 20 Jan., 1838)-              "         "
         - Roger Rollo Hunter
         (seated 27 Feb., 1838)
```

29. Prescott County

1800 - 1808 with Glengarry.

1808 separate riding under 48 Geo. III c.11.

```
   1808 - 5 - Thomas Mears
   1812 - 6 -    "         "
   1816 - 7 - John Macdonell
```

1820 combined with Russell as one member riding under 1 Geo. IV c.2.

Prescott and Russell

```
   1820 - 8 - William Hamilton
            (declared not elected 24 Mar., 1821).
          - David Pattie
            (seated 24 Mar., 1821).
   1824 - 9 - Donald Macdonell
   1828 - 10 -    "         "
   1830 - 11 -    "         "
```

1834 Prescott separated from Russell and made a two member riding under 1 Geo. IV c.2. (1820).

Prescott

```
   1834 - 12 - Alexander Macdonell         - Charles Waters
            (+16 Feb., 1835)
          - John Chester (2 Apr., 1835)
   1836 - 13 - John Kearns                 - Richard P. Hotham
```

30. Prince Edward County

1792 by Proclamation of 16 July includes former Township of Adolphus in Lennox.

```
   1792 - 1 - Philip Dorland (19 Sept. 1792 refused oath as a Quaker).
            - Peter Vanalstine ( 1 June, 1793 takes seat).
   1797 - 2 - David McGregor Rogers
```

1800 county separate riding under 40 Geo. III C.3.

```
   1800 - 3 - Ebenezer Washburn
   1804 - 4 -    "         "
```

1808 Township of Ameliasburgh transferred to Hastings 48 Geo. III c. 11.

    1808 - 5 - James Wilson (3 Mar., 1810 unseated)

            - John Stinson (1 Feb., 1811 seated)

    1812 - 6 -   "   "

    1816 - 7 - James Cotter

1820 county a separate riding under 1 Geo. IV c.2. - 2 seats

    1820 - 8 - James Wilson   -   Paul Peterson

    1824 - 9 -   "   "   -   "   "

    1828 - 10 -   "   "   -   "   "

    1830 - 11 - Asa Werden   -   John Roblin

    1834 - 12 James Wilson   -   John P. Roblin

    1836 - 13 - James R. Armstrong   -   Charles Bockus (or

                                                        Bochus)

31. Russell County

1800 - 20 - with Stormont

1820 - 34 - with Prescott

1834 separate riding under provisions of 1 Geo. IV c.2 (1820)

    1834 - 12 - Thomas MacKay

    1836 - 13 -   "   "

32. Simcoe County

1800 -08 - with Durham and East Riding York

1808 - 20 - with East Riding York

1820 - 28 - with York

1828 Separate riding under 1 Geo. IV c.2. (1820)

    1828 - 10 - John Cawthra

    1830 - 11 - William Beverley Robinson

1834 2 members under same

    1834 - 12 - William B. Robinson - Samuel Lount

    1836 - 13 -   "   "   - Charles Wickens

33. Stormont County

1792 created by Proclamation of 16 July

    1792 - 1 - Jeremiah French

    1797 - 2 - Robert Isaac Dey Gray

1800 40 Geo. III c.3. Stormont combined with Russell in one member riding.

Stormont and Russell

    1800 - 3 - Robert Isaac Dey Gray

    1804 - 4 -   "   "   "   "   (Oct., 1804+)

              D'Arcy Boulton Sr. (5 Feb., 1806 seated)

    1808 - 5 - John Brownell   (Dec., 1809+)

              Abraham Marsh (18 Sept., 1810 elected, 1 Feb., 1811

                  seated)

    1812 - 6 - John Beikie

    1816 - 7 - Philip Vankoughnet

1820 1 Geo. IV c.2. Stormont separated from Russell and made two member riding

    Stormont

    1820 - 8 - Philip Vankoughnet   -   Archibald McLean

    1824 - 9 -   "   "   -   "   "

    1828 - 10 - Ambrose Blacklock   -   "   "

    1830 - 11 - Philip Vankoughnet   -   "   "

    1834 - 12 - William Bruce   -   Donald AE. Macdonell

    1836 - 13 - Archibald McLean   -   "   "

              (4 Mar., 1837)

              Alexander McLean

              (20 Dec., 1837 seated)

34. Suffolk County

1792 combined with Essex as riding by Proclamation of 16 July

    Suffolk and Essex

    1792 - 1 - David William Smith

    1797 - 2 - John Cornwall

1798 county abolished by 38 Geo. III c.5.

35. Wentworth County

1792 - 1817 see York W. Riding and Lincoln

1817 one member under 57 Geo. III c.1.

    1817 - 7 - James Durand (Durand was expelled for an attack on the
                  House (7 Mar. 1817), but re-elected (15 May
                  1817[G] and was seated 6 Feb., 1818)

1820 2 members under 1 Geo. IV c.2

    1820 - 8 - George Hamilton   -   John Willson

    1824 - 9 -   "   "   -   "   "

1828 - 10 -	"	"	-	" "
1830 - 11 -	Allan MacNab		-	" "
1834 - 12 -	Harmannus Smith		-	Jacob Rymal
1836 - 13 -	Allan MacNab		-	Michael Aikman

36. York County

1792 - 1800 with Durham and 1st riding Lincoln

1800 under 40 Geo. III c.3, York divided into two Ridings Durham, East Riding York and Simcoe (see Durham)

West Riding York, part 1st Riding Lincoln and Haldimand (two members)

West Riding York, 1st Riding Lincoln and Haldimand

1800 - 3 - Robert Nelles   -   Richard Beasley

1804 - 4 - Solomon Hill   -   Joseph Willcocks

1808 divided into two ridings East Riding York and Simcoe, and West Riding York

East Riding York and Simcoe

1808 - 5 - Thomas B. Gough

1812 - 6 - Thomas Ridout

1816 - 7 - Peter Robinson

West Riding York

1808 - 5 - Richard Beasley (unseated 1809)

        John Willson (seated 1 Feb., 1810)

1812 - 6 - "   "   (ill 19 Feb., 1814)

        Abraham Markle (deserted)

        James Durand (present 7 Feb., 1816)

1816 - 7 - see Halton and Wentworth

1820 riding with Simcoe under 1 Geo. IV c.2.

York and Simcoe

1820 - 8 - Peter Robinson   -   William Warren Baldwin

1824 - 9 - William Thompson   -   Ely Playter (Left

                                            province but seat

                                            declared not vacant

                                            17 Feb., 1827)

1828 Simcoe separated by 1 Geo. IV c.2. (1820)

York

1828 - 10 - Jesse Ketchum   -   William L. Mackenzie

        1830 - 11 -   "   "   -   "   "

                                            (This was the
                                            parliament from which
                                            W. L. Mackenzie was
                                            expelled five times
                                            but re-elected each
                                            time)

   1833 York County divided into four ridings each with one member by 3 Wm.
        IV c.15.

   ### 1st Riding

        1834 - 12 - David Gibson

        1836 - 13 -   "   "   (expelled - fled 15 Jan. 1838)

                - John W. Gamble (seated 5 Feb. 1838)

   ### 2nd Riding

        1834 - 12 - William Lyon Mackenzie

        1836 - 13 - Edward W. Thompson

   ### 3rd Riding

        1834 - 12 - Thomas D. Morrison, M.D.

        1836 - 13 -   "   "   (fled-new writ 28 Mar., 1839)

                - James Edward Small (seated 29 Apr. 1839)

   ### 4th Riding

        1834 - 12 - John McIntosh

        1836 - 13 -   "   "

37. Town of York (City of Toronto, 1834)

   1792 - 1820 see York County

   1820 separate riding under 1 Geo. IV c.2.

        1820 - 8 - John Beverley Robinson

        1824 - 9 -   "   "   "

        1828 - 10 -   "   "   "

        1829 - 10 - Robert Baldwin

        1830 - 11 - William Botsford Jarvis

        1834 - 12 - James Edward Small

        1836 - 13 - William Henry Draper

d. Speakers of the House of Assembly

Parliament	Speakers		Dates	
1	John Macdonell		1792 -	1796
2	David William Smith	16 May,	1797 -	5 June, 1800
	Samuel Street	5 June,	1800 -	7 July, 1800
3	David William Smith	30 May,	1801 -	1802
	Richard Beasley		1803 -	1804
4	Alexander Macdonell	1 Feb.,	1805 -	1807
5	Samuel Street	3 Feb.,	1809^G -	1811
6 - 7	Allan McLean		1812 -	1820
8	Levius Peters Sherwood		1821 -	1824
9	John Willson		1825 -	1828
10	Marshall Spring Bidwell	9 Jan.,	1829^G -	1830
11	Archibald McLean	8 Jan.,	1831^G -	1834
12	Marshall Spring Bidwell		1835 -	1836
13	Archibald McLean	9 Nov.,	1836 -	4 Mar., 1837
	Allan Napier MacNab	19 June,	1837 -	28 Dec., 1837
	Henry Ruttan (pro tem.)	28 Dec.,	1837 -	24 Jan., 1838
	Allan Napier MacNab	24 Jan.,	1838 -	10 Feb., 1841

e. Staff of the House of Assembly
1. Clerks

Angus Macdonell (Collachie)	12 Dec.,	1792^A -	30 May, 1801
Donald McLean (or Maclean)	12 Mar.,	1801 -	May, 1813
Grant Powell	18 May,	1813 -	4 May, 1827
James FitzGibbon	4 May,	1827 -	10 Feb., 1841

2. Clerks of the Crown in Chancery

The official in charge of issuing the writs for elections.

John Small	22 May,	1793 -	
David Burns			- 6 Feb., 1806+
Samuel Peters Jarvis	17 May,	1817 -	(1837)

3. Chaplains

The office seems to have been passed back and forth at times.

Rev. Robert Addison		1792 -	6 Oct., 1829+
Rev. George Okill Stuart	7 Nov.,	1807 -	1812?
Rev. Thomas Phillips	21 Dec.,	1829^G -	31 Oct., 1834

4. Sergeants-at-Arms

George Lane	12 Sept.,	1792	-	1 Feb.,	1810
Thomas Ridout	17 July,	1798	-		
- Thomas Hamilton (Deputy)	2 Feb.,	1810^A	-		
William Stanton	1 Jan.,	1811	-	1 Feb.,	1812
- Stephen Jarvis (Acting)	4 Feb.,	1812^A	-		
Allan MacNab	May,	1813	-	17 Oct.,	1828+
David Archibald MacNab	15 Oct.,	1828	-	10 Feb.,	1841
- William Hepburn (Deputy)	6 Nov.,	1832^A	-	13 Feb.,	1833
- Andrew Stewart (Deputy)	5 Dec.,	1839^A	-		

5. Librarians

George Mayer	1792	-	1823
Robert Baldwin Sullivan	(1828)	- 14 Mar.,	1836
Alpheus Todd	(1837)	-	
Jasper Brewer	(1838)	-	
William Winder	(1838)	-	1855

6. Doorkeepers

Hugh Mclean	17 July,	1798	-	
Hugh Cameron	22 May,	1801	-	
Thomas Ridout Johnson	8 Sept.,	1804	-	
William Knott Sr.	27 Sept.,	1816	-	1833+
Hugh McLennan	15 Oct.,	1833^g	-	(1835)

Part IV
The Judiciary and The Legal Profession

A. The Judiciary
a. Introduction

One of the main difficulties faced by the early Loyalist settlers was the lack of court facilities, the nearest courts being at Montreal. After what is now southern Ontario was divided into four districts by the Proclamation of 24 July, 1788, some attempt was made to provide for the colonists' needs by setting up a Court of Common Pleas in each district; but the system did not work too well because of a lack of lawyers and the difficulties created by French civil law. In 1792 the first English law in matters of property and civil rights (32 Geo. III. c.1), was passed and two years later Governor Simcoe and Chief Justice Osgoode completely revised the court system and created a high court for the province in the Court of the King's Bench (34 Geo. III, c.2.). At the same time the Courts of Common Pleas were abolished. The King's Bench remained the superior court of the province throughout the Upper Canadian period. in 1835 the judges of the King's Bench were made independent of the Crown, that is, henceforth they held office on "good behaviour" rather than "at the pleasure of His Majesty" and were thus freed from potential political control.

For minor matters the justices of the peace (or magistrates) meeting in the Courts of Quarter Sessions had judicial as well as administrative authority. In 1792 the magistrates were empowered to set up Courts of Requests (roughly Division Courts) by 32 Geo. III, c.6. These could try minor cases (up to 40 shillings Quebec currency). They continued throughout the Upper Canadian period.

The magistrates have not been listed as some 1700 of them were commissioned by regular "commissions of the peace" and others (sometimes overlapping) by commissions of association.

After the abolition of the Court of Common Pleas a District Court was set up in each district (34 Geo. III, c.3) for cases of moderate importance not involving title to land (40 shillings to £15). The District Courts are the ancestors of the modern County and Judicial District Courts. For the settlement of estates a provincial Court of Probate and district Surrogate Courts were established in 1793 (33 Geo. III, c.8).

There was no Court of Chancery—the body in charge of equity cases—until 1837. The Lieutenant-Governor was automatically the Chancellor of the province and some minor officials were appointed to administer chancery matters. After 1837 there was a formal court under a Vice-Chancellor (7 Wm. IV, c.2).

There were four court terms in the year:
Hilary   - 3rd Monday in January.
Easter   - Monday next after April 16.
Trinity   - 3rd Monday in July.
Michaelmas   - 1st Monday in October.

b. The Courts of Common Pleas

When the first four districts were established in 1788 each was provided with a Court of Common Pleas with unlimited civil, but no criminal, jurisdiction. Criminal cases were sent to Montreal. Each district court was to have three judges, who were appointed from among the leading citizens of the region, as there were no lawyers in the western part of the Province of Quebec. Because of the protests of the merchants in the Detroit area, and the fact that two of the three judges who were appointed refused to sit, William Dummer Powell, a lawyer in Montreal, was sent out as the sole judge of the District of Hesse (later the Western District), which included that centre.

After the formation of Upper Canada in 1791 criminal cases could no longer be taken to Montreal, and from 1792 on English common law replaced French civil law (32 Geo. III c.l.). During this period commissions for judges continued to be issued for the individual districts; but some judges were commissioned for the province generally. Finally, in 1794, the Courts of Common Pleas were abolished by the Judicature Act (34 Geo. III c.2) which set up a new high court for the entire province, the Court of the King's Bench. Thus these initial courts had an existence of six years only.

The early Courts of Common Pleas should not be confused with the new Court of Common Pleas which was established on 1 Jan., 1850. This was a court of concurrent jurisdiction with the King's Bench with authority across the province. It was created because of the increasing number of cases which had to be heard.

As many of the judges of Common Pleas do not appear in the "General Index of Commissions" the following table is a combination of the names on existing commissions and the judges listed in such studies as the various works of Justice William R. Riddell on the subject. Some of the judges who were commissioned never acted (marked NA on table), and some of the judges who were most prominent in the courts may never have been commissioned.

1. Lunenburgh (Eastern) District - sitting at Cornwall, Osnabruck, Stormont and New Johnstown

Judges

Richard Duncan	24 July, 1788	-	28 Feb., 1793
Edward Jessup	24 July, 1788	-	Sept., 1790
Alexander McDonnell	24 July, 1788	-	
John McDonell	7 Jan., 1790	-	1794
John Munro	Dec., 1792	-	1794

Clerk

Jacob Farrand	24 July, 1788	-

2. Mecklenburg (Midland) District - sittings at Kingston, and once at Adolphustown

Judges

John Stuart	24 July, 1788	-
Neil McLean	24 July, 1788	-
James Clarke	24 July, 1788 -	8 July, 1789
Richard Cartwright Jr.	16 Oct., 1788	-
James McDonell	14 Oct., 1790	-
Hector McLean	15 Oct., 1790	-

Clerk

Peter Clarke   26 July, 1788 -

3. Nassau (Home) District - sittings probably at Newark

Judges

John Butler	24 July, 1788	-
Robert Hamilton	24 July, 1788	-
Jesse Pawling	NA	22 Oct., 1788

(commissioned in error for Benjamin Pawling and appointed a coroner instead)

Benjamin Pawling	24 Oct., 1788	-
Peter Tenbrook (Ten Broeck) NA	24 Oct., 1788	-
Nathaniel Pettitt	24 Oct., 1788	-

Clerks

Philip Fry	24 July, 1788 -
Ralfe Clench	17 June, 1790 -

4. Hesse (Western) District - sittings at L'Assumption (Sand-wich).

Jacques Duperron Baby Sr.	NA	1788 -	Sept., 1788
William Robertson	NA	24 July, 1788 -	Sept., 1788
Alexander McKee	NA	24 July, 1788 -	(1788)
William Dummer Powell (sole judge)		2 Feb., 1789 -	1794

Upper Canada Generally -

William Dummer Powell	31 Dec., 1791 -
Peter Russell	27 June, 1793 -

c. The Court of the King's Bench

The high court of the province was established by 34 Geo. III, c.2, 1794. It originally consisted of a chief justice and two puisne (associate) justices, but the number of puisne judges was increased to four by 7 Wm. IV c.1, 1837.

1. Chief Justices

William Osgoode	31 Dec., 1791 -	24 Feb., 1794
John Elmsley	21 Nov., 1796 -	13 Oct., 1802
Henry Allcock	7 Oct., 1802 -	1 July, 1805
Thomas Scott	22 Jan., 1806 -	1816
William Dummer Powell	1 Oct., 1816 -	1825
Sir William Campbell	17 Oct., 1825 -	1829
Sir John Beverley Robinson	13 July, 1829 -	14 Mar., 1862

2. Puisné (Associate) Judges

William Dummer Powell	31 Dec., 1791 -	1 Oct., 1816
Peter Russell	15 July, 1795 -	30 Nov., 1798?
Henry Allcock	30 Nov., 1798 -	1 Oct., 1802
Thomas Cochrane	25 July, 1803 -	7 Oct., 1804+
Robert Thorpe	1 Jan., 1805 -	30 Oct., 1807
William Campbell	18 Nov., 1811 -	17 Oct., 1825
D'Arcy Boulton Sr.	12 Feb., 1818 -	4 Apr., 1827
Levius Peters Sherwood	17 Oct., 1825 -	18 Apr., 1839
James Buchanan Macaulay	3 July, 1827 -	26 Sept., 1827
John Walpole Willis	26 Sept., 1827 -	26 June, 1828
Christopher A. Hagerman	26 June, 1828 -	13 July, 1829
James Buchanan Macaulay	13 July, 1829 -	14 Dec., 1849
Archibald McLean	23 Mar., 1837 -	31 Dec., 1849
Jonas Jones	23 Mar., 1837 -	30 July, 1848+
Christopher A. Hagerman	15 Feb., 1840 -	12 May, 1847+

3. Clerks of the Crown and of the Common Pleas

The official who was in charge of the administrative side of the court's work both in York and on the assizes.

David Burns	31 Dec., 1791 -	c15 Feb., 1806+
John Beikie (deputy)		
Dr. William Warren Baldwin (acting)	1806	
John Small	12 Mar., 1806 -	10 Aug., 1825
Charles Coxwell Small	10 Aug., 1825 -	17 Mar., 1864+

4. Reporters

In the early days there was no reporter to arrange the publication of the court's decisions for the use of the legal profession. Provision was made for such an official under 4 Geo. IV, c.3, 1823, the reporter being appointed by the governor. The system failed to produce regular reports and in 1840 the Law Society was given the authority to appoint the reporter under 3 Vic., c.2, 1840.

Thomas Taylor	9 July, 1823^G	-
Simon Ebenezer Washburn	4 May, 1829	-
William Henry Draper	12 Nov., 1829^G -	13 Mar., 1837
Henry Sherwood	1837 -	2 Nov., 1840
John Hillyard Cameron	7 Nov., 1840 -	1846

d. The Court of Chancery

In the early years there was no Court of Chancery in the province. Technically the Lieutenant-Governor as Keeper of the Great Seal of the province was Chancellor and could preside over a court of equity (4 Eliz. I, c. 18, 1562). The Master in Chancery and minor officials handled the administration of chancery cases under the general jurisdiction of the Court of the King's Bench.

In 1837, after many years of discussion, a Court of Chancery was finally established with a vice-chancellor acting for the governor (7 Wm. 4, c.2). Since only solicitors could appear before such a court all barristers and attornies in the province were declared to be also solicitors.

1. Vice-Chancellors

Robert Sympson Jameson	23 Mar., 1837	-	31 Dec., 1849

2. Masters in Chancery

John McGill	22 May, 1793	-	
David Burns	(1803)	-	
William Warren Baldwin	5 Feb., 1806	-	(1815)
D'Arcy Boulton Jr.	22 Oct., 1828	-	(1835)
John G. Spragge	20 June, 1837^G	-	

3. Registrars

John Small	22 May, 1793	-	
William Hepburn	22 May, 1837^G	-	(1839)
J. G. Spragge	13 July, 1844	-	

4. Sergeants at Arms

William Botsford Jarvis	12 June, 1838	-

e. The Court of Probate

A Court of Probate and Surrogate Courts in each district were established by 33 Geo. III, c.8, 1793. Generally, the Court of Probate had jurisdiction over estates that were over a certain value or located in several districts and the Surrogate Courts handled wills limited to a single district. (See under districts for Surrogate Court Judges). The Probate Court was abolished under the Surrogate Court Act of 1858, the Surrogate Courts assuming its functions.

1. Official Principals

AEneas Shaw	7 Apr., 1794 -	
David Burns	22 May, 1796 -	6 Feb., 1806+
Donald McLean	26 May, 1806 -	
Grant Powell	Apr., 1813 -	10 June, 1838+
William Hepburn	11 Dec., 1838 -	
Secker Brough	13 July, 1844 -	

2. Registrars

Alexander Burns	22 May, 1796 -	
Joseph Willcocks (dismissed)	9 May, 1803 -	10 Apr., 1807
Miles McDonell	11 Apr., 1807 -	
William Warren Baldwin	19 Nov., 1808^G -	
Stephen Heward	28 Dec., 1816^G -	
James FitzGibbon	8 Sept., 1828 -	**1842**
Charles FitzGibbon	11 Apr., 1842 -	

B. The Legal Profession

a. Introduction

In the years immediately following the creation of the first courts in Upper Canada there were only two trained lawyers in the province: William Dummer Powell, the judge of the Western District; and Walter Roe who practised in the Detroit area. The other men who practised before the courts were, like the other judges, untrained in the law. They were permitted to practise under "letters of Procuration". With the coming of Chief Justice William Osgoode and Attorny-General John White the number of men with legal training in the province was doubled.

After the establishment of the Court of the King's Bench in 1794 some drastic action was necessary. To create the nucleus of a legal profession, Simcoe was authorized to grant sixteen selected men without legal training a license to practise as advocates or attorneys. These were appointed in 1794-96, mostly from the official circle.

In 1797, under the aegis of White, the Legislature passed the first act regulating the legal profession in the province (37 Geo. III, c.13). This not only arranged for the training of lawyers in the colony, but also made provision for a Law Society of Upper Canada to regulate the legal profession. Shortly after it was passed the lawyers met at Newark on 17 July, 1797, and established the society with 15 initial members. Administration was placed in the hands of a Treasurer and board of Benchers, who were self-perpetuating until 1871. The act has been amended at various times, the most important change being in 1822 when a parallel body with the same name was incorporated so the Law Society could hold land.

With the establishment of a governing body, and the regulation of legal training, the legal profession in Upper Canada rapidly became one of the most influential groups in the province. It is for this reason that complete tables of the members are provided, for the lawyers constantly appear in all aspects of both the local and the provincial government.

b. Treasurers of the Law Society of Upper Canada, 1797-1841

The treasurer was the chief official of The Law Society of Upper Canada. He changed office at one of the four court terms in which the year was divided: Hilary, Easter, Trinity and Michaelmas.

John White	T. 1797 - T. 1798
Robert I. D. Grey	T. 1798 - E. 1801
Angus Macdonell	E. 1801 - E. 1805
Thomas Scott	E. 1805 - H. 1806
D'Arcy Boulton (1st)	H. 1806 - M. 1811
Dr. William Warren Baldwin (1st)	M. 1811 - M. 1815
D'Arcy Boulton (2nd)	M. 1815 - E. 1818
(Sir) John Beverly Robinson (1st)	E. 1818 - M. 1819
Henry John Boulton (1st)	M. 1819 - M. 1820
Dr. W. W. Baldwin (2nd)	M. 1820 - M. 1821
J. B. Robinson (2nd)	M. 1821 - M. 1822
Henry John Boulton (2nd)	M. 1822 - M. 1824
Dr. W. W. Baldwin (3rd)	M. 1824 - H. 1828
J. B. Robinson (3rd)	H. 1828 - M. 1829
George Ridout	M. 1829 - H. 1832
Dr. W. W. Baldwin (4th)	H. 1832 - H. 1836
Robert Baldwin Sullivan	H. 1836 - M. 1836
Robert Simpson Jameson (1st)	M. 1836 - M. 1841
Livius Peters Sherwood	M. 1841 - M. 1843
William Henry Draper	M. 1843 - M. 1845
R. S. Jameson (2nd)	M. 1845 - M. 1846
Henry John Boulton (3rd)	M. 1846 - M. 1847
Robert Baldwin (1st)	M. 1847 - M. 1848
James Edward Small	M. 1848 - M. 1849

c. Attorneys

The title formerly used for the lawyer who carried on proceedings before the common law courts (in Upper Canada The King's Bench). He could not be a barrister unless enrolled separately. In a few cases the exact date of admission is uncertain.

Name	Date of Admission
A	
Armstrong, Christopher	3 May 1834
Ackland, Gideon	27 June 1836
Armour, J. G.	11 June 1838
Ainslie, Adam	12 June 1839
Armour, Robert	9 June 1840
Asken, W. H. Z.	3 Nov. 1840
B	
Beardsley, B. C.	26 May 1796
Boulton, D'Arcy, Sr.	22 Jan. 1803
Baldwin, W. W.	22 Jan. 1803
Boulton, D'Arcy, Jr.	10 Mar. 1807
Bostwick, Henry	13 Jan. 1808
Breakenridge, J.	13 July 1816
Boulton, Henry John	5 Nov. 1816
Butler, T.	16 July 1817
Boulton, George S.	2 July 1818
Bidwell, M. S.	13 Apr. 1821
Buell, A. N.	5 Nov. 1821
Barry, Robert	14 Nov. 1821
Boulton, James	15 Nov. 1822
Boswell, John	24 Apr. 1823
Bethune, Donald	9 July 1823
Burrell, M.	19 Jan. 1825
Baldwin, Robert	23 June 1825
Burns, R. E.	8 Jan. 1827
Boswell, G. M.	21 Apr. 1828
Beaseley, Charles	6 Nov. 1828
Bogart, John	5 Jan. 1830
Beasley, R. G.	12 Nov. 1832
Ball, J.	7 Nov. 1833
Burton, E.	14 Nov. 1833
Burk, C. F.	11 Nov. 1834
Baldwin, Henry, Jr.	15 Nov. 1834
Bethune, Angus	3 Feb. 1835
Burnham, E.	21 Apr. 1835
Barrett, Read	14 Nov. 1835
Boulton, W. H.	14 Nov. 1835
Boswell, William	20 June 1836
Benson, C. O.	25 June 1836
Bell, D. M.	19 Nov. 1836
Blackstone, H. W.	13 Feb. 1837
Boulton, D. E.	19 Aug. 1837
Blake, W. H.	10 Feb. 1838
Bonnycastle, H. W. J.	10 Jan. 1839
Brough, Secker	4 Nov. 1839
Burns, Thomas	5 Nov. 1839
Brock, George	3 Feb. 1840
Burnham, Z.	8 June 1840
Baby, W. D.	5 Aug. 1840
Becher, Henry C. R.	2 Nov. 1840
Burton, G. W.	21 June 1841
Boomer, George	6 Aug. 1841
Billings, J.	13 Nov. 1841

C

Clark, James	7 Jan. 1794
Cameron, Alex	9 Jan. 1808
Cartwright, J.	6 July 1808
Cozen, W.	18 Nov. 1820
Cassady, Henry	5 July 1822
Clive, Robert	19 Jan. 1825
Chewett, Alex	20 Apr. 1825
Cartwright, John S.	7 Nov. 1825
Campbell, W. A.	1 May 1827
Campbell, E. G.	28 Dec. 1829
Claus, Warren	22 June 1830
Cummings, George A.	10 Nov. 1835
Covert, Henry	1 July 1836
Chrysler, G. M.	6 Feb. 1837
Cameron, John	22 Apr. 1837
Cansy, Peter John	16 Feb. 1838
Cameron, J. H.	7 Aug. 1838
Crooks, R. P.	4 Feb. 1839
Crawford, John	10 June 1839
Cahill, James	10 June 1839
Crayton, F.	22 June 1839
Cleverley, F.	5 Feb. 1840
Campbell, A.	13 Jan. 1841
Campbell, S. B.	14 June 1841

D

Dickson, William	22 Jan. 1803
Dickson, Robert	8 Jan. 1821
Dickson, William	6 Nov. 1822
Draper, W. H.	11 Nov. 1828
Dalton, Thomas	10 Jan. 1829
Dougall, B.	
Dickson, W. H.	28 Dec. 1829
Doyle, James	19 Apr. 1830
Duggan, George	16 Nov. 1833
Davis, Joseph	4 Nov. 1835
Duggan, R. C.	8 Nov. 1836
Dobbs, A. H.	4 Dec. 1837
Denison, G. T.	10 June 1839
Duggan, John	
Duff, Alex	2 Nov. 1840

E

Elliott, William	22 Jan. 1803
Elliott, John	12 June 1837
Eccles, Henry	3 Aug. 1840

F

Farrand, Jacob	20 Oct. 1794
Farrand, J. L.	13 Jan. 1806
Fairfield, B. J. Jr.	16 July 1819
Fairfield, D. L.	4 Jan. 1827
Ford, David B. C.	15 Nov. 1827
Foster, C. A.	
Freel, Peter	2 May 1832
Forsyth, J. R.	16 June 1834
Forward, W. A.	17 June 1835
Foster, Colley	13 Feb. 1837
Fowley, Harvey	12 Feb. 1838
Fergusson, A. J.	11 Feb. 1839
Freeman, S. B.	8 Jan. 1840
Fraser, Douglas	1 Feb. 1841
Fairbanks, S. B.	3 Feb. 1841
FitzGibbon, W. W.	3 Feb. 1841
Foley, B.	9 Aug. 1841
FitzGerald, W. J.	13 Aug. 1841

G

Grey, Robert I. D.	22 Oct. 1794
Givens, James	27 Apr. 1827
Gamble, C.	23 Apr. 1832
Grant, Alex	16 June 1834
Glassford, George	27 June 1836
Gwynne, John W.	19 Jan. 1837
Gowan, J. R.	4 Feb. 1839
Geddes, W. A.	10 June 1839
Gellehar, P.	22 June 1839
Geddes, James	6 Aug. 1840
Givens, A.	9 Feb. 1841

H

Hagerman, Nicholas	20 Oct. 1794
Hagerman, C. A.	16 Jan. 1813
Hagerman, Dan	6 Nov. 1815
Hotham, P. P.	2 Nov. 1824
Hawley, P.	16 Nov. 1827
Hagerman, J. A.	10 Jan. 1829
Hirchmer, Joseph R.	10 Jan. 1829
Heward, C. R.	
Hubbell, James	8 Nov. 1830
Heward, H. C.	5 May 1832
Hatt, John O.	1 May 1833
Hamilton, Robert	8 Nov. 1833
Hall, C. L.	13 Nov. 1833
Hubbell, E. J.	16 June 1834
Hamilton, Joseph	24 June 1834
Heward, Henry	27 Apr. 1835
Hitchings, E.	8 June 1836
Hector, John	7 Feb. 1839
Holland, R. L.	5 Aug. 1839
Horton, W.	6 Aug. 1839
Hagarty, J. H.	8 June 1840
Hall, E. B.	6 Nov. 1840
Hamilton, M.	19 June 1841
Hagarty, Henry	3 Aug. 1841

I and J

Jones, Jonathan	6 Nov. 1811
Jones, Jonas	6 Nov. 1812
Jones, David	9 Apr. 1815
Jarvis, Samuel	5 July 1815
Jones, Daniel Jr.	5 July 1815
Jarvis, George S.	14 Nov. 1820
Jones, Israel F.	22 Apr. 1829
Jessop, James	3 July 1830
Jones, Stewart	9 Nov. 1832
Jameson, R. S.	22 Apr. 1834
Jones, Ormond	23 Apr. 1834

K

King, James	6 Nov. 1827
Kirkpatrick, Thomas	3 Nov. 1828
Kirkpatrick, Stafford F.	27 June 1834
Kornish, William	27 Apr. 1835
Keele, William Conway	17 Apr. 1837
Kirchoffer, N.	11 Feb. 1840
Keer, Thomas	2 Nov. 1840

L

Lyons, John	13 Nov. 1824
Low, John	7 Nov. 1827

Law, John	10 Feb. 1834
Low, Philip	3 Nov. 1835
Lyons, George B.	13 June 1838
Loring, W. G.	18 Aug. 1838
Lapenotière, W.	7 Nov. 1838
Lewis, J. B. Jr.	15 Nov. 1839
Latham, H.	14 June 1841

M

Mallock, George	15 Nov. 1822
Muirhead J. B.	16 July 1823
Merrill, Samuel	7 Nov. 1823
Murney, William	27 Apr. 1830
Mulholland, B.	27 Apr. 1830
Murney, Edmund	5 Nov. 1833
Meyers, A. H.	8 Nov. 1833
Miller, W.	5 Nov. 1834
Miller, John	5 Nov. 1834
Milne, A. S.	3 Nov. 1835
Morrison, J. C.	5 Feb. 1838
Moore, John	13 Aug. 1838
Murney, Wellington	4 Feb. 1839
Miller, R. B.	10 June 1839
Muttlebury, E. C.	22 June 1839
Moore, Thomas	11 Feb. 1840
Maddock, J. F.	15 Feb. 1840
Miller, Richard	3 Aug. 1840
Merrick, T. H.	11 Nov. 1840
Mowat, O.	5 Nov. 1841

Mc

McDonald, Angus	7 July 1794
McLean, Allan	7 July 1794
McDonald, John	6 July 1808
McLean, A.	7 Apr. 1813
Macaulay, J. B.	1 Nov. 1819
Macaulay, Robert	17 Apr. 1820
Macaulay, George	29 Apr. 1822
McMartin, Daniel	3 May 1823
McLean, James A.	
MacNab, A. N.	11 Nov. 1826
Mackenzie, George	4 Jan. 1828
Macaulay, J. H.	4 Jan. 1828
McDonald, Alexander	3 Nov. 1828
McDonald, John R.	5 Nov. 1828
McLean, Robert C. A.	5 Nov. 1828
McPherson, L.	5 Nov. 1828
McDonald, George	19 Apr. 1830
McDonell, Rolland	8 Feb. 1832
McIntosh, James	2 May 1832
McKeyes, B.	3 May 1832
McDonald, Allan	12 Nov. 1832
McMillen, A. J.	12 Nov. 1832
Macdonald, J. A.	5 Feb. 1835
McPherson, A.	23 June 1836
McQueen, D. O.	27 Apr. 1837
Macnamara, M. J.	4 Dec. 1837
Macaulay, D. W. B.	14 Aug. 1838
Macdonald, John	4 Nov. 1839
Macdonald, John S.	3 Feb. 1840

N

Nicholls, James, Jr.	21 Jan. 1824
Notman, William	10 Jan. 1827

O

Oliver, Charles .... 19 Apr. 1830
O'Reilly, Miles .... 22 June 1830
O'Reilly, H. R. .... 4 Nov. 1835

P

Powell, W. D. Jr. .... 3 Nov. 1795
Phillips, Davenport .... 6 Nov. 1795
Peters, Charles J. .... 4 Jan. 1796
Peters, W. B. .... 26 May 1796
Powell, John .... 22 Jan. 1803
Price, J. H. .... 24 June 1833
Powell, John .... 3 Nov. 1834
Price, John .... 15 Aug. 1838
Pringle, J. F. .... 10 Nov. 1838
Powell, W. D. .... 6 Nov. 1839
Phillpotts, G. A. .... 13 Aug. 1841

R

Ridout, George .... 4 Jan. 1813
Robinson, J. B. .... 4 Jan. 1813
Richardson, F. X. .... 14 Nov. 1820
Rolph, George .... 6 Jan. 1821
Rolph, John .... 7 Nov. 1821
Radenhurst, Thomas .... 21 Apr. 1824
Robinson, R. C. .... 19 Jan. 1825
Richardson, Charles .... 30 June 1826
Ridout, John .... 22 Apr. 1828
Rapelje, P. W. .... 23 June 1828
Raymond, L. D. .... 19 June 1835
Robertson, S. F. .... 28 Apr. 1836
Richardson, P. W. .... 29 Apr. 1836
Roberts, B. W. .... 16 June 1837
Richards, W. B. .... 24 June 1837
Ridout, Edward T. .... 18 Aug. 1838
Ross, John .... 17 June 1839
Robertson, James .... 21 June 1839
Raymond, E. B. .... 3 Nov. 1840

S

Smith, D. W. .... 7 Jan. 1794
Stewart, Alex .... 6 Nov. 1795
Sherwood, Samuel .... 26 May 1796
Sherwood, L. P. .... 22 Jan. 1803
Small, J. R. .... 6 Apr. 1808
Strick, J. B. .... 7 July 1819
Small, James E. .... 13 Jan. 1821
Stewart, Alex .... 14 Apr. 1821
Samson, J. H. .... 3 Nov. 1823
Smith, D. W. .... 7 Nov. 1823
Small, C. C. .... 21 Apr. 1824
Salmon, W. .... 7 Nov. 1827
Sullivan, R. B. .... 22 Apr. 1828
Sherwood, Henry ....
Spragge, J. G. .... 14 Nov. 1828
Secord, Charles B. .... 28 Jan. 1829
Stuart, John .... 8 Feb. 1832
Strachan, G. C. .... 1 May 1833
Sherwood, G. .... 24 June 1833
Smith, Henry D. .... 4 Nov. 1833
Smith, James .... 20 June 1834
Stanton, G. H. .... 4 Nov. 1835
Smith, John S. .... 2 July 1836
Scott, James .... 19 Nov. 1836
Strachan, John .... 12 June 1837

Steele, R. F.	12 Dec.	1837
Street, Thomas C.	12 Feb.	1838
Strachan, James McGill	16 Feb.	1838
Sullivan, A. B.	6 Aug.	1838
Start, John	7 Aug.	1838
Smart, W. J.	22 June	1839
Stevenson, J. G.	22 June	1839
Stuart, Charles	6 Aug.	1839
Stewart, John	4 Aug.	1840
Secord. E. W.	3 Nov.	1840

T

Tickell, R. B.	7 June	1794
Tinbrook, Jno	17 Jan.	1801
Thompson, Timothy	20 July	1801
Taylor, Thomas	8 Jan.	1819
Taylor, T. H.		
Taylor, J. J.	12 Nov.	1832
Tiffany, G. S.	8 Feb.	1833
Taylor, R. W.	27 June	1833
Taylor, J. F.	30 Apr.	1835
Throop, W. H.	5 Feb.	1838
Talbot, R.	13 June	1841
Turner, Robert J.	19 Aug.	1841

W

Weeks, William	1 Apr.	1798
Walker, William	10 Jan.	1800
Walker, Edward	10 Jan.	1800
Wilkinson, W. B.	18 Apr.	1801
Ward, Thomas	15 July	1802
Walker, Hamilton	5 July	1811
Washburn, Daniel	12 Apr.	1815
Washburn, Simon	14 Jan.	1820
Whitehead, F. M.	14 Jan.	1822
Wilkinson, Alexander	2 Nov.	1824
Winterbottom, W. B.	31 Dec.	1827
Wilson, Adam	8 Feb.	1830
Wallbridge, L.	11 Feb.	1830
Woods, James	30 Apr.	1830
Wallis, William	8 Nov.	1830
Ward, G. C.	24 June	1833
Wills, W. B.	5 Nov.	1833
Wilson, John	5 Nov.	1834
Walker, John	7 Nov.	1836
Warren, T. G.	13 Feb.	1837
Wilkes, F. T.	12 June	1837
Wills, G. D.	6 Aug.	1839
Wilson, H. B.	17 June	1841

d. Barristers

In English law only the barrister could actually plead before the bar in any common law court. In Upper Canada almost all lawyers were barristers. A roll of barristers was kept by the Law Society, but some barristers' names were not recorded on it. They are listed in Table 2 below.

1. On the Barristers' Roll of the Law Society of Upper Canada, Osgoode Hall

Trinity Term, 37 Geo. III. 1797

    John White
    Robert Isaac Dey Gray
    Walter Roe
    Angus MacDonell
    James Clark
    Christopher Robinson
    Allan McLean
    William Dummer Powell, Jr.
    Alexander Stewart
    Nicholas Hagerman
    Bart. Crannell Beardsley
    Timothy Thompson
    Jacob Farrand
    Samuel Sherwood
    John McKay

Trinity Term, 39 Geo. III 1799

    William Weekes

Easter Term, 41 Geo. III. 1801.

    James Woods

Trinity Term, 41 Geo. III 1801

    Thomas Scott

Hilary Term, 43 Geo. III 1803

    Levius Peter Sherwood

Easter Term, 43 Geo. III 1803

    William Birdseye Peters
    William Dickson
    D'Arcy Boulton
    John Powell
    William Elliot
    William Warren Baldwin
    John Tenbroeck
    Walter Butler Wilkinson

Hilary Term, 46 Geo. III, 1806

    John Lowe Farrand

Hilary Term, 47 Geo. III, 1807

    D'Arcy Boulton, Jr.

Michaelmas Term, 48 Geo.III, 1807

    William Firth

Hilary Term, 48 Geo. III, 1808

    Alexander Cameron
    Henry Bostwick
    Thomas Ward

Easter Term, 48 Geo. III, 1808

    John Robert Small

Trinity Term, 48 Geo. III, 1808

    James Cartwright
    John McDonell

Hilary Term, 50 Geo. III, 1810

    Edward Walker

Trinity Term, 51 Geo. III, 1811

    Hamilton Walker

Michaelmas Term, 52 Geo. III, 1811

    Jonathan Jones

Hilary Term, 55 Geo. III, 1815

    John Beverley Robinson
    George Ridout
    Jonas Jones
    Christopher A. Hagerman
    David Jones

Easter Term, 55 Geo. III. 1815

    Archibald McLean

Trinity Term, 55 Geo. III, 1815

    Samuel Peters Jarvis
    Daniel Jones, jr.

Michaelmas Term, 56 Geo. III, 1815

    Daniel Hagerman

Michaelmas Term, 57 Geo. III, 1816

    Henry John Boulton

Easter Term, 57 Geo. III, 1817

    John Breakenridge

Trinity Term, 57 Geo. III, 1817

    Thomas Butler

Michaelmas Term, 59 Geo. III, 1818

    George Strange Boulton

Hilary Term, 59 Geo. III, 1819

    Thomas Taylor

Trinity Term, 59 Geo. III, 1819

    Benjamin Fairfield

Trinity Term, 1 Geo. IV, 1820

    Robert Macaulay
    Simon Washburn

Hilary Term, I Geo. IV, 1821

    Robert Dickson
    James Edward Small

Easter Term, 2 Geo. IV, 1821

    Marshall Spring Bidwell
    Alexander Stewart

Trinity Term, 2 Geo. IV, 1821

    George Rolph

Michaelmas Term, 2 Geo. IV, 1821

    Andrew Norton Buell
    John Rolph
    Robert Berrie

Hilary Term, 2 & 3 Geo. IV, 1822

    James Buchanan Macaulay

Easter Term, 3 Geo. IV, 1822

    George Macaulay

Michaelmas Term, 3 Geo. IV. 1822

    William Dickson, Jr.

Hilary Term, 3 & 4 Geo. IV, 1823

    George Stephen Jarvis

Easter Term, 4 Geo. IV, 1823

    Daniel McMartin

Trinity Term, 4 Geo. IV, 1823

    Donald Bethune
    John Muirhead

Michaelmas Term, 4 Geo. IV, 1823

    James Hunter Samson
    Daniel Farley
    Marcus Fayette Whitehead
    David William Smith
    Samuel Merill, jr.

Hilary Term, 4 & 5 Geo. IV, 1824

    James Nickalls, jr.
    James Boulton

Easter Term, 5 Geo. IV, 1824
    Charles Coxwell Small
    Thomas Maybee Radenhurst

Trinity Term, 5 Geo. IV, 1824

    Henry Cassady.

Michaelmas Term 5 Geo. IV, 1824

    George Malloch

Hilary Term, 5 & 6 Geo. IV, 1825

    Robert Cline
    Richard Cartwright Robinson
    Marcus Burritt

Easter Term, 6 Geo. IV, 1825

    Alexander Chewitt

Trinity Term, 6 Geo. IV, 1825

    Robert Baldwin
    John Boswell

Michaelmas Term, 6 Geo. IV, 1825

    John Solomon Cartwright
    Joseph Allan McLean

Trinity Term, 7 Geo. IV, 1826.

    Charles Richardson

Michaelmas Term, 7 Geo. IV, 1826

    Alexander Wilkinson
    John Lyons
    Allan Napier MacNab

Hilary Term, 7 Geo. IV, 1827

    Robert Easton Burns
    William Notman

Michaelmas Term 8 Geo. 1827

    William Salmon
    John Low
    George Boswell
    William Alexander Campbell
    David B. Ogden Ford
    James King
    Philo Hawley

Hilary Term, 8 Geo. IV, 1827 & 1828

    James Givens

Easter Term, 9 Geo. IV, 1828

    John Small
    Donovan Ridout
    Simon Macaulay
    George Mackenzie
    Alexander Y. McDonell

Trinity Term, 9 Geo. IV, 1828

    William Henry Draper
    Peter Rapelje
    David Lockwood Fairfield

Michaelmas Term, 9 Geo. IV, 1828

    Henry Sherwood
    Joseph Nicholas Hagerman
    Thomas Kirkpatrick

Robert Baldwin Sullivan
John Godfrey Spragge
Charles Baby
John R. McDonell
Robert McLean
Lowther Pennington McPherson

Hilary Term, 9 Geo. IV, 1828 & 1829

    Thomas Dalton, jr.
    Joseph Kerby Herchimer

Easter Term, 10 Geo. IV, 1829

    Israel Jones

Michaelmas Term, 10 Geo. IV, 1829

    Benjamin Dougall
    Charles Robinson Heward
    Colley Alexander Foster

Hilary Term, 10 Geo. IV, 1829, 1830

    Edward Clark Campbell
    Walter H. Dickson
    John Bogert

Easter Term, 11 Geo. IV, 1830

    James Doyle
    George McDonell
    Charles Oliver
    William Friend Murney
    James Woods

Trinity Term 11 Geo. IV, &1 Wm. IV, 1830

    Warren Claus
    Miles O'Reilly
    William Bowers Winterbottom
    Thomas Horatio Taylor
    Charles Badeux Secord
    James Jessup

Michaelmas Term, 1 Wm. IV, 1830

    William Wallis
    James Hubbell
    John Stuart

Easter Term, 2 Wm. IV, 1832

    Roland McDonald
    Peter Freel
    James McIntosh
    Burrage Y. McKyes

Trinity Term, 2 & 3 Wm. IV, 1832

    Joseph Clarke Gamble
    Henry Christopher Heward

Michaelmas Term, 3 Wm. IV, 1832

    Michael Barrett
    Richard G. Beasley

Hilary Term, 3 & 4 Wm. IV, 1833

    Allan McDonell

Trinity Term, 4 Wm. IV, 1833

    Robert S. Jameson
    George S. Tiffany
    John O. Hatt

Michaelmas Term, 4 Wm. IV, 1833

    George Sherwood
    William B. Wells
    John Bell
    George C. Strachan
    Charles L. Hall

Hilary Term, 4 Wm. IV, 1834

    Edmund Murney
    John Law
    Henry Smith
    Adam H. Meyers

Easter Term, 4 Wm. IV, 1834

    John G. Malloch
    John C. Ward

Trinity Term, 4 & 5 Wm. IV, 1834

    John R. Forsyth
    Christopher Armstrong
    Osmond Jones
    James Smith

Michaelmas Term, 5 Wm. IV, 1834

    John P. Carey
    Stafford F. Kirkpatrick

Hilary Term, 5 Wm. IV, 1835

    Henry Baldwin, jr.
    Ephraim J. Hubbell
    John Miller
    Angus Bethune

Easter Term, 5 Wm. IV, 1835

    John Powell
    John Wilson

Trinity Term, 5 & 6 Wm. IV. 1835

    Wm. A. Forward
    Lorenzo D. Raymond

Hilary Term, 6 Wm. IV, 1836

    Wm. Miller
    Charles Durand
    Wm. H. Boulton
    John A. Macdonald

Easter Term, 6 Wm. IV, 1836

    Philip Low
    Francis G. Stanton

Trinity Term, 6 & 7 Wm. IV, 1836
    Alexander Grant

Michaelmas Term, 7 Wm. IV. 1836

    Edward Hitchings
    Charles O. Benson
    Hamilton O'Reilly
    Arthur Acland
    John S. Smith

Hilary Term, 7 Wm. IV. 1837

    Joseph Davis
    Henry W. Blackstone
    Richard O. Duggan
    Colly Foster
    Archibald Gilkison

Easter Term, 7 Wm. IV. 1837

    Alexander S. Milne

Trinity Term, 1 Vic. 1837

    George Duggan, jr.
    Gideon Acland
    John Strachan, jr.
    John W. Gwynne

Michaelmas Term, 1 Vic. 1837

    Brownlow W. Roberts
    D'Arcy E. Boulton
    George A. Cumming
    Reade Burritt
    Wm. B. Richards
    Frederick T. Wilkes

Hilary Term, 1 Vic. 1838

    Wm. Boswell
    Alan Cameron
    Richard F. Steele

Easter Term, 1 Vic. 1838
    Wm. Cayley
    Henry Tyrhitt
    Robert Hervey, jr.
    Thomas C. Street
    Wm. H. Blake.

Trinity Term, 2 Vic. 1838

    James C. P. Esten
    James M. Strachan
    James G. Armour
    Robert H. Throope

Michaelmas Term, 2 Vic. 1838

    John H. Cameron
    Donald W. B. Macaulay
    John Prince

Hilary Term, 2 Vic. 1839

    Jacob F. Pringle
    Augustus B. Sullivan

Easter Term, 2 Vic. 1839

    William C. Loring
    Adam J. Fergusson
    Lewis Walbridge
    Joseph C. Morrison

Trinity Term, 3 Vic. 1839

    John Crawford
    John Hector
    Adam Wilson
    William A. Geddes

Michaelmas Term, 3 Vic 1839

    Charles Stuart
    James R. Gowan
    David S. McQueen
    Geroge B. Lyon
    John Ross
    Samuel B. Harrison

Hilary Term, 3 Vic. 1840

    George T. Denison, Jr.
    Frederick C. Muttlebury
    Wm. D. Powell
    James Cahill
    Robert P. Crooks
    William Horton
    Wm. Smart, Jr.

Easter Term, 3 Vic. 1840

    John Delmege
    Simon F. Robertson
    Secker Brough
    Nesbitt Kirchoffer
    Thomas Moore
    John B. Lewis

Trinity Term, 4 Vic. 1840

    George D. Wells
    John G. Stevenson
    Samuel Black Freeman
    Wellington Murney
    George W. Brock
    John Duggan
    John S. Macdonald
    Henry Allen

Michaelmas Term, 4 Vic. 1840

    John H. Hagarty
    Elias Burnham

Hilary Term, 4 Vic. 1841

    Richard Miller
    Alexander Duff

Michaelmas Term, 5 Vic. 1841

    William W. Fitzgibbon
    Frederick Cleverly
    Henry C. R. Becher
    James Robertson
    Terence H. Mirrick

2. Barristers Whose Names are not upon the Rolls of the Court

Christopher Robinson	1797.	John Muirhead	1823.
John McKay	1797.	Samuel Merrill	1823.
Walter Roe	1797.	Geroge Mallock	1824.
Thomas Scott	1801.	Simon McAuley	1828.
James Wood	1801.	Charles Baby	1828.
William B. Peters	1803.	J. C. Herchmer	1828.
Walter B. Wilkinson	1803.	Michael Barrett	1832.
Daniel Farley	1823.		

e. Notaries Public

There is no complete list extant of notaries public in Upper Canada. In the early years they were commissioned, but this system was not continued. The two following tables, which overlap slightly, show those notaries who were commissioned and those Upper Canadian appointees who were still alive in 1856. The duties of the notary, then as now, included such legal matters as certifying deeds and contracts, and recording the fact that a person had sworn that something was true. They were not necessarily lawyers.

1. Notaries Public granted Commissions

Adhemar St. Martin	3 June, 1793
Thomas Ridout	12 July, 1794
Bartholemew Crannell Beardsley	10 July, 1798
Walter Roe	5 Aug., 1798
Peter La Force	16 June, 1800
Thomas Sparham	22 July, 1800
Thomas Ward	16 July, 1802
Benjamin Geale	17 Apr., 1819
John W. Ferguson	17 Apr., 1819
Matthew Olley	12 July, 1830
Thomas Gallon	20 Dec., 1830

2. Notaries Public appointed prior to 1842 and Still Living in 1856

A

Asken, John H. L.	24 Apr., 1841
Asken, Thomas	Dec., 1837

B

Babington, Benjamin	23 Nov., 1837
Baldwin, Henry	2 Dec., 1834
Beekman, Robert	25 July, 1838
Bell, John	26 Feb., 1834
Benjamin, George	18 Feb., 1836
Berczy, Charles	21 Feb., 1834
Bethune, Angus	21 Mar., 1838
Black, James	20 Aug., 1828
Boulton, D'Arcy E.	11 Nov., 1837
Boulton, James	26 Feb., 1834
Boulton, William H.	5 Sept.,1837
Boswell, William	4 Oct., 1834
Brock, George	19 June, 1840
Brown, Richard	25 June, 1839
Burk, George T.	27 Sept.,1831
Burnes, Robert Easton	29 Sept.,1831
Burns, Thomas	14 Mar., 1838
Burritt, Read	17 July, 1833
Burwell, John	6 Oct., 1825

C

Cameron, Allan	5 Sept.,	1837
Cameron, John H.	15 Dec.,	1838
Campbell, Edward C.	28 July,	1833
Chatterton, Richard D.	27 Aug.,	1834
Chewit, Alexander	30 Dec.,	1831
Christie, Alexander J.	8 Sept.,	1835
Chrysler, George Mosely	18 Nov.,	1836
Clarke, John	14 Dec.,	1821
Clarke, P.T.	25 Oct.,	1836
Cooke, James	26 Nov.,	1833
Cornish, William King	28 Mar.,	1831
Crofton, Walter C.	29 Oct.,	1832
Crooks, Robert Pilkington	9 Mar.,	1836

D

Daly, Charles	24 Nov.,	1836
Deacon, Robert	5 Nov.,	1833
Dickson, Robert	16 Dec.,	1825
Dougall, James	29 Jan.,	1837
Doyle, John S.	8 July,	1841
Duffy, Edward	7 Dec.,	1836
Duggan, George, Jr.	18 Dec.,	1833
Duggan, Richard Oliver	13 Jan.,	1837
Dupuy, Hilary	15 Jan.,	1838
Dyett, George	11 Mar.,	1835

E

Elliott, William	19 Mar.,	1818
Ewart, James Bell	7 Jan.,	1833
Ewart, William	25 Apr.,	1834

F

Farrell, Thomas P.	16 Dec.,	1825
Ferguson, John	29 Sept.,	1809
Ferguson, John W.	17 Apr.,	1819
Fortune, Joseph	28 Mar.,	1816
Foster, Colley A.	14 Jan.,	1830
Franklin, Francis	14 June,	1837
Fraser, Douglas	18 Feb.,	1837

G

Gamble, Clark	23 Mar.,	1833
Gauvreau, Charles	28 Nov.,	1810
Geale, Benjamin	17 Apr.,	1819
Gilkison, Archibald	23 Jan.,	1837
Givins, James	3 Aug.,	1833
Goldsmith, Edward	12 Aug.,	1831
Goodeve, George Mills	7 Apr.,	1840
Goodwin, James C.	19 Mar.,	1840
Gordon, Alexander	31 Oct.,	1838
Gowan, James Robert	15 Dec.,	1839
Grant, Alexander	19 May,	1834
Grundy, George	16 Nov.,	1840

H

Hall, Charles Lethura	13 Feb.,	1835
Hall, P. F.	13 June,	1820
Hartwell, Joseph K.	10 Dec.,	1825
Hamilton, James	18 Oct.,	1834
Hamilton, John	24 June,	1834
Headlam, Robert	11 Jan.,	1840
Hensleigh, Henry John	2 Nov.,	1835
Hewson, Francis	16 Nov.,	1840
Hill, Francis M.	7 Apr.,	1840
Hincks, Francis	8 May,	1837
Hodgert, James	6 July,	1835
Horne, John G.	13 Feb.,	1837
Horne, R. C.	16 Sept.,	1833

Howard, John G. .... 9 Feb., 1841
Hume, James .... 26 Nov., 1834
Huntley, John J. .... 19 Feb., 1836

I

Ireland, George T. F. .... 25 Mar., 1818

J

Jellett, Morgan .... 18 Aug., 1836
Johnson, Charles .... 22 Aug., 1834
Jones, Jonas A. .... 28 Oct., 1818

K

Keating, John W. .... 13 Jan., 1836
Keays, James .... 1 Sept. 1830
Keele, W. Conway .... 21 Nov., 1835
Kennedy, William S. .... 20 Oct., 1832
Kevill, James .... 28 Jan., 1835
King, James .... 30 Nov., 1827
Kirchoffer, Nesbitt .... 29 Feb., 1840
Knowlson, John .... 22 Mar., 1840

L

La Force, Peter .... 16 June, 1800
Lapenotiere, William .... 11 Nov., 1834
Larne, Andrew .... 7 Oct., 1839
Leslie, Anthony .... 7 Feb., 1835
Lewis, John B. .... 15 Jan., 1838
Lewis, Joseph C. .... 16 Mar., 1835
Lockhart, Andrew .... 9 Feb., 1841
Loring, William C. .... 15 Nov., 1838
Lyon, George B. .... 17 Mar., 1834

M

MacNab, Sir Allan N. .... 8 July, 1826
Madock, John F. 21 Oct.,1839
Mair, Thomas 24 Sept.,1834
Maionville, Alexis .... 28 Feb., 1818
Mallock, George .... 23 Mar., 1832
Mallock, John G. .... 30 Jan., 1837
McDonald, Rolland .... 14 Jan., 1836
McDonell, Allan .... 30 Dec., 1836
McFarlane, James .... 14 Dec., 1821
McFarlane, John .... 16 May, 1822
McGregor, Duncan .... 25 Feb., 1823
McKenny, Amos .... 19 Mar., 1818
McLean, Archibald .... 23 July, 1833
McMicken, Gilbert .... 2 Nov., 1838
McMillan, William C. 14 Sept.,1837
McNabb, Alexander .... 14 May, 1840
McQueen, David S. .... 24 Feb., 1841
Miller, John .... 5 Dec., 1837
Miller, Robert Bell .... 6 Dec., 1839
Miller, William .... 14 May., 1839
Morrison, Joseph C. .... 15 Feb., 1838
Murphy, Thomas .... 7 July, 1827
Mylne, John .... 3 Feb., 1840

N

Nichol, William .... 20 Dec., 1820
Noel, John .... 30 Aug., 1834
Notman, William .... 7 Jan., 1833

O

O'Reilly, Miles .... 29 May, 1832

P

Parker, Thomas .... 30 May, 1833
Patton, John .... 29 Nov., 1832

Peterson, Henry W. .... 19 Apr., 1839
Phelps, Thomas C. .... 26 Nov., 1833
Phipps, William Brown .... 19 Dec., 1836
Powell, John .... 2 Dec., 1834

R

Raymond, Lorenzo D. .... 8 Apr., 1837
Ridout, Charles .... 16 Oct., 1827
Ridout, John .... 16 Aug., 1833
Robertson, Simon F. 24 Sept.,1834
Robins, Redford .... 17 Jan. 1838
Rorke, Joseph .... 18 Jan., 1836
Rorke, William .... 12 Dec., 1836
Rorke, Samuel .... 14 June, 1839
Ross, Charles L. 18 Sept.,1838

S

Sache, Charles Henry .... 3 Dec., 1831
Scott, John .... 9 Feb., 1831
Secord, Charles B. .... 8 Mar., 1830
Simpson, William .... 10 Aug., 1824
Small, James Edward .... 28 July, 1831
Smith, Henry .... 27 Dec., 1826
Smith, Henry .... 8 Mar., 1827
Smith, James .... 20 June, 1839
Smith, John Shuter .... 5 Mar., 1825
Smith, John Shuter .... 28 Apr., 1835
Smith, Robert .... 3 Jan., 1823
Smith, William .... 18 Dec., 1829
Somerville, John .... 17 June, 1837
Stanton, Robert .... 28 Feb., 1823
Steven, Andrew .... 12 Jan., 1830
Steven, Andrew .... 10 Aug., 1833
Stevenson, James .... 1 Mar., 1838
Stokoe, Thomas 22 Sept.,1838
Strachan, John .... 20 July, 1837
Strathy, John .... 18 May, 1836
Street, George Charles .... 13 May, 1837
Street, William W. .... 31 May, 1841
Stuart, Charles .... 29 Apr., 1840

T

Taylor, John F. .... 3 Dec., 1834
Tazewell, Oliver .... 31 Dec., 1830
Tench, Frederick, B. .... 16 May, 1837
Throop, Benjamin .... 16 Feb., 1837
Throop, Robert Henry .... 7 Feb., 1838
Tiffany, George S. .... 11 Feb., 1839
Traveller, Reuben .... 20 Dec., 1841
Turner, Alfred .... 7 July, 1834

W

Walker, Hamilton .... 31 Oct., 1818
Walker, John .... 22 Feb., 1836
Wallbridge, Lewis .... 18 Nov., 1839
Walton, George .... 23 Jan., 1836
Walton, John .... 16 July, 1840
Ward, Thomas
Warren, Thomas Dickson .... 11 May, 1841
Wenham, Joseph 24 Sept.,1834
Whitman, Stephen .... 17 Apr., 1837
Wilkes, Frederick Thomas .... 6 Apr., 1838
Wilks, James .... 23 Mar., 1842
Willcocks, Arthur L. .... 12 Apr., 1830
Willson, George .... 12 Jan., 1837
Wilson, Andrew .... 15 Dec., 1838
Wilson, John .... 5 Nov., 1840
Wilson, William Mercer .... 25 July, 1840
Wright, Francis H. .... 24 Mar., 1836

f. Solicitors

In the old English legal system a solicitor was a lawyer who appeared in chancery cases, and, as there was no Court of Chancery in Upper Canada before 1837, no solicitors were required in the province. When the Court of Chancery was established all attorneys and barristers were automatically declared solicitors. A separate Solicitors' Roll was begun for the province but it was little used before about 1844-45.

John Ford Maddock	22 June, 1837
Robert J. Turner	19 Aug., 1841
George Williams	15 Aug., 1844

g. Queen's Counsels

Allan Napier MacNab	21 Jan., 1838
John S. Cartwright	22 Jan., 1838
Henry Sherwood	23 Jan., 1838

Part V
Local and Municipal Government, 1788-1849

A. Townships

a. Introduction

The townships were the first unit of local government to be created with the arrival of the Loyalists in 1783-84. As the population spread out, and new areas were surveyed more townships were added and old ones sometimes subdivided. Most of these still exist and form the base unit of local government today. Further townships were created after 1849.

The 1788 districts and the 1792 counties were created without regard to township boundaries and as a result there was considerable overlapping. In 1800 the boundaries of the various divisions were regularized; after that each township was contained in a single county and each county in a single district. The local organizational setup until 1849 was thus: township, county and district. (see below)

The following lists are based on the extensive research on township development done by Professor Robert W. Wightman of the Department of Geography of the University of Western Ontario, who has kindly given permission for the use of this data. Townships where the survey was begun after 1850 are not included. The county names as of 1874, when the last counties were created, have been added for ease in location.

The evolution of the townships and their various transfers from one county to another, boundary changes and divisions is too extensive a matter to attempt to incorporate here; but some of the major township divisions are noted under the districts.

Under 33 Geo. III c. 2 (1793) towns were allowed to hold town meetings and elect their own officials such as a warden, clerk, assessors and collectors, but their activities were closely supervised by the Quarter Sessions of the District. Although much has been written concerning the demand for elective institutions following the New England pattern the difficulty of getting individuals to serve is demonstrated by the penalty clauses of the Act.

After the beginning of town incorporations in 1832 more local autonomy was extended to townships under 5 Wm. IV. c. 8 (1835); but after the Rebellion of 1837 this was suspended and repealed by 1 Vic. c. 21 (1838), although the actual repeal clause was omitted by clerical error. (This was very Upper Canadian).

Elective local governments finally came with the District Councils Act of 1841. (See introduction to Districts and list of legislation).

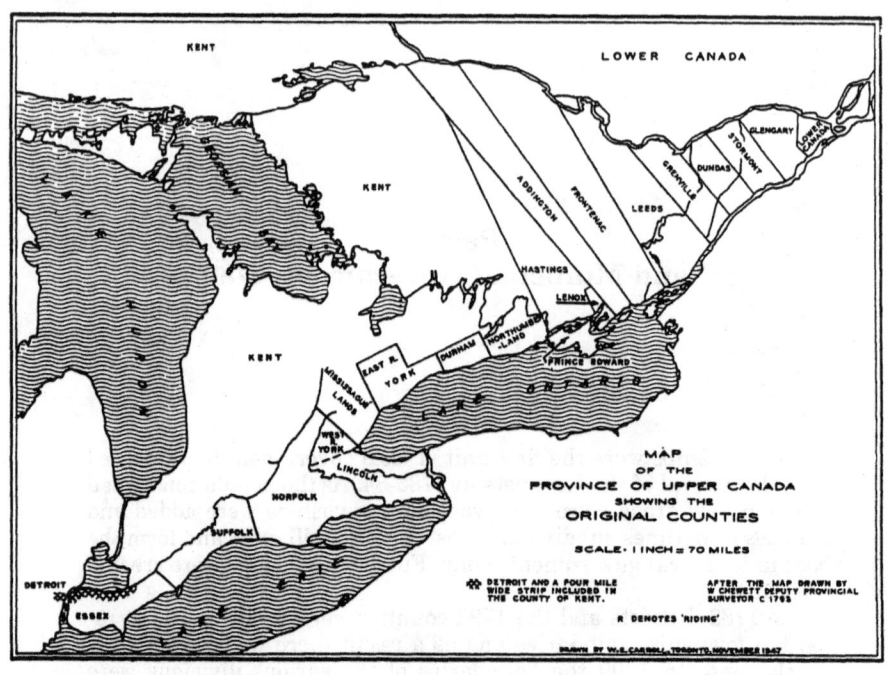

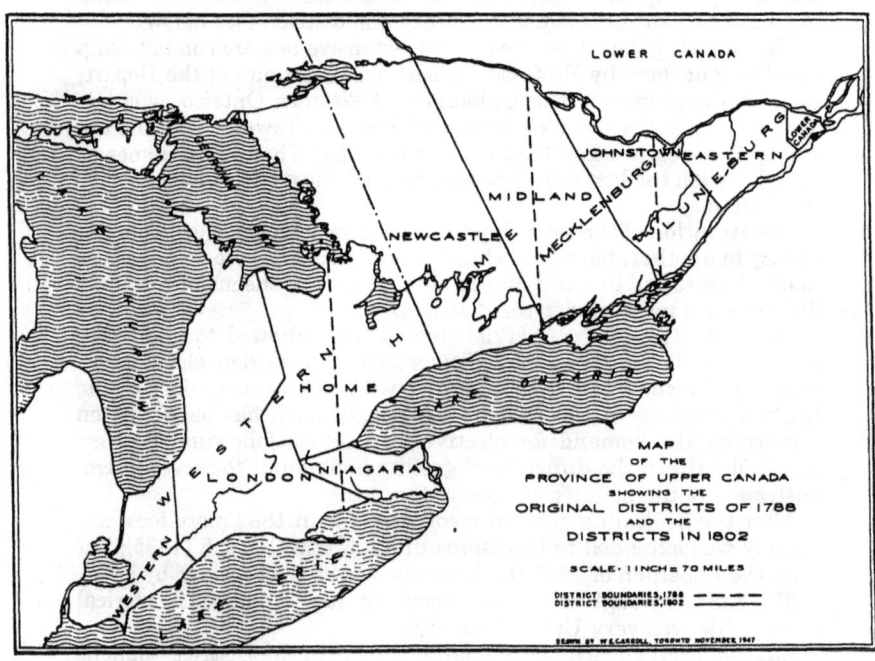

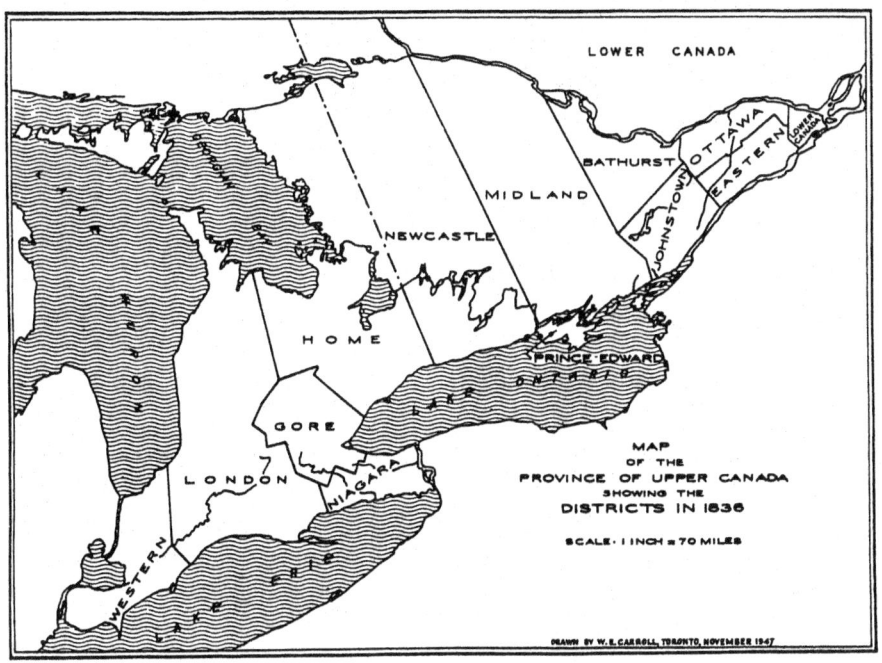

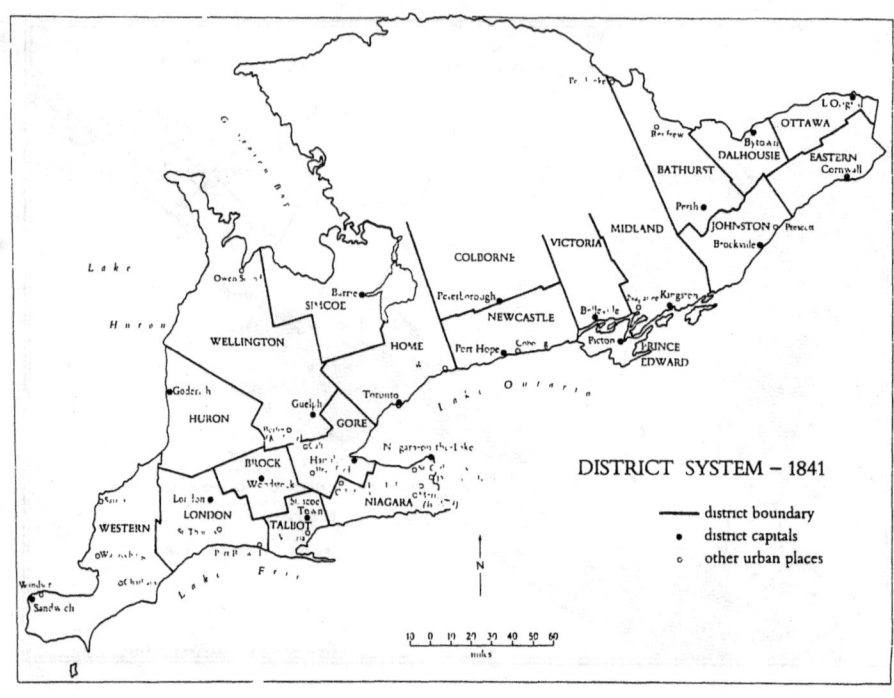

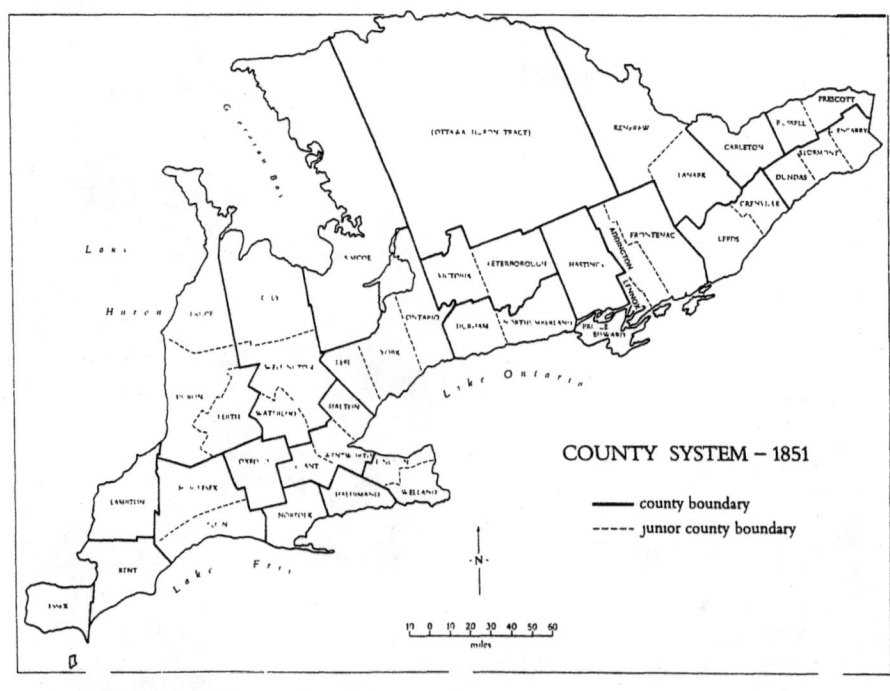

b. Lists of Townships

Township	Date of Indian Alien.	Date of First Township Survey	Date of First Legal Settler	Area in Acres	County
Adelaide	1825	1831	1832	44300	Middlesex
Adjala	1818	1820	1825	46400	Simcoe
Admaston	1819	1842	1842	78000	Renfrew
Adolphustown	1783	1783	1784	10800	Lennox & Addington
Albemarle	1853	1853	1857	56789	Bruce
Albion	1818	1819	1819	56200	Peel
Aldborough	1790	1797	1804	80000	Elgin
Alfred	1783	1795	1800	45400	Prescott
Alnwick	1784	1811	1836	20000	Northumberland
Amabel	1855	1855	1856	66544	Bruce
Amaranth	1818	1823	1827	63844	Dufferin
Ameliasburg	1793	1785	1787	42745	Prince Edward
Amherst Island	1783	1790	1803	14700	Lennox & Addington
Ancaster	1784	1793	1795	45500	Wentworth
Anderdon	1833	1835	1838	31334	Essex
Anglesea	1819	1852	1852	67200	Lennox & Addington
Arran	1836	1851	1852	54833	Bruce
Artemesia	1818	1848	1849	70000	Grey
Arthur	1836	1840	1840	68823	Wellington
Ashfield	1825	1836	1837	64800	Huron
Asphodel	1818	1820	1825	39600	Peterborough
Athol	1783	1784	1788	22973	Prince Edward
Augusta	1783	1783	1784	75905	Grenville
Bagot	1819	1842	1842	70000	Renfrew
Barrie	1819	1857	1859	68600	Frontenac
Barton	1784	1791	1791	14800	Wentworth
Bastard	1783	1794	1795	57064	Leeds
Bathurst	1819	1816	1816	62600	Lanark
Bayham	1793	1799	1811	60000	Elgin
Beckwith	1819	1816	1817	62600	Lanark
Bedford	1783	1824	1831	85700	Frontenac
Belmont	1818	1828	1836	70000	Peterborough
Bentinck	1836	1851	1851	76662	Grey
Bertie	1781	1784	1784	36400	Welland
Beverley	1793	1793	1795	70200	Wentworth
Bexley	1819	1833	1840	28000	Victoria
Biddulph	1825	1836	1836	39899	Middlesex
Binbrook	1784	1789	1789	28000	Wentworth
Blandford	1793	1797	1799	29714	Oxford
Blanshard	1825	1839	1840	49259	Perth
Blenheim	1793	1798	1798	67200	Brant
Blithefield	1819	1842	1842	30750	Renfrew
Bosanquet	1825	1835	1838	72626	Lambton
Brant	1836	1850	1854	71205	Bruce
Brantford	1793	1830	1831	78400	Brant

Township	Date of Indian Alien.	Date of First Township Survey	Date of First Legal Settler	Area in Acres	County
Brighton	1784	1792	1792	48004	Northumberland
Brock	1784	1817	1821	67200	Ontario
Bromley	1819	1842	1842	50000	Renfrew
Brooke	1819	1832	1833	74600	Lambton
Bruce	1836	1847	1854	67522	Bruce
Burford	1793	1798	1798	67200	Brant
Burgess	1783	1794	1815	39200	Lanark
Burleigh	1818	1834	1861	74400	Peterborough
Caistor	1784	1795	1795	34400	Lincoln
Caledon	1818	1819	1820	69000	Peel
Caledonia	1783	1806	1815	46700	Prescott
Cambridge	1783	1821	1830	60000	Russell
Camden (eastern)	1790	1808	1808	91868	Lennox & Addington
Camden (western)	1790	1794	1794	26800	Kent
Canborough	1783	1801	1803	21547	Haldimand
Caradoc	1819	1820	1822	76400	Middlesex
Carrick	1836	1852	1854	59525	Bruce
Cartwright	1784	1816	1834	37284	Durham
Cavan	1784	1816	1817	64400	Durham
Cayuga (North and South)	1793	1831	1832	50500	Haldimand
Charlottenburg	1783	1783	1784	81044	Glengarry
Charlotteville	1793	1793	1795	57753	Norfolk
Chatham	1790	1794	1794	83139	Kent
Chinguacousy	1805	1818	1818	81600	Peel
Clarence	1783	1791	1804	70000	Russell
Clarendon	1819	1862	1862	75000	Frontenac
Clarke	1784	1793	1796	72000	Durham
Clinton	1784	1786	1786	25200	Lincoln
Colborne	1825	1835	1835	33740	Huron
Colchester	1790	1787	1787	65282	Essex
Collingwood	1818	1833	1834	68900	Grey
Cornwall	1783	1783	1784	65600	Stormont
Cramahe	1784	1793	1797	68600	Northumberland
Crosby South	1783	1795	1800	50200	Leeds
Crosby North	1783	1806	1820	70653	Leeds
Crowland	1784	1795	1795	19193	Welland
Culross	1836	1849	1854	58095	Bruce
Cumberland	1783	1791	1801	74227	Russell
Dalhousie	1819	1820	1820	62600	Lanark
Darling	1819	1820	1820	62600	Lanark
Darlington	1784	1793	1794	73400	Durham
Dawn	1819	1821	1821	79200	Lambton
Delaware	1790	1798	1798	27600	Middlesex
Derby	1836	1842	1842	40236	Grey
Dereham	1793	1799	1813	67200	Oxford
Dorchester South	1793	1795	1815	43200	Elgin
Dorchester North	1793	1795	1810	50679	Middlesex
Douro	1818	1823	1823	41000	Peterborough

Township	Date of Indian Alien.	Date of First Township Survey	Date of First Legal Settler	Area in Acres	County
Dover	1790	1792	1792	81000	Kent
Downie	1825	1832	1834	48463	Perth
Drummond	1819	1816	1816	62600	Lanark
Dumfries North	1793	1817	1817	47000	Waterloo
Dumfries South	1793	1817	1817	47000	Brant
Dummer	1818	1823	1831	73000	Peterborough
Dunn	1793	1833	1835	18000	Haldimand
Dunwich	1790	1797	1803	69710	Elgin
Easthope North	1825	1832	1839	43691	Perth
Easthope South	1825	1832	1832	24683	Perth
Eastnor	1855	1856	1869	51576	Bruce
Edwardsburg	1783	1783	1784	70364	Grenville
Egremont	1836	1846	1848	76262	Grey
Ekfrid	1819	1820	1831	56150	Middlesex
Elderslie	1836	1851	1852	55775	Bruce
Elizabethtown	1783	1783	1784	78200	Leeds
Eldon	1818	1826	1828	66800	Victoria
Ellice	1825	1832	1832	54397	Perth
Elma	1825	1848	1853	67500	Perth
Elmsley North	1783	1795	1816	34000	Lanark
Elmsley South	1783	1795	1810	26000	Leeds
Elzevir	1819	1821	1839	68200	Hastings
Emily	1818	1818	1819	64000	Victoria
Enniskillen	1819	1833	1836	86600	Lambton
Ennismore	1818	1825	1825	19600	Peterborough
Eramosa	1818	1819	1820	44600	Wellington
Erin	1818	1819	1820	70400	Wellington
Ernestown	1783	1783	1784	62800	Lennox & Addington
Escott	1783	1788	1790	25300	Leeds
Essa	1818	1820	1826	68000	Simcoe
Esquesing	1818	1819	1819	70400	Halton
Etobicoke	1784	1795	1800	30000	York
Euphemia	1819	1822	1825	39497	Lambton
Euphrasia	1818	1836	1842	72000	Grey
Fenelon	1818	1822	1831	68600	Victoria
Finch	1783	1794	1805	53945	Stormont
Fitzroy	1819	1822	1822	62400	Carlton
Flamborough East	1784	1793	1800	33800	Wentworth
Flamborough West	1784	1793	1793	31200	Wentworth
Flos	1815	1822	1825	64400	Simcoe
Fredericksburg (North and South)	1783	1783	1784	63231	Lennox & Addington
Fullarton	1825	1832	1832	41057	Perth
Gainsborough	1784	1794	1794	39933	Lincoln
Garafraxa East	1818	1821	1826	42398	Dufferin
Garafraxa West	1818	1821	1823	46967	Wellington
Georgina	1784	1817	1819	41000	York
Glanford	1784	1794	1794	23539	Wentworth

Township	Date of Indian Alien.	Date of First Township Survey	Date of First Legal Settler	Area in Acres	County
Glenelg	1836	1848	1848	68969	Grey
Gloucester	1783	1792	1809	84500	Carleton
Goderich	1825	1828	1828	55698	Huron
Gosfield	1790	1787	1787	59600	Essex
Goulbourne	1819	1818	1818	66034	Carleton
Gower South	1783	1793	1802	21736	Leeds & Grenville
Gower North	1783	1795	1820	34320	Carleton
Grantham	1784	1784	1784	23400	Lincoln
Greenock	1836	1852	1854	64853	Bruce
Grey	1825	1847	1854	63935	Huron
Grimsby	1784	1788	1788	34057	Lincoln
Grimsthorpe	1819	1868	1868	68200	Hastings
Guelph	1793	1828	1828	42000	Wellington
Gwillimbury North	1784	1803	1803	29011	York
Gwillimbury East	1784	1800	1803	58000	York
Gwillimbury West	1818	1819	1820	46244	Simcoe
Haldimand	1784	1792	1797	77000	Northumberland
Hallowell	1783	1785	1788	43660	Prince Edward
Hamilton	1784	1792	1798	68000	Northumberland
Harvey	1818	1824	1830	107200	Peterborough
Harwich	1790	1794	1795	88400	Kent
Hawkesbury East	1783	1795	1796	54905	Prescott
Hawkesbury West	1783	1795	1800	40940	Prescott
Hay	1825	1838	1838	53448	Huron
Hibbert	1825	1832	1840	41476	Perth
Hillier	1783	1785	1790	31700	Prince Edward
Hinchinbrooke	1783	1824	1838	73500	Frontenac
Holland	1836	1848	1849	77347	Grey
Hope	1784	1793	1793	67000	Durham
Horton	1819	1825	1826	41600	Renfrew
Houghton	1793	1799	1820	38800	Norfolk
Howard	1790	1794	1794	58789	Kent
Howe Island	1783	1833	1833	8460	Frontenac
Howick	1836	1847	1854	67228	Huron
Hullet	1825	1835	1836	53822	Huron
Humberstone	1784	1789	1789	31200	Welland
Hungerford	1783	1797	1826	96920	Hastings
Huntingdon	1783	1797	1816	56000	Hastings
Huntley	1819	1823	1823	62600	Carleton
Huron	1836	1847	1852	58201	Bruce
Innisfil	1818	1820	1820	69000	Simcoe
Kaladar	1819	1822	1845	67200	Lennox & Addington
Kennebec	1819	1824	1850	68600	Frontenac
Kenyon	1783	1792	1792	77826	Glengarry
Keppel	1855	1855	1856	87491	Grey
Kincardine	1836	1847	1851	60556	Bruce
King	1784	1800	1800	86014	York
Kingston	1783	1783	1783	66039	Frontenac

Township	Date of Indian Alien.	Date of First Township Survey	Date of First Legal Settler	Area in Acres	County
Kinloss	1836	1851	1852	45794	Bruce
Kitley	1783	1795	1797	50400	Leeds
Lake	1819	1822	1860	68200	Hastings
Lanark	1819	1819	1820	62600	Lanark
Lancaster	1783	1783	1784	57279	Glengarry
Lansdowne	1783	1788	1789	59000	Leeds
Lavant	1819	1822	1828	55800	Lanark
Leeds	1783	1788	1789	48000	Leeds
Lindsay	1855	1856	1870	64284	Bruce
Lobo	1819	1820	1820	48600	Middlesex
Lochiel	1783	1795	1795	71730	Glengarry
Logan	1825	1832	1837	53773	Perth
London	1796	1810	1818	105200	Middlesex
Longueuil	1783	1795	1798	23620	Prescott
Loughborough	1783	1804	1805	55300	Frontenac
Louth	1784	1786	1787	19600	Lincoln
Luther East	1818	1837	1850	45000	Dufferin
Luther West	1818	1837	1853	45000	Wellington
McGillivray	1825	1835	1835	66506	Middlesex
McKillop	1825	1835	1835	52140	Huron
McNab	1819	1824	1824	68000	Renfrew
Madoc	1819	1820	1821	70400	Hastings
Maidstone	1790	1790	1791	47400	Essex
Malahide	1793	1799	1811	62899	Elgin
Malden	1790	1786	1786	22000	Essex
Manvers	1784	1816	1830	70000	Durham
Mara	1819	1821	1830	64200	Ontario
March	1819	1820	1820	28200	Carleton
Mariposa	1818	1820	1827	73927	Victoria
Markham	1784	1794	1794	69500	York
Marlborough	1783	1791	1793	64000	Carleton
Marmora	1819	1819·	1820	68200	Hastings
Maryborough	1825	1849	1849	57074	Wellington
Marysburg (North and South)	1783	1784	1785	46441	Prince Edward
Matchedash	1785	1836	1842	47400	Simcoe
Matilda	1783	1783	1784	63200	Dundas
Medonte	1815	1820	1832	73379	Simcoe
Melancthon	1818	1830	1831	76800	Dufferin
Mersea	1790	1799	1801	59400	Essex
Metcalfe	1819	1831	1832	36149	Middlesex
Methuen	1818	1823	1857	72000	Peterborough
Middleton	1793	1806	1815	45400	Norfolk
Minto	1836	1853	1853	74000	Wellington
Monaghan South	1784	1817	1818	18700	Northumberland
Monaghan North	1818	1818	1818	15300	Peterborough
Mono	1818	1823	1824	70400	Dufferin
Montague	1783	1793	1798	64800	Lanark

Township	Date of Indian Alien.	Date of First Township Survey	Date of First Legal Settler	Area in Acres	County
Moore	1825	1829	1829	73328	Lambton
Mornington	1825	1848	1848	50724	Perth
Morris	1825	1849	1852	55747	Huron
Mosa	1819	1820	1820	49600	Middlesex
Moulton	1793	1825	1825	31000	Haldimand
Mountain	1783	1795	1803	57600	Dundas
Mulmer	1818	1823	1825	70400	Dufferin
Murray	1784	1792	1792	48704	Northumberland
Nassagaweya	1818	1819	1820	44800	Halton
Nelson	1795	1806	1806	45474	Halton
Nepean	1783	1794	1805	65000	Carleton
Niagara	1781	1782	1782	22600	Lincoln
Nichol	1793	1819	1823	28000	Wellington
Nissouri West	1825	1818	1818	49500	Middlesex
Nissouri East	1825	1818	1820	46452	Oxford
Normanby	1836	1845	1845	69120	Grey
Norwich South	1793	1799	1808	33833	Oxford
Norwich North	1793	1799	1810	36000	Oxford
Nottawassaga	1818	1832	1834	90000	Simcoe
Oakland	1793	1796	1799	10800	Brant
Olden	1819	1827	1850	67200	Frontenac
Oneida	1793	1842	1842	37550	Haldimand
Onondaga	1793	1842	1842	22282	Brant
Ops	1818	1825	1829	60000	Victoria
Orford	1790	1794	1794	53000	Kent
Orillia	1765	1820	1832	74200	Simcoe
Oro	1815	1820	1820	74600	Simcoe
Osgoode	1783	1792	1822	91433	Carleton
Osnabruck	1783	1783	1784	62800	Stormont
Oso	1819	1826	1848	47800	Frontenac
Osprey	1818	1849	1849	70677	Grey
Otonabee	1818	1819	1820	70000	Peterborough
Oxford East	1793	1796	1796	34700	Oxford
Oxford West	1793	1797	1797	25735	Oxford
Oxford North	1796	1799	1802	20004	Oxford
Oxford (on Rideau River))	1783	1795	1800	59481	Grenville
Pakenham	1819	1822	1823	64000	Lanark
Palmerston	1819	1861	1861	67200	Frontenac
Peel	1793	1843	1846	73858	Wellington
Pelham	1784	1794	1794	29000	Welland
Pembroke	1819	1836	1836	8600	Renfrew
Percy	1784	1794	1800	55000	Northumberland
Pickering	1784	1791	1798	73200	Ontario
Pilkington	1793	1808	1819	29202	Wellington
Pittsburg	1783	1787	1789	48251	Frontenac
Plantagenet North	1783	1792	1802	51500	Prescott
Plantagenet South	1783	1820	1821	49600	Prescott
Plympton	1825	1829	1833	76400	Lambton

Township	Date of Indian Alien.	Date of First Township Survey	Date of First Legal Settler	Area in Acres	County
Portland	1783	1787	1789	57000	Frontenac
Proton	1818	1840	1843	87000	Grey
Puslinch	1793	1828	1829	59800	Wellington
Rainham	1793	1795	1795	26600	Haldimand
Raleigh	1790	1792	1792	72400	Kent
Rama	1819	1834	1835	25148	Ontario
Ramsay	1819	1821	1821	62600	Lanark
Rawdon	1783	1797	1803	67400	Hastings
Reach	1784	1809	1815	65800	Ontario
Richmond	1783	1785	1785	51200	Lennox & Addington
Rochester	1790	1790	1790	35200	Essex
Romney	1790	1799	1808	27400	Kent
Ross	1819	1836	1836	53900	Renfrew
Roxborough	1783	1793	1807	71554	Stormont
Russell	1783	1794	1829	47000	Russell
St. Edmunds	1855	1857	1871	57811	Bruce
St. Vincent	1818	1833	1834	65000	Grey
Saltfleet	1784	1791	1791	28000	Wentworth
Sandwich	1790	1792	1793	73000	Essex
Sarawak	1842	1851	1851	10730	Grey
Sarnia	1823	1829	1832	39115	Lambton
Saugeen	1836	1851	1852	46434	Bruce
Scarborough	1784	1791	1796	45000	York
Scott	1784	1805	1830	49400	Ontario
Scugog	1784	1816	1836	10800	Ontario
Seneca	1793	1842	1842	42000	Haldimand
Seymour	1784	1819	1819	73832	Northumberland
Sheffield	1783	1822	1825	82000	Lennox & Addington
Sherbrooke	1793	1820	1820	4593	Haldimand
Sherbrooke North	1819	1821	1821	16400	Lanark
Sherbrooke South	1819	1817	1821	44000	Lanark
Sidney	1783	1787	1787	71381	Hastings
Smith	1818	1818	1818	61200	Peterborough
Sombra	1796	1820	1821	91200	Lambton
Somerville	1819	1835	1857	70000	Victoria
Sophiasburg	1783	1783	1788	43252	Prince Edward
Southwold	1790	1799	1811	72608	Elgin
Stafford	1819	1841	1841	21650	Renfrew
Stamford	1781	1784	1784	21622	Welland
Stanley	1825	1835	1835	45251	Huron
Stephen	1825	1831	1834	54725	Huron
Storrington	1783	1807	1807	56507	Frontenac
Sullivan	1836	1843	1844	73791	Grey
Sunnidale	1818	1831	1833	55200	Simcoe
Sydenham	1836	1840	1840	80381	Grey
Tay	1795	1811	1816	50400	Simcoe
Tecumseth	1818	1820	1822	67200	Simcoe
Thorah	1819	1820	1822	39400	Ontario
Thorold	1784	1794	1794	25200	Welland
Thurlow	1783	1792	1792	59000	Hastings

Township	Date of Indian Alien.	Date of First Township Survey	Date of First Legal Settler	Area in Acres	County
Tilbury East	1790	1792	1792	53134	Kent
Tilbury West	1790	1790	1791	49600	Essex
Tiny	1795	1821	1821	81000	Simcoe
Torbolton	1819	1823	1824	25966	Carleton
Toronto	1805	1806	1806	67200	Peel
Toronto Gore	1805	1819	1819	19200	Peel
Tosoronto	1818	1816	1826	44800	Simcoe
Townsend	1793	1795	1796	66400	Norfolk
Trafalgar	1795	1806	1806	69000	Halton
Tuckersmith	1825	1835	1835	41436	Huron
Tudor	1819	1857	1857	68200	Hastings
Turnberry	1836	1852	1854	34800	Huron
Tuscarora	1793	1842	1842	40322	Brant
Tyendinaga	1793	1820	1820	92800	Hastings
Usborne	1825	1839	1839	43373	Huron
Uxbridge	1784	1805	1806	51812	Ontario
Vaughan	1784	1793	1796	68000	York
Verulum	1818	1831	1832	86016	Victoria
Vespra	1815	1820	1820	66400	Simcoe
Wainfleet	1784	1791	1791	50200	Welland
Wallace	1825	1852	1855	53773	Perth
Walpole	1793	1795	1795	67200	Haldimand
Walsingham	1793	1798	1795	87814	Norfolk
Warwick	1825	1832	1832	74800	Lambton
Waterloo	1793	1800	1800	94400	Waterloo
Wawanosh	1825	1836	1840	83593	Huron
Wellesley	1793	1843	1843	66863	Waterloo
Westmeath	1819	1836	1836	70000	Renfrew
Westminster	1790	1809	1811	63447	Middlesex
Whitby	1784	1791	1794	69000	Ontario
Whitchurch	1784	1800	1800	59743	York
Williams East	1825	1832	1833	38737	Middlesex
Williams West	1825	1832	1833	35350	Middlesex
Williamsburg	1783	1783	1784	62800	Dundas
Willoughby	1781	1785	1785	18639	Welland
Wilmot	1793	1824	1824	62000	Waterloo
Winchester	1783	1795	1800	58444	Dundas
Windham	1793	1795	1795	66538	Norfolk
Wolfe Island	1783	1790	1792	31361	Frontenac
Wolford	1783	1795	1796	49200	Grenville
Woodhouse	1793	1795	1795	34200	Norfolk
Woolwich	1793	1806	1807	58000	Waterloo
Yarmouth	1790	1799	1804	71784	Elgin
Yonge	1783	1794	1796	60561	Leeds
York	1784	1791	1793	64399	York
Zone	1790	1794	1794	29000	Kent
Zorra East	1825	1820	1824	57000	Oxford
Zorra West	1825	1820	1830	56400	Oxford

B. Counties

a. Introduction

Prior to 1849 the county was not a unit of local government, that function being reserved to the district. The early county had three basic functions: as a riding, as the organizational division for the militia, and for land registration purposes. Originally, a county was much smaller than a district. In 1792, when Simcoe first divided the province into counties in preparation for the elections to the first Provincial Parliament, there were 19 counties and only four districts. The nomenclature the governor used showed little imagination. Beginning in the extreme west, the first county was named Kent and then the names of the successive counties northward up the east coast of England were followed until finally Northumberland was reached—a pattern that has since been obscured by the creation of new counties and the suppression of Suffolk.

As the years went on new counties were established as the population grew until by 1851, the year after the county replaced the district as the basic unit of local government, the present county distribution of southern Ontario was virtually complete. Once established a county normally retained its boundaries, but a certain amount of transferring townships did take place. It is sometimes difficult to be certain of the exact date at which a county was created, particularly as it might be combined with other counties either as a riding or for administrative purposes. Also, the wording of many of the early statutes is not too clear. Peterborough is created by both 7 Wm. IV c.115 s.2 (1837) and 8 Vic. c.7 s.5 (1845) and Waterloo by 7 Wm. IV c.116 s.28 (1837) and 8 Vic. c.7 s.5 (1845).

In the tables that follow the first shows the various Upper Canada acts which arranged the riding pattern of the province, and at the same time legally established new counties. The second is a list of the counties for reference, including the post-1841 creations. Then follow tables of the two officials who were appointed on a county basis; the lieutenants whose primary task was heading the militia and the registrars. It has been impossible to list all the militia officers as even an incomplete list would be twice as long as the tables of the other Upper Canadian officials put together.

Care must be taken not to confuse the names of counties and districts, or of the various counties. Normally counties and districts were named separately, but in several cases the name was the same for both county and district: Prince Edward, Simcoe, Huron, and the provisional District of Kent. In the case of Huron, however, the county only formed part of the district. Also, the counties of Wellington and Victoria, created in 1851, should not be confused with the districts of the same name which were suppressed in 1849; nor should the former county of Ontario, also established in 1851, be confused with the county of the same name which existed from 1792 to 1800. The earlier Ontario consisted of certain islands in the Kingston region.

b. Legislation Establishing Counties and Ridings to 1841

1792 Proclamation of 16 July -- Governor Simcoe divides the province into 19 counties and 15 ridings: Dundas; Durham, York & Lincoln 1st Riding; Glengarry 1st Riding; Glengarry 2nd Riding; Grenville; Kent; Leeds & Frontenac; Lennox, Hastings & Northumberland; Lincoln 2nd Riding; Lincoln 3rd Riding; Lincoln 4th Riding & Norfolk; Ontario and Addington; Prince Edward; Stormont; Suffolk & Essex. As Kent had two members there were 16 seats in the Legislature.

1800 40 Geo III c.3 (4 July). Representation reorganized and increased to 19. One member: Stormont & Russell; Dundas; Grenville; Leeds; Frontenac; Prince Edward; Lennox & Addington; Hastings & Northumberland; Durham, E. Riding York and Simcoe; Oxford, Middlesex & Norfolk; and Kent. Two members: Glengarry & Prescott; W. Riding York, 1st Riding Lincoln & Haldimand; 2nd, 3rd & 4th Ridings Lincoln; and Essex.

1808 48 Geo III c.11 (16 Mar.), Act of 1800 repealed and six new ridings created raising representation to 25.
One member: Prescott; Stormont & Russell; Dundas; Grenville; Leeds; Frontenac; Prince Edward (except Ameliasburg); Hastings (including Ameliasburg); Northumberland & Durham; East Riding York & Simcoe; West Riding York; part 1st Riding Lincoln and part Haldimand; other part same; 2nd Riding Lincoln; 3rd Riding Lincoln; 4th Riding Lincoln; Oxford & Middlesex; Norfolk; and Kent.
Two members: Glengarry; Lennox & Addington; and Essex.

1817 57 Geo III c.1 (8 Feb.). Wentworth and Halton one member each.

1820 60 Geo III c.2 renumbered 1 Geo IV c.2 (7 Mar.). Repealed all former acts. Every town of 1000 souls to have one member provided quarter sessions were held there. Every country of 1000 souls should have one member, and 4000 souls two members. University to have one member when organized. Result parliament of 1821 had 40 members representing 25 counties and two towns. Repealed by Act of Union of 1840.

1824 4 Geo IV c.5 (19 Jan). Divides Carleton into Lanark and Carleton, but limits representation to same maximum as if one county.

1832 2 Wm IV c.18 (28 Jan.). Amends 4 Geo IV c.5 (1824) to remove limit on representation of Carleton and Lanark.

1833 3 Wm IV c.16 (13 Feb.). Divides York into 4 ridings as follows: (by Township)
1st Riding: York, Etobicoke, Vaughan, King.
2nd Riding: Caledon, Chinquacousy, Toronto, Toronto Gore, Albion (now County Peel).
3rd Riding: Scarborough, Markham, Pickering and Whitby.
4th Riding: East & North Gwillimbury, Scott, Georgina, Brock, Reach, Whitchurch, and Uxbridge.

The Act also provides that future York and Lincoln (now in Regional Municipality of Niagara) elections be by riding, each riding having one member. The Lincoln ridings were not reorganized.

c. List of Counties with Dates of Creation

County	Created	Statute	District (in 1849)

Post-1841 creations are shown in parenthesis.

Where modern Regional Municipalities exist they are shown in square brackets following the district, but their boundaries are frequently different.

Addington	1792	Proclamation of 16 July	Midland
	1800	Incorporated with Lennox 38 Geo III c.5, s.15.	
(Brant	1851	14 & 15 Vic. c.5)	--
(Bruce	1849	12 Vic. c.96)	Huron
Carleton	1800	38 Geo III c.5 s.9	Dalhousie [Ottawa-Carleton]
(Dufferin	1874	Ont., 37 Vic. c.31)	--
Dundas	1792	Proclamation of 16 July	Eastern
Durham	1792	" " " "	Newcastle [Durham]
(Elgin	1851	14 & 15 Vic. c.5)	--
Essex	1792	Proclamation of 16 July	Western
Frontenac	1792	" " " "	Midland
Glengarry	1792	" " " "	Eastern
Grenville	1792	" " " "	Johnstown
(Grey	1851	14 & 15 Vic. c.5)	--
Haldimand	1800	38 Geo III c.5 s.31	Niagara [Haldimand-Norfolk]
(Haliburton	1874	37 Vic. c.65 [provisional])	--
Halton	1816	56 Geo III c.19	Gore [Halton]
Hastings	1792	Proclamation of 16 July	Victoria
Huron	1835	4 Wm IV c.55 s.1	Huron
Kent	1792	Proclamation of 16 July	Kent/Western
(Lambton	1849	12 Vic. c.78)	--
Lanark	1824	5 Geo IV c.5 s.2	Bathurst
Leeds	1792	Proclamation of 16 July	Johnstown
Lennox	1792	" " " "	Midland
	1800	Incorporated with Addington 38 Geo III c.5 s.15	
Lincoln	1792	Proclamation of 16 July	Niagara [Niagara]
Middlesex	1800	38 Geo c.5 s.36	London
Norfolk	1792	Proclamation of 16 July	Talbot [Haldimand-Norfolk]
Northumberland	1792	" " " "	Newcastle

Ontario (1)	1792	" " " "	--
	1800	abolished 38 Geo III c.5 s.11-13	--
(Ontario (2)	1851	14 & 15 Vic. c.5)	Durham [Durham]
Oxford	1800	38 Geo III c.5 s.35	**Brock (Oxford)**
(Peel	1851	14 & 15 Vic. c.5)	-- [Peel]
Peterborough	1838	7 Wm IV c.115 s.2	Colborne
(Perth	1849	12 Vic. c.96)	Huron
Prescott	1800	38 Geo III c.5 s.4	Ottawa
Prince Edward	1792	Proclamation of 16 July	Prince Edward
(Renfrew	1845	8 Vic. c.7)	Bathurst
Russell	1800	38 Geo III c.5 s.5	Ottawa
Simcoe	1800	38 Geo III c.5 s.23	Simcoe
Stormont	1792	Proclamation of 16 July	Eastern
Suffolk	1792	" " " "	
	1800	abolished 38 Geo III c.5 (s.40?)	--
(Victoria	1851	14 & 15 Vic. c.5)	--
Waterloo	1838	7 Wm IV c.116 s. 28	Wellington [Waterloo]
(Welland	1845	8 Vic. c.7 s.5)	Niagara [Niagara]
(Wellington	1851	14 & 15 Vic. c.5)	Wellington
Wentworth	1816	56 Geo III c.19	Gore [Hamilton-Wentworth]
York	1792	Proclamation of 16 July	Home [York and Metropolitan Toronto]

d. Lieutenants of Counties

The county lieutenancy was an office intended to roughly parallel the lord lieutenancy of counties in Great Britain. It was another example of the attempt of Grenville and Simcoe to establish an aristocratic form of government in the colony. Lieutenants were to be justices of the peace and were to play an influential role in militia and magistrates' appointments.

Although lieutenants were to be appointed as soon as counties became sufficiently populous to warrant such an official, there is no evidence that appointments were ever made for many counties. The experiment was not a success; after 1807 no new lieutenants were commissioned. Technically the incumbents held office for life, although they can have had little authority after the military reorganizations during the War of 1812.

Addington
William Johnston   5 May, 1795 -

Dundas
Richard Duncan   2 Nov., 1792 -

Durham
Robert Baldwin Sr.   27 Aug., 1800 -   1816+

Essex
Alexander McKee   2 Nov., 1792 - 13 Jan., 1799+
Alexander Grant Sr.   23 Aug., 1799 -
Francis Baby   1 Aug., 1807 -
Alexander Grant Sr.   17 Dec., 1807 -   May, 1813+

Frontenac
Richard Cartwright Jr.   2 Nov., 1792 - 27 July, 1815+

Glengarry
John Macdonell (Aberchalder)   2 Nov., 1792 - 21 Nov., 1809+

Grenville
Peter Drummond   5 June, 1794 -

Hastings
John Ferguson   23 Nov., 1798 -

Kent
Jacques Duperron Baby   2 Nov., 1792 - 19 Feb., 1833+

Leeds
James Breckenridge   12 May, 1795 -

Lennox
Hazelton Spencer   23 June, 1794 -   Feb., 1813+

Lincoln
John Butler   2 Nov., 1792 - 13 May, 1796+
Robert Hamilton   20 July, 1796 - 8 Mar., 1811+

Middlesex
Thomas Talbot   8 Nov., 1803 - 5 Feb., 1853+

Norfolk
Samuel Ryerse   17 July, 1797 -   1812+

Northumberland

Alexander Chisholm	24 July, 1801 -

Oxford

William Claus	28 June, 1802 - 12 Nov., 1826+

Prescott

William Fortune	20 Feb., 1801 -

Prince Edward

Peter Van Alstine	2 Nov., 1792 -
Archibald Macdonell	11 Aug., 1800 -

Stormont

James Gray	2 Nov., 1792 -
Archibald Macdonell	24 Oct., 1796 -
John Macdonell	10 May, 1805 -

York

AEneas Shaw	29 Aug., 1796 -
David William Smith	3 Dec., 1798 -
John McGill	27 Apr., 1805 - 31 Dec., 1834+

e. Registrars of Counties

Originally each of the four districts of Upper Canada had a land board; but to facilitate land granting these were split into local boards by Simcoe in a circular dated 21 October, 1792. Each board had authority over one or more counties. In 1795 an act was passed (35 Geo. III c.5) which provided for the establishment of land registry offices throughout the province. Registrars were appointed for counties, however, particularly in the early period, a registrar could hold office for more than one county in the same district: e.g. Stormont, Dundas and Glengarry (the Eastern District).

The following table is a combination of the registrars who received commissions (with two 1827 exceptions all before 1841 were dated 1796-1803) and those whose appointment appeared in the *Gazette*. Thus it can only be partially complete.

The date of creation of the county is shown after the county name, but a registrar was not necessarily appointed at that time.

Carleton (1800)

Levius Peters Sherwood	29 May, 1801 - 17 Oct.,	1825
Alexander McMillan	9 Dec., 1825 -	(1842)
George Thew Burke	(1846) -	(1849)

Dundas (1792)

Alexander Campbell	1795 -	1801
Jacob Farrand	20 May, 1801 - 11 May,	1803+

154

John Low Farrand	25 May, 1803	- 29 June, 1814+
John McLean	5 Feb., 1815^G-	
Archibald McLean	10 Feb., 1817	- 13 June, 1837
Alexander McDonell	11 Sept.,1837 -	1867

Durham (1792)

Thomas Ward	15 Nov., 1808 -	(1846)
George C. Ward	(1847)-	(1849)

Essex (1792)

Rev. Richard Pollard	Sept.,1794 -	6 Nov., 1824+
John Hands	24 Jan., 1825^G-	29 Dec., 1830+
James Askin	13 Apr., 1831 -	(1858)

Frontenac (1792)

Allan McLean	4 June, 1796 -	(1839)
Charles Stuart	7 Nov., 1840 -	(1849)

Glengarry (1792)

Jacob Farrand	1795 -	11 May, 1803+
John Low Farrand	25 May, 1803	- 29 June, 1814+
Archibald McLean	1814 -	
John McDonell	1816 -	Apr.,1833$^+$
Walter Cameron	18 May, 1833 -	1837
Alexander Fraser	7 Oct., 1837^G-	1853

Grenville (1792)

Alexander Campbell	1795 -	1801
Levius Peters Sherwood	20 May, 1801 -	(1827)
Andrew Patton		1830
John Patton	17 May, 1830 -	(1849)

Haldimand (1800)

J. Powell		1827+
John Lyons	12 May, 1827 -	(1839)
Agnew P. Farrell	9 Aug., 1844 -	(1849)

Halton (1816)

James Durand	(1821)-	22 Mar., 1833+
Thomas Racey	1 May, 1833 -	(1849)

Hastings (1792)

Allan McLean	4 June, 1796 -	(1846)
George Benjamin	(1847)-	(1849)

Huron (1835)

Robert Graham Dunlop	30 May, 1835 -	28 Feb., 1841+
John Galt	31 May, 1841 -	(1849)

Kent (1792)

Rev. Richard Pollard	Sept.,1794 -	6 Nov., 1824+
James Richardson	25 Jan., 1825^G-	1827
John Beverley Robinson	12 Nov., 1829 -	
Robert Rist (?)	1829 -	
William Jones	15 Dec., 1829 -	1849
Henry Glass	13 Jan., 1849 -	1851

Lanark (1824)

George T. Burke	23 May, 1824 -	(1839)
Alexander McMillan	(1846) -	(1849)

Leeds (1792)

Alexander Campbell	1795 -	1801
Levius Peters Sherwood	20 May, 1801 -	17 Oct., 1825
Sir Daniel Jones	10 Dec., 1825 -	23 Aug., 1838+
David Jones	22 Sept.,1838 -	(1849)

Lennox (and Addington) (1792)

Allan McLean	4 June, 1796 -	(1839)
Isaac Fraser	(1846) -	(1849)

Lincoln (1792)

John Powell	(1821) -	1827+
John Lyons	12 May, 1827^G-	(1844)
John Powell	9 Aug., 1844 -	(1849)

Middlesex (1800)

Thomas Hornor	11 July, 1800 -	
Mahlon Burwell	20 Dec., 1809 -	1843
Hercules Burwell	1843 -	(1849)

Norfolk (1792)

Thomas Welch (Walsh)	1796 -	1810
Francis Leigh Walsh	4 Apr., 1810 -	1884

Northumberland (1792)

D. McGregor Rogers	(1821) -	1824+
George Strange Boulton	17 July, 1824^G-	13 Feb., 1869+

Oxford (1800)

Thomas Hornor	11 July, 1800 -	1834+
James Ingersoll	12 Nov., 1834 -	9 Aug., 1886+

Peterborough (1838)

Charles Rubidge	9 Dec., 1841 -	(1849)

Prescott (1800) (with Russell)

Joseph Fortune	19 July 1800 -	1821
R. P. Hotham	17 Dec., 1821^G -	10 Oct., 1840+
Thomas Fortye	9 Dec., 1841 -	
George D. Reed	16 Aug., 1824 -	(1849)

Prince Edward (1792)

Allan McLean	4 June, 1796-	(1847?)
Andrew Dickson	3 Sept., 1842-	
John P. Roblin	(1848)-	(1849)

Renfrew (1845)

James Morris	(1847)-	(1849)

Russell (1800)

- see Prescott -

Simcoe (1800)

Stephen Jarvis	(1821)-	1827
George Lount	20 Aug., 1827 -	(1849)

Stormont (1792)

Jacob Farrand	1795 -	11 May, 1803+
John Low Farrand	25 May, 1803 -	29 June, 1814+
John McLean	5 Feb., 1815^G-	
Archibald McLean	10 Feb., 1817 -	23 Mar., 1837
John McLean	28 June, 1837 -	1852

Waterloo (1838)

H. W. Peterson	(1841)-	(1849)

Welland (1845)

John Powell	(1847)-	(1849)

Wentworth (1816)

James Durand	4 Apr., 1816^G-	22 Mar., 1833+
David A. MacNab	12 Apr., 1833 -	29 Feb., 1840+
Sir Allan Napier MacNab	23 Mar., 1840 -	
Alexander Stewart	8 Nov., 1844 -	(1846)

York (1792)

Thomas Ridout	14 Sept.,1796 -	
Stephen Jarvis	(1821)-	1827
Samuel Smith Ridout	14 May, 1827 -	1855+

C. Districts

[See Table I p. 198 for the development of the district system]

a. Introduction

The District was the basic unit of local government throughout the Upper Canadian period, the original four districts in Upper Canada—Lunenburgh, Mecklenburg, Nassau and Hesse—being established in 1788 and gradually subdivided as the population increased until there were 20 and one provisional district in 1849. Four of the new districts were set up in a general territorial revision in 1798, and no less than eight in 1837-43 (Table c. below). In 1847 shortly before the abolition of the district in favour of the county, legislation was passed creating a District of Kent but the process was never completed.

Until 1841 the government of the district was on an autocractic basis except for a brief period before the Rebellion; the Justices of the Peace meeting in a Court of Quarter Sessions four times a year both to try legal cases and supervise the administration of the area. The justices and most of the officials were legally appointed by the Lieutenant-Governor and were responsible only to the government at York/Toronto, although from the point of view of practical politics the central government normally paid careful attention to local interests and family connections in making the appointments. From 1793 each township was allowed to elect its own officials for minor local matters (33 Geo. III, c.2), but they had little authority and were always under the supervision of the magistrates. More local autonomy gradually developed in the towns especially after 1832 when incorporations began. (Table D. below).

In 1841 this whole system was changed by the first district councils Act (Table b. below) which brought in an elected council to replace the administrative powers of the Magistrates of the Quarter Sessions. In 1846 the central government gave up the rights of appointment it had retained over the officials of the council, which body basically assumed the form it has today. In 1850 with the abolition of the districts the District Council became the County Council. (Table b. below).

The most important of the local officials—who are listed in the following tables—and their duties, were as follows:

— *Clerk of the Peace*—Attended Court of Quarter Sessions, gave notice of its being holden or adjourned, kept its records, and handled all the administrative work connected with it. Presented and received bills for the Grand Jury and recorded its verdict.

— *Sheriff*—Executed all processes issuing from the King's Courts of Justice, issued writs, called juries, made arrests, executed sentences, kept jails, and attended the Quarter Sessions.

— *Treasurer*—Received and kept all moneys belonging to the district, kept financial records, and made payments as directed. Appointed by the Quarter Sessions.

— *District Court Judge*—An experienced barrister who presided over the District Courts which were roughly equivalent to the County Courts today. There often was more than one district judge at a time. The *Clerk* kept the court records.

— *Surrogate Court Judge*—Granted probates of wills and letters of administration in the district. Estates that involved property of any amount or in more than one district normally fell under the jurisdiction of the provincial Court of Probate. The *Registrar* kept the records of the court and provided official copies of wills.

—*Inspectors of Licences*—Were appointed by the Lieutenant-Governor for the districts, and were normally not commissioned. Their duties were the licensing of houses of public entertainment, stores, retailing spirituous liquors, inns, ale and beer houses and eating-places. Though minor, the post was a lucrative one which was frequently held by prominent individuals as a "secondary" appointment. Complete lists are virtually impossible to reconstruct.

— *District Schoolmasters*—District schools were established under 47 George III c.6, passed 10 March, 1807, which provided for one school per district, usually located at the district town. A board of school trustees of not less than five in number was appointed for each district by the Lieutenant-Governor and limited funding provided. The trustees, who were usually leading justices of the peace and officials of the district, appointed and removed the schoolmaster as they saw fit, so complete lists are very difficult to establish. Often the schoolmaster was a minister (CE = Church of England, P = Presbyterian, etc.). The schools were a sort of high-elementary combination which gradually evolved into the present secondary school structure in the middle and late nineteenth century.

— *Warden*—The chairman of the District Council after 1841. He was appointed by the provincial government till 1846 and then elected by the councillors from among their number. Usually after 1846 he held office for only one year.

— *Clerk of the District Council*—Another new official after 1841. Kept the council records and made them available to the public as required. After 1846 held appointment at the pleasure of the council.

The following tables include all legislation relating to the districts. Together with the notes on the counties above they provide a picture of the territorial arrangements of Upper Canada. The transfers of counties between the districts are shown, but except in extraordinary cases it has been impossible to list the names of all townships involved. Special transfers of townships, however, are noted, as are acts dividing existing townships—which are rare except in Prince Edward County.

The tables of officials are as complete as possible, but are still quite fragmentary for the reasons noted in the introduction. The lists of Sheriffs, Judges, Surrogates, and Wardens from 1841 to 1846 are probably most complete. Information on the treasurers and some clerks is difficult to obtain.

b. General Legislation Relating to Districts

1788   Proclamation of 24 July. Lord Dorchester creates five new districts, Gaspe in modern Quebec and Lunenburg, Mecklenburg, Nassau and Hesse covering what is now southern Ontario.

1792   32 Geo. III, c.8 (15 Oct). Four districts renamed Eastern, Midland, Home and Western respectively.

1798   38 Geo. III, c.5 (Proclaimed 1 Jan., 1800). Complete territorial redistribution. Several new districts created and old ones redefined.

1800-1841   New districts created by individual legislation, but no general redistribution.

1837   7 Wm. IV c.11. General restatement of Quarter Sessions times and places of meeting.

1841   4 & 5 Vic. c.10 (27 Aug.). Effective 1 Jan., 1842, District Councils established to replace Courts of Quarter Sessions for administrative purposes. Councils to consist of a Warden, appointed by the governor, and a body of councillors elected by the townships. Townships with less than 300 inhabitant householders elect one councillor, with over 300 elect two councillors. Councillors to have a three-year-term, one third retiring each year. Meetings of Council to be held quarterly. Governor to appoint the district Clerk (From a list of three submitted by the Council) and the district Treasurer.

1845   8 Vic. c.7 (10 Feb.) Defines limits of all districts and creates certain new townships.

1846   9 Vic. c.40 (9 June). Each district council shall elect its own Warden annually from among the Council members. Wardens can be re-elected. District Treasurer to be appointed by Council for a three year renewable term. District Clerk to be appointed by Council; Clerk of the Peace to be eligible for the office. Council normally to meet only half-yearly (February and October).

1846   9 Vic. c.46 (23 May). Amends 8 Vic. c.7; redefines Counties of Carleton and Grenville.

1849   12 Vic. c.78 (30 May). Effective 31 Dec., 1849 all districts abolished as in many cases are identical with counties, and English system of counties established. Where district consists of more than one county it is to be replaced by a Union of Counties. Under Sec. 10 such unions can be abolished by order-in-council when population of smaller county reaches 15,000 and two-thirds of reeves petition for change.

1849   12 Vic. c.79 (30 May). Amends above especially in regard to Union of Essex, Kent and Lambton.

1849   12 Vic. c.80 (30 May). Repeats various acts relating to local and municipal authorities.

1849   12 Vic. c.81 (30 May). (Municipal Act or Baldwin act). Classifies municipal corporations and provides for the erection of new ones. Six categories:

         I. Townships   IV. Incorporated Villages
        II. Counties   V. Towns
       III. Police Villages   VI. Cities

1850   13 & 14 Vic. c.64 (10 Aug.). Provides schedule of two types of villages (called town) that was left off above and corrects errors.

c. Key List of Districts

N.B. Dates are those of first act and the actual proclamation of district if it was later.

Date	District	Town	Out of
1821 (1822)	Bathurst	Perth	Johnstown
1837 (1839)	Brock	Woodstock	London
1838 (1841)	Colborne	Peterborough	Newcastle
1838 (1842)	Dalhousie	Bytown	Bathurst, Johnstown and Ottawa
1788	Eastern	New Johnstown and later Cornwall	-
1816	Gore	Hamilton	York and Niagara
-	Hesse - see Western	-	
1788	Home	Newark (renamed; Niagara-on-the-Lake) and later York/Toronto	
1838 (1841)	Huron	Goderich	London
1798 (1800)	Johnstown	Johnstown and later Brockville	Eastern
1847 (----)	Kent	Chatham	Western
1798 (1800)	London	Charlotteville and later Vittoria and London	Home and Western
-	Lunenburgh -see Eastern	-	
-	Mecklenburg - see Midland	-	
1788	Midland	Kingston	
-	Nassau - see Home	-	
1798 (1802)	Newcastle	Newcastle and Cobourg	Home
1798 (1800)	Niagara	Niagara-on-the-Lake	Home
1816	Ottawa	L'Original	Eastern
1831 (1834)	Prince Edward	Picton	Midland
1821 (1843)	Simcoe	Barrie	Home
1837	Talbot	Simcoe	London
1837 (1839)	Victoria	Belleville	Midland
1838 (1840)	Wellington	Guelph	Gore and Home
1788	Western	Sandwich	-

d. Districts with Legislation and Officials

Dates after name show actual proclamation as a district.

1. Bathurst District 1822

i. Legislation.

1821 2 Geo. IV c.3 s.4 (14 Apr.). Governor empowered to separate Carleton County from the Johnstown District when he sees fit.

1822 Proclamation of 13 Nov. Carleton County declared a separate district by the name of Bathurst.

1823 4 Geo. IV c.2. s.3 (29 Jan.). Provides for district court and school system and makes Perth the district town.

1824 5 Geo. IV c.5.(19 Jan.). Divides district into two counties, Lanark and Carleton, and limits their representation in the Legislative Assembly.

1838 1 Vic. c.25 (6 Mar.). County of Carleton transferred to the new district of Dalhousie. County of Lanark reorganized so that it includes part of Carleton, and also some townships from the Johnstown District.

1846 9 Vic. c.46 (23 May). Divides North Gower Township assigning part south of the Rideau River to South Gower Township in Grenville County, Johnstown District.

1849 12 Vic. c.94 (30 May). Transfer of certain unorganized lands from Midland District to Bathurst District. (What is now the interior of Renfrew County).

ii. Officials

Clerks of the Peace

G. H. Reade	9 Jan., 1823^G -	(1839)
John Macdonald	24 Oct., 1843 -	(1846)
W. F. R. Berford	(1848) -	(1849)

Sheriffs

James Henry Powell	6 Dec., 1822 - 13 Nov., 1831	
John Ambrose Hume Powell	14 Nov., 1831 -	
John Fitzwilliam Berford	3 Dec., 1832 -	
John Ambrose Hume Powell	2 May, 1834 -	(1839)
Andrew Dickson	5 July, 1843 - 17 Apr., 1852	

Treasurers

John Watson	(1823)-	Sept. 1832+
John McKay	(1833)-	(1839)
Thomas M. Radenhurst	23 Dec., 1841 -	(1849)

District Court Judges

Jonas Jones	6 Dec., 1822 -	(1837)
Hamilton Walker	18 Nov., 1823 -	(1827)

Donald Bethune	22 Nov.,	1826 -	(1837)
Alexander Thorn	23 Apr.,	1835 -	
George Malloch	29 Sept.,	1837 -	(1839)
Thomas Radenhurst	29 Dec.,	1841 -	
Christopher Armstrong	20 Jan.,	1842 -	
John Glass Malloch	18 Aug.,	1842 -	(1846)
James Hubbell	8 Sept.,	1848 -	

District Court Clerks

Charles Henry Sache	3 Jan.,	1823 -	(1849)

Surrogate Court Judges

Jonas Jones	6 Dec.,	1822 -	
Jonas or Josias Taylor	25 July,	1835 -	
Ephraim Jones Hubbell	5 Dec.,	1835 -	
John Glass Malloch		(1846)-	
Daniel McMartin	5 Feb.,	1848 -	(1849)

Surrogate Court Registrars

Henry Bradfield	30 Dec.,	1822^G-	1830
Joseph Taylor	24 June,	1830 -	(1837)
Charles Henry Sache		(1839)-	(1849)

Inspectors of Licences

Anthony Lesslie	31 Dec.,	1822 -	(1836)

Schoolmasters

Vacant		(1821)-	
John Stewart	1 July,	1823 -	(1828)
William Kay	1 July,	1835 -	(1836)
John Brown			(1848)

Wardens

Alexander MacMillan	23 Dec.,	1841 -	
Daniel McMartin		(1846)-	
Robert Bell		(1848)-	1850

Clerks of the District Council

Robert Moffatt	1 Mar.,	1842 -	(1848)

2. Brock District 1839

i. Legislation

1837 7 Wm. IV c.30 (4 Mar.) Certain townships of London District to be turned into new district of Brock as soon as court house and jail built. District town to be Woodstock. Magistrates may borrow £6,000 for building. All townships in district to be in County of Oxford.

1839 2 Vic. c.29 (11 May) Extends time for additional tax to be paid for court house and jail.

1839 30 Nov., Proclamation of district.

1849 12 Vic. c.78 (30 May) Abolished. County of Oxford succeeds.

ii. Officials

Clerks of the Peace

William Lapenotiere	30 Jan., 1840^G -	(1849)

Sheriffs

James Carroll	7 Mar., 1840 -	(1849)

Treasurers

Hugh C. Barwick	10 Feb., 1842 -	(1849)

District Court Judges

John Arnold	5 Feb., 1840 -
David Shank McQueen	26 May, 1845 - 6 June, 1885+

District Court Clerks

J. G. Vansittart	30 Jan., 1840^G -	
Richard Foquett	3 July, 1847^G -	(1849)

Surrogate Court Judges

John Arnold	1 Aug., 1840 -	
William Lapenotiere	22 Oct., 1845 -	(1849)

Surrogate Court Registrars

John George Vansittart	10 Aug., 1840 -	(1849)

Inspectors of Licences

J. G. Vansittart	26 Feb., 1848 -

Schoolmasters

Timothy Shyne	(Feb., 1841)	-
J. Somerville		(1848)

Wardens

Peter Boyle de Blaquiere	23 Dec., 1841 -	(1849)
Solomon Lossing	30 Mar., 1843 - 24 June, 1844+	
George Washington Whitehead	27 June, 1845 -	

Daniel McMartin (Acting?)	7 Aug., 1845 -	
George Washington Whitehead	Feb., 1846 -	
Jared Vining	Feb., 1847 -	(1849)

Clerks of the District Council

William Lapenotiere	1 Mar., 1842 -	(1849)

3. Colborne District 1841

i. Legislation

1838 7 Wm. IV c.115 (Proclaimed 20 Apr.). North part of Newcastle made a separate district with Peterborough as district town. District to be coterminus with new County of Peterborough. Court house and jail to be built first. £6,000 loan authorized.

1839 2 Vic. c.31. (11 May). Extends time for special tax, to pay for court house and jail. Bill No. 1154-(Act suspended). Proposal to divide County Peterborough into County Colborne (those townships formerly in Northumberland in Newcastle district), and County Mansfield (those townships formerly in Durham County, Newcastle district). In 1851 those townships which would have formed Mansfield were separated as the township of Victoria by 14 and 15 Vic. c.5.

1841 14 Oct., Proclamation of district.

1849 12 Vic. c.78 (30 May). Abolished. County of Peterborough succeeds.

ii. Officials

Clerks of the Peace

W. H. Wrighton	9 Dec., 1841 -	(1856)

Sheriffs

Wilson S. Conger	9 Dec., 1841 -	(1849)

Treasurers

John Gilchrist	10 Feb., 1842 -	
Frederick Ferguson	21 Apr., 1845 -	(1849)

District Court Judges

Burrage Yale McKyes	10 Dec., 1841 -	1846
George B. Hall	8 Dec., 1847 -	(1849)

District Court Clerks

Thomas Fortye	9 Dec., 1841 -	(1849)

Surrogate Court Judges

Burrage Yale McKyes	10 Dec., 1841 -	(1846)
George B. Hall	1 May, 1848 -	(1849)

Surrogate Court Registrars

Thomas Fortye	9 Dec., 1841 -	(1849)

Inspectors of Licences

Unknown

Schoolmasters

Rev. R. J. C. Taylor   (1848)

Wardens

George A. Hill   23 Dec., 1841 -   (1849)

John Langton   (1848) -   1850

Clerks of the District Council

John Darcus   1 Mar., 1842

Walter Sheridan   17 Sept., 1844 -   (1849)

4. Dalhousie District 1842

i. Legislation

1838 1 Vic. c.25 (6 Mar.). Transfers certain townships from the Bathurst, Ottawa and Johnstown Districts to form a new district to be proclaimed as soon as jail and court facilities available. District to be called Dalhousie and district town to be Bytown (renamed Ottawa, 1855). Magistrates authorized to borrow £2,500 for buildings. County of Carleton reorganized to be coterminous with district.

1839 2 Vic. c.26 (11 May). Clarifies selection of site for buildings in Bytown.

1840 3 Vic. c.45 (10 Feb.). Additional tax for jail and court house erection.

1841 4 & 5 Vic. c.76 (18 Sept.). Authorized the borrowing of an additional £6,000 for erection of jail and court house.

1842 19 Mar., Proclamatin of district.

1849 12 Vic. c.78 (30 May). Abolished, County of Carleton succeeds.

ii. Officials

Clerks of the Peace

Alexander J. Christie   12 May, 1842 -   1843+

F. C. Powell   23 Nov., 1843 -   (1849)

Sheriffs

Edward Malloch   25 June, 1842 -   1846

Simon Fraser   9 Jan., 1846 -   (1849)

Treasurers

Daniel O'Connor   22 June, 1842 -   (1849)

District Court Judges

Christopher Armstrong   7 May,   1842 -   (1846)

Ephraim Jones Hubbell   27 May, 1844 -

District Court Clerks

Braddish Billings, Jr.   9 May,   1842 -   (1849)

Surrogate Court Judges

Christopher Armstrong	7 May, 1842 –	(1849)

Surrogate Court Registrars

Braddish Billings, Jr.	9 May, 1842 –	(1849)

Inspector of Licences

Unknown

Schoolmasters

Vacant	(1821)	
Rev. J. Robb		(1848)

Wardens

Thomas McKay	12 May, 1842 –	1846
Hamnet Pinhey	19 Jan., 1846 –	(1849)

Clerks of the District Court

Godfrey Phipps Baker	2 Sept.,1842 –	(1846)
Charles Hamnet Pinhey	(1848)–	(1849)

5. Eastern District (Lunenburgh) 1788

i. Legislation

1788 Proclamation of 24 July, using the spelling "Luneburg", whereas the later statute used "Lunenburgh", Lord Dorchester divides modern southern Ontario into four districts. Lunenburgh comprised the area east of a line running due north from the mouth of the Gananoque River.

1792 32 Geo. III c.8 (15 Oct.). Provided name change from Lunenburgh to Eastern District (sec. 2). District town to be New Johnstown (s. 8).

1794 34 Geo. III c.10 (9 July). Provides for second jail and court house to be erected at Cornwall.

1798 38 Geo. III c.5. s.1-10 (Proclaimed 1 Jan., 1800). Act for better division of province. Reorganized Eastern District so that it consisted of counties of Glengarry, Stormount, Dundas, Prescott and Russell. Counties of Grenville, Leeds and Carleton separated to become the Johnstown District.

1801 41 Geo. III c.6. s.2 (9 July). Courts to be held at Cornwall.

1816 56 Geo. III c.2 (22 Mar.). Counties of Prescott and Russell separated to form Ottawa District.

1818 59 Geo. III c.3 (27 Nov.). Township Lancaster in Glengarry County divided into Townships of Lancaster and Lochiel.

1827 8 Geo. IV c.15 (17 Feb.). Provides for raising a loan of £4,000 for new jail and court house at Cornwall.

1830 11 Geo. IV c.29 (6 Mar.). Magistrates can borrow £3,500 for new jail and court house.

1833 3 Wm. IV c.4 (13 Feb.). Authorizes additional £2,000 loan.

1849 12 Vic. c.78 (30 May). Abolished district. United counties of Stormont, Dundas and Glengarry succeed.

ii. **Officials**

Clerks of the Peace

Jacob Farrand		1798 - 11 May, 1803+
John Low Farrand	25 May,	1803 - 29 June, 1814+
John McLean	5 Feb.,	1815^G
Archibald McLean	14 May,	1817^G - 23 Mar., 1837
James Pringle	10 May.,	1837- 1858

Sheriffs

Cornelius Munro		1792 -
Neil McLean	5 Dec.,	1808 -
John Kerr	9 Feb.,	1816 -
Donald Macdonell (of Greenfield)	13 Aug.,	1819 - (1837)
Alexander McMartin	18 Dec.,	1839 -
Donald MacDonell	8 Apr.,	1848 - (1849)

Treasurers

Robert McGregor		(1799)- (1800)
Neil McLean		1806 - 3 July, 1832+
Alexander McLean		1832 - (1846)
R. Macdonald		(1847)- (1849)

District Court Judges

Richard Wilkinson	4 July,	1794 -
Samuel Anderson	2 Aug.,	1796 - 1814
David Sheek	12 Mar.,	1811 - 1822
Levius P. Sherwood	19 Mar.,	1821 - 17 Oct., 1825
David Jones	21 Dec.,	1825 - 1841
Hamilton Walker	21 Dec.,	1825 - ?
Daniel Jones	23 Nov.,	1826 - (1837)
George Stephen Jarvis	6 Jan.,	1842 - 1878

District Court Clerks

Alexander Campbell		1794 - 1800
J. Donovan		1800 - 1809
George Anderson	17 Nov.,	1809 - 1850

Surrogate Court Judges

Richard Wilkinson	3 Sept.,	1793 -
Ephraim Jones	7 June,	1796 -

Samuel Anderson	1 Jan., 1800 –	1812
John Low Farrand	1812 –	1814
David Sheek	1814 –	1821
Neil McLean	31 Jan., 1822 –	1832
John McDonald (of Gart)	31 May, 1833 –	1844
Robert Cline	7 Aug., 1845 –	1847
George McDonell	24 Jan., 1848 –	1857

Surrogate Court Registrars

Robert I. D. Gray	5 Sept., 1793 –	1796
Samuel Sherwood	7 June, 1796 –	
Joseph Anderson	1 Jan., 1800 –	
Richard Warffe	1811 –	1817
Archibald McLean	3 Apr., 1817 –	1837
Alexander McLean	1837 –	(1849)

Inspectors of Licences

Neil McLean	23 Apr., 1803 –	(1831)
Philip Vankoughnet	10 Oct., 1832^G –	(1836)

Schoolmasters

Rev. John Strachan, CE.	1807 –	1812
Rev. John Bethune, CE.	(1812) –	6 May 1814
Rev. W. D. Baldwyn	May 1814 –	6 Nov., 1815
Rev. Joseph Johnston, CE.	27 Oct., 1817 –	
Vacant	(1818) –	
Rev. John Leeds, CE.	(1818) –	(1823)
Henry James (temporary)	10 Jan., 1823 –	
Rev. Harry Leith, CE.	2 Feb., 1823 –	(1824)
Rev. Hugh Urquhart, P.	3 Jan., 1827 –	(1836)
Wm. Kay		(1848)

(Uncertain date) – James Fulton (pre 1830)

Wardens

Alexander Fraser	23 Dec., 1841 –	1849

Clerks of the District Council

James Pringle	6 June, 1842 –	1851

6. Gore District 1816

i. Legislation

1816 56 Geo. III c.19 (22 Mar.). Parts of the West Riding of the County of York (Home District) and parts of the 1st Riding of the County of Lincoln and the County of Haldimand (Niagara District) separated to form the Gore District, which was divided into two new counties, Wentworth and Halton. Hamilton to be the district town. Operation of district to start immediately.

1827 8 Geo. IV c.13 (17 Feb.). Provided for magistrates to borrow £4,000 to complete court house and jail at Hamilton.

1838 7 Wm. IV c.116 (Proclaimed 20 Apr.). Parts of County Halton, with parts of Simcoe from Home District, created into Wellington District.

1843 7 Vic. c.40 (9 Dec.). Defines boundary between Gore and Niagara (see Niagara for details).

1849 12 Vic. c.78 (30 May). Abolished. United counties of Wentworth and Hamilton succeed.

ii. Officials

Clerks of the Peace

George Rolph	(1818)-	(1828)
John Burwell (pro tem)	(1827)-	(1828)
Robert Berrie (Dismissed)	18 May, 1829 -	10 Mar., 1841
Arthur Gifford	3 Apr., 1841 -	25 Aug., 1844+
Samuel B. Freeman	20 Sept., 1844 -	(1849)

Sheriffs

John Symington	4 Apr., 1816^G-	
Titus Geer Simons	15 Apr., 1816 -	1824
William Munson Jarvis	7 May, 1824 -	(1837)
Allan McDonell	(1839)-	
Edward Cartwright Thomas	17 Mar., 1843 -	(1875)

Treasurers

George Hamilton	(1821)-	(1827)
Elijah Secord	(1831)-	1834
Henry Beasley	1834 -	1846
James Kirkpatrick	1846 -	1876

District Court Judges

Richard Hatt	13 Apr., 1816 -	
Thomas Taylor	4 Nov., 1819 -	Dec., 1838+
Miles O'Reilly	28 Mar., 1837 -	(1849)

District Court Clerks

George Rolph	4 Apr., 1816^G -	1824
John Law	24 Oct., 1823 -	
Andrew Stuart	29 July, 1844 -	(1849)

Surrogate Court Judges

Richard Hatt	27 Sept., 1816^G -	
Thomas Taylor	7 Nov., 1819 -	(1831)
John Wilson	21 June, 1838 -	
William Dummer Powell	26 Mar., 1847 -	
William Allan Harvey	1 May, 1847 -	
Samuel B. Freeman	4 Jan., 1848 -	(1849)

Surrogate Court Registrars

George Rolph	4 Apr., 1816^G -	(1849)

Inspectors of Licences

John Wilson (Willson)	1 Apr., 1816 -	(1836)

Schoolmasters

Richard Cochrel	(pre-1830 uncertain date)	
Rev. Ralph Leeming, CE	(182) -	
John Law	1 June, 1821 -	(1829)
Stephen Randal	5 Dec., 1827 -	
Rev. M. Y. Stark	7 June, 1834 -	
John Rae A.M.	13 Dec., 1834 -	(1836)
-Asst. William Tassie	1836 -	
George Elmslie		(1848)

Wardens

John Wetenhall	23 Dec., 1841 -	
Samuel Clarke	1847 -	1849

District Council Clerks

Dr. Edward C. Thomas	1 Mar., 1842 -	
Henry W. Jackson	15 Mar., 1843 -	
James Durand	1847 -	1850

7. Home District [Nassau] 1788

i. Legislation

1788 Proclamation of 24 July. Lord Dorchester divides present southern Ontario into four districts. Nassau is area between lines running due north from the mouth of the Trent River and the tip of Long Point on Lake Erie.

1792 32 Geo. III c.8. s.4. (15 Oct.). Name of district changed from Nassau to Home.

1798 38 Geo. III c.8. (Promulgated 1 Jan., 1800). Reorganized the districts. Sections 19-24 provided Home District would consist of counties of Northumberland, Durham, East and West Ridings of York and Simcoe. Section 25 provided Northumberland and Durham would be separate district called Newcastle when population reached 1000 and six townships. Sections 27 - 32 set up District of Niagara separate from Home District consisting of the four Ridings of Lincoln, and Haldimand. Sections 33-37 created District of London composed of counties of Norfolk, Oxford, and Middlesex, formerly part in Home and part in Western District.

1801 41 Geo. III c.6. (9 July). District town York.

1816 56 Geo. II c.19. s.2. (22 Mar.). Part of the West Riding of York separated and joined with parts of the Niagara District to form the Gore District. The township of Toronto transferred to the east Riding of York.

1821 2 Geo. III c.3 s.7-8. (14 Apr.). Establishes County of Simcoe and provides governor could declare it a separate district by proclamation when he saw fit. See also 7 Wm. IV c.32 (1837).

1821 2 Geo. IV c.16 (14 Apr.). Quarter Sessions in future on 3rd Tues. in Jan., Apr., July, and 2nd Tues. in Oct.

1823 4 Geo. IV c.24 (19 Mar.). Provides for magistrates to borrow £4,000 to erect new jail and court house at York.

1823 4 Geo. IV c.30 (19 Mar.). Quarter Sessions in future on Tues. of week following term of the King's Bench.

1825 6 George IV c.4 (13 Apr.). Provides for additional £2,000 loan for same purpose.

1837 7 Wm. IV c.32 (4 Mar.). Governor can erect County of Simcoe into a separate district when jail and court house constructed at Barrie, to be district town. Certain townships of Simcoe transferred to York and Waterloo.

1837 7 Wm. IV c.40 (4 Mar.). Authorizes building of jail and court house at Barrie.

1838 7 Wm. IV c.116 (20 Apr.). Parts of Simcoe County and parts of Halton in Gore District erected into Wellington District.

1839 2 Vic. c.44 (11 May). Authorizes loan of £15,000 for jail and court house.

1849 12 Vic. c.78 (30 May). Abolished. County of York succeeds (including future counties of Peel and Ontario).

1853 16 Vic. c.96 (22 Apr.). Township of Georgina transferred from Ontario to York.

ii. Officials

The partition of the Home District in 1800 left the old district town of Niagara in the new District of Niagara and most of the local officials remained there with new officials being appointed at York.

Clerks of the Peace

Ralfe Clench	2 June, 1792 -	1 Jan., 1800
Thomas Ridout	1 Jan, 1800 -	
Stephen Heward	(1818) -	1828+
Simon Ebenezer Washburn	14 Oct., 1828^G -	29 Sept., 1837+
George Gurnett	7 Oct., 1837^G -	17 Nov., 1861+

Sheriffs

Alexander Macdonell (Collachie)	1 Mar., 1792 -	1804
Joseph Willcocks (Dismissed)	4 Sept., 1804 -	10 Apr., 1807
Miles McDonell	10 Apr., 1809 -	
John Beikie	2 May, 1810 -	1815
Samuel Smith Ridout	26 Apr., 1815 -	1827
William Botsford Jarvis	1 May, 1827 -	26 July, 1864+

Treasurers

William Allan	(1805) -	10 June, 1829
Francis Thomas Billings	May, 1829 -	(1841)
James Scott Howard	11 Jan., 1846 -	(1863)

District Court Judges

Prior to 1800 the judges were largely legal officials of the provincial government who were also commissioned for the District Court.

John White	4 July, 1794 -	1 Jan., 1800
Robert Isaac Dey Gray	7 June, 1796 -	1 Jan., 1800
Alexander Stuart	15 Sept., 1797 -	1 Jan., 1800
William Dummer Powell	6 Aug., 1798 -	1 Jan., 1800
Henry Allcock	19 Jan., 1799 -	1 Jan., 1800
William Willcocks	1 Jan., 1800 -	(1809)
Dr. William Warren Baldwin (Dismissed)	22 July, 1809 -	17 July 1836
Dr. Grant Powell	15 Oct., 1818 -	10 June, 1838+
John Powell	11 Sept. 1835 -	1844
Robert Easton Burns	19 Aug., 1844 -	(1847)
Samuel Bealey Harrison	19 Aug., 1844 -	1867+

District Court Clerks

Stephen Heward	(1818) -	1828+
C. R. Heward		Nov., 1832
Henry C. Heward	22 Nov., 1832 -	(1839)
Walter McKenzie	(1846) -	

Surrogate Court Judges

Dr. Robert Kerr	1793 -	1 Jan., 1800
William Willcocks	31 Jan., 1800 -	1813+
Robert Baldwin Sr.		1816+
Dr. William William Baldwin (Dismissed)	28 Dec., 1816 -	17 July, 1836
John Godfrey Spragge	16 July, 1836^G -	
William Hume Blake	1 July, 1841 -	
Samuel Bealey Harrison	4 Jan., 1845 -	23 July, 1867+

Surrogate Court Registrars

Richard Barnes Tickell	1794 -	June, 1795+
Alexander MacNab	1795 -	
Ralph Clench	13 Apr., 1798 -	1 Jan., 1800
William Chewett	1 Jan., 1800 -	(1846)

Inspectors of Licences

William Allan	3 Mar., 1803 -	(1827)
Alexander McDonell	Nov., 1828 -	1841
James McDonell	8 July, 1841^G -	

Schoolmasters

Rev. George Okill Stuart, CE	1807 -	1812
Rev. John Strachan, CE	1812 -	1823
Rev. William R. Brown, CE	1823 -	
Rev. Samuel Armour		
Rev. Dr. Thomas Phillips, CE	31 May, 1825 -	(1827)
-Asst. George Anthony Barber		
Rev. David Macaulay, CE	16 Mar., 1835 -	(1836)
M. C. Crombie		(1848)

Wardens

Edward William Thompson	23 Dec., 1841 -	(1846)
Michael P. Empey	(1848) -	

Clerks District Council

John Elliott	1 Mar., 1842 -	(1870)

8. Huron District 1841

i. Legislation

1838 1 Vic. c.26 (6 Mar.). Authorizes the governor to separate the County of Huron from the District of London and create it a separate district as soon as a court house and jail are erected at Goderich. Magistrates in the Huron area may raise £6,000 for construction purposes.

1839 2 Vic. c.30 (11 May). Deals with the time necessary to determine the contribution Huron County should make to London District costs as long as it is part of that district.

1840 3 Vic. c.38 (10 Feb.). Attaches Ashfield and other townships in the range to the north to Huron in anticipation of the creation of the new district.

1841 Proclamation of 14 October. County of Huron incorporated as the District of Huron.

1846 9 Vic. c.47 (23 May). All the land to the north of the District of Huron (stretching up to Lake Huron and Georgian Bay), which is not already part of the Districts of Wellington or Simcoe, shall belong to Huron.

1849 12 Vic. c.78 (30 May). Provides for the abolition of the district effective 1 Jan., 1850.

1849 12 Vic. c.96 (30 May). Divides district (in anticipation of future abolition) into three counties: Huron, Perth and Bruce. These are to form a Union of Counties as soon as the District ceases to exist.

ii. Officials

Clerks of the Peace

Daniel Lizars	16 Oct. 1841 -	(1846)

Sheriffs

Henry Hyndman	16 Oct.,1841 - 19 Sept.,	1844+
John McDonald	21 Apr.,1845 - 31 July,	1873+

Treasurers

Henry Rainsford	9 Feb.,1842 - Apr.,	1846
George Brown Jr.	20 May, 1846 -	(1858)

District Court Judges

Arthur Acland	6 Dec., 1841 -	1853+

District Court Clerks

John Colville	16 Oct., 1841 -

Surrogate Court Judges

Arthur Acland	6 Dec., 1841 -	1853+

Surrogate Court Registrars

John Colville	16 Oct., 1841 -	(1846)
T. McQueen		

Inspectors of Licences

Charles Widder	8 Dec., 1841[G] -

Schoolmasters

John Haldane	(1848)

Wardens

Dr. William Dunlop	23 Dec., 1841 -	1846
Thomas Mercer Jones	3 Apr., 1846 -	
William Chalk	27 Feb., 1847 - 22 Jan.,	1855

Clerks of the District Council

Daniel Lizars (acting)	12 Jan., 1842 - 6 May,	1842
David Don	12 Apr., 1842 -	1850+

9. Johnstown District 1800

i. Legislation

1798 38 Geo. III c.5 s.7-10 (Proclaimed 1 Jan., 1800). An Act for the better division of the province separated counties of Grenville, Leeds and Carleton, and made them into the Johnstown District.

1801 41 Geo. III c.6 s.2. (9 July). District courts to be held at Johnstown.

1808 48 Geo. III c.15 (16 Mar.). Authorized transfer of district town from Johnstown to the first concession of Elizabethtown Township (Brockville), and erection of new court house and jail there.

1816 56 Geo. III c.1 (22 Mar.). Quarter Sessions in future on 2nd Tues. in Jan., Apr., July and Oct. (Act also applied to London District).

1821 2 Geo. IV c.3. s.4. (14 Apr.). Provides that the governor may declare the county of Carleton a separate district by proclamation when he sees fit.

1822 Proclamation of 13 Nov., Carleton County declared a separate district by the name of Bathurst.

1824 4 Geo. IV c.35 (19 Jan.). Authorizes repair or rebuilding of court house and jail at Brockville.

1838 1 Vic. c.38 (6 Mar.). Authorizes loan of £7,500, for new land, court house and jail at Brockville.

1838 1 Vic. c.25 (6 Mar.). Certain townships transferred to Bathurst and new District of Dalhousie.

1846 9 Vic.c.16 (23 May). Divides North Gower Township assigning part south of Rideau River to South Gower Township of County Grenville.

1849 12 Vic. c.78 (30 May). District abolished. United Counties of Leeds and Grenville succeed on 1 Jan., 1850.

1849 12 Vic. c.99 (30 May). Divides Townships of Leeds and Lansdowne.

ii. Officials

Clerks of the Peace

Edward Jessup	1 Jan., 1800 -	Feb., 1816+
Hamilton Walker	(1818) -	1830+
James Jessup	15 Sept., 1830 -	(1849)

Sheriffs

Thomas Fraser	1 Jan., 1800 -	
William Fraser	23 Apr., 1803 -	(1808)
John Stuart	26 May, 1813 -	(1827)
Adiel Sherwood	4 July, 1829 -	1864+

Treasurers

Charles Jones	(1805)-	
Adiel Sherwood	1813 -	(1841)
Andrew Norton Buell	7 Feb., 1842 -	
James L. Schofield	(1847)-	(1849)

District Court Judges

Solomon Jones	1 Jan., 1800 -	(1821)
Levius Peters Sherwood	15 Nov., 1820 - 17 Oct.,	1825
Hamilton Walker	18 Nov., 1823 -	(1828)
C. A. Hagerman	27 June, 1826 - 26 June,	1828
Jonas Jones	18 Oct., 1828 -	1836
James Jessup	22 Oct., 1836 -	1837
George Stephen Jarvis	30 June, 1837 - 6 Jan.,	1842
George Malloch	20 Jan., 1842 -	(1849)

District Court Clerks

Charles Jones (Dismissed)	1800 -	1808
Jonathan Jones	1808 -	
George Malloch	(1821)-	(1831)
T. D. Campbell	13 May, 1816 -	(1849)

Surrogate Court Judges

Ephraim Jones	1 Jan., 1800 -	1802+
Levius Peters Sherwood	(1818)-	(1824)
Jonas Jones	31 Dec., 1824 - 23 Mar.,	1837
Ormond Jones	18 Aug., 1837 -	
George Malloch	20 Oct., 1845 -	(1849)

Surrogate Court Registrars

Samuel Sherwood	1 Jan., 1800 -	
George Malloch	17 Aug., 1820 - 15 June,	1838
James Jessup	27 July, 1838 -	(1839)

Inspectors of Licences

Oliver Everts	11 Nov., 1802 -	(1831)?
John Weaterhead	30 Oct., 1828 -	(1836)

Schoolmasters

William Pitt		Spring, 1814
Rev. John Bethune, CE	27 May, 1814 -	(1821)
Rev. Rossington Elms, CE	1823 -	
Rev. John Leeds, CE	(1824) -	
James Padfield (later Rev. of C.E.)	15 Mar., 1827 -	
Hugh Bushby	(1828) -	Mar., 1834
Rev. John Smith A.M.	31 Mar., 1834 -	(1836)
Rev. Henry Caswell	Nov., 1838 -	(1838)
James Windcot (Windcat)		(1848)

Wardens

Hon. William Morris	23 Dec., 1841 -	
Richard F. Steele	25 June, 1845 -	
Ogle R. Gowan	(1848) -	1850

Clerks of the District Council

James Jessup	1 Mar., 1842 -	(1849)

10. Kent District

Legislation was passed for the creation of this district; but because the district system was abolished it never became a completely separate entity. See Western District for further details.

i. Legislation

1847 10 & 11 Vic. c.39(9 July). County of Kent (except Township of West Tilbury, which is to go to Essex) to be separated from the Western District and become a separate district as soon as court house and jail erected. District councillors of the area may borrow £3,000 for construction purposes. Chatham to be district town.

1848 28 Feb., Order-in-Council to put act into effect (Proclaimed?).

1849 12 Vic. c.78(30 May). Substitutes United Counties of Essex and Kent for Western District effective 1 Jan., 1850.

1849 12 Vic., c.79(30 May). Changes future organization to United Counties of Essex, Kent, and Lambton.

1849 12 Vic., c.80(30 May). Repeals most sections of 10 & 11 Vic. c.39.

ii. Officials

No officials were appointed, however, the district councillors apparently began to operate as a separate body de facto at Chatham, 17 Aug., 1847.

Chairmen of the Provisional Council

George Duck   1847   -   1848

Lionel H. Johnson   1849   -

11. London District 1800

i. Legislation

1798 38 Geo. III c.5 s.33-37 (Proclaimed 1 Jan., 1800). Establishes the London District which is to consist of the Counties of Norfolk, Oxford, and Middlesex, which were formerly parts of the Home and Western Districts.

1801 41 Geo. III c.6 s.2 (9 July). Courts to be held at Charlotteville in the Township of Charlotteville.

1815 55 Geo. III c.3 (14 Apr.). Quarter Sessions moved from Charlotteville to Tisdale's Mills (renamed Vittoria 1818).

1816 56 Geo. III c.1 (22 Mar.). Quarter Sessions in future on 2nd Tues. in Jan., Apr., July and Oct. (Act also applied to Johnston District).

1821 2 Geo. III c.3 (14 Apr.). Townships of Mosa, Ekfrid, Caradoc and Lobo attached to Middlesex and Dorchester extended east.

1826 7 Geo. IV c.13 (30 Jan.). As the court house and jail at Vittoria have been burnt down, and that town is inconveniently located to provide for the needs of the district, the district town shall be moved to the reservation made at the Forks of the Thames (London) in the County of Middlesex. The Townships of Rainham and Walpole, which would be remote from the new district town, shall be transferred to the County of Haldimand in the Niagara District.

1826 7 Geo. IV c.14 (30 Jan.). Provides for the survey of a new town in the Townships of London and Westminister (London), and the erection of a court house and jail at that location.

1835 4 Wm. IV c.55 (5 May). Creates County of Huron out of certain new townships, and adds Adelaide Township to Middlesex and others to Kent.

1837 7 Wm. IV c.30 (4 Mar.). Authorizes the separation of certain townships to form the District of Brock.

1837 7 Wm. IV c.33 (4 Mar.). County of Norfolk to become District of Talbot.

1838 1 Vic. c.26 (6 Mar.). Authorizes the separation of the County of Huron as the District of Huron as soon as court facilities are erected.

1838 1 Vic. c.37 (6 Mar.). Authorizes loan of £4000 to build new jail.

1840 3 Vic. c.38 (10 Feb.). Ashfield and other townships in the range north of Huron to be transferred to that county and district.

1842 6 Vic. c.21 (12 Oct.). Middlesex County Registry Office moved from Dunwich Township in Elgin County to London.

1845 8 Vic. c.7 (10 Feb.). Metcalfe Township formed out of parts of Adelaide and Ekfrid. Williams Township transferred from Huron to Middlesex.

1849 12 Vic. c.78 (30 May). District abolished, County of Middlesex to succeed.

1851 14 & 15 Vic. c.5 (2 Aug.). Elgin County separated from Middlesex when jail and court house erected. Nissouri and Dorchester Townships divided. Counties split effective 1 Jan., 1854.

1859 22 Vic. c.81 (4 May). Williams Township divided into East and West Williams, effective 1 Jan., 1860.

1862 25 Vic. c.28 (9 June). Biddulph and McGillivray Townships attached to Middlesex instead of Huron, effective 1 Jan., 1863.

ii. Officials

Clerks of the Peace

Thomas Welch (Walsh)	1 Jan.,	1800 -	9 Sept.,	1806
Richard William Dease	9 Sept.	1806^S-		(1819)
John Baptiste Askin	30 Sept.	1820 -	15 Nov.,	1869+

Sheriffs

Joseph Ryerson	1 Jan.,	1800 -	16 Nov.,	1805
John Bostwick	16 Nov.,	1805^S-		(1817)
Abraham A. Rapelje	2 Sept.,	1818 -		1837
James Hamilton	7 Aug.,	1837 -	27 Mar.,	1858+

Treasurers

Dan Millard	12 Apr.,	1800 -	10 Mar.,	1802
Joseph Ryerson	10 Mar.,	1802 -	16 July,	1808
Aaron Collver	16 July,	1808 -		
Henry Van Allen		(1814)-		(1818)
John Harris	7 Jan.,	1821 -	25 Aug.,	1850+

District Court Judges

Samuel Ryerse	1 Jan.,	1800 -		
Thomas Welch	2 Apr.,	1810 -		
Dr. Thomas Rolfe	5 Mar.,	1811 -	Mar.,	1814+
James Mitchell	26 May,	1814 -		(1835)
William Young	16 June,	1835 -	20 Jan.,	1837+
Rowland Williams	20 Mar.,	1839 -		+
Henry Allen (Dismissed)	28 June,	1841 -	Oct.,	1846
James Givens	6 Feb.,	1847 -	15 Sept.,	1849
James Edward Small	22 Oct.,	1849 -	27 May,	1869+

District Court Clerks

Thomas Welch	1 Jan.,	1800 -	9 Sept.,	1806
Richard William Dease	9 Sept.,	1806^S-		(1819?)
John Baptiste Askin	8 Aug.,	1820 -	15 Nov.,	(1869)

Surrogate Court Judges

Samuel Ryerse		(1804)-		
Thomas Welch		1810 -		1814?

Philip Sovereign		1814?-	
James Mitchell		(1821)-	1839
Rowland Williams	6 July,	1839 -	1839
John Brooks Crowe	24 Oct.,	1839 -	
Henry Allen	28 June,	1841 -	(1849)

Surrogate Court Registrars

Thomas Welch (or Walsh)	1 Jan.,	1800 -	1810
Francis Leigh Walsh	29 May,	1810 - 10 Jan.,	1838
Henry Corry Becher	14 June,	1839 -	(1849)

Inspectors of Licences

George Ryerson		(1818)-	1821
James Mitchell	6 May,	1821 -	(1836)
Joseph B. Clench	2 Feb.,	1839 -	(1848)

Schoolmasters

James Mitchell		(1818)-	(1821)
Rev. George Ryerson, CE		(1824)-	
Rev. Eli Chadwick, Cong'l.	1 Jan.,	1827 -	(1836)
Rev. Francis Wright		1837?-	1841?
Rev. Benjamin Bayley		1841 -	(1848)

Wardens

John Wilson	23 Dec.,	1841 -		
John Stewart Buchanan	9 July,	1845 -		1846
William E. Niles	Feb.,	1847 -	Jan.,	1851

Clerks of the District Council

James B. Strathey	1 Mar.,	1842 -	1851

12. Midland District [Mecklenburg] 1788

1. Legislation

1788 Proclamation of 24 July. Lord Dorchester divides present South Ontario into four districts. Mecklenburg is the area between lines running due north from the mouth of the Gananoque River on the east and the mouth of the Trent River on the west.

1792 32 George III c.8 (15 Oct.) Section 3. Changed name from Mecklenburg to Midland. Section 11 provided Kingston district town.

1798 39 George III c.5. s.11-18 (Proclaimed 1 Jan., 1800). Redivided the province. The Midland district townships redistributed, abolishing the county of Ontario and uniting the counties of Lennox and Addington. District to consist of this last county plus Frontenac, Hastings, and Prince Edward.

1801 41 George IV c.6. s.2 (9 July). Courts to be held alternately at Adolphustown and Kingston.

1822 2 George IV c.21 (17 Jan.). Authorizes magistrates to borrow up to £3,000 to erect jail and court house in Kingston.

1824 4 George VI c.32 (19 Jan.). Authorizes additional £1,000.

1831 1 Wm. IV c.6 (16 Mar.). County of Prince Edward to be proclaimed a separate district as soon as the governor satisfied that adequate jail and court house facilities have been erected. Picton to be district town.

1837 7 Wm. IV c.31 (4 Mar.). County of Hastings to be a separate district [Victoria] with Belleville as district town.

1839 2 Vic. c.43 (11 May). Authorizes magistrates to borrow £1,000 for wall around jail and court house.

1840 3 Vic. c.44 (10 Feb.). Reorganizes debt and approves loan of £3,500.

1849 12 Vic. c.78 (30 May). Abolished. United counties Frontenac, Lennox and Addington succeed.

1849 12 Vic. c.94 (30 May). Transfer of territory from Midland to Bathurst.

ii. Officials

Clerks of the Peace

Allan McLean	Sept.,	1794 –	(1808)
Charles Stuart			1816+
John McLean	6 Jan.,	1817 –	
Allan McLean		(1818) –	(1827)
James Nickalls (or Nichol) Jr.	15 May,	1830 –	(1849)

Sheriffs

Allan McLean	29 July,	1792 –	
William Coffin	13 July,	1792 –	1804+
Charles Stuart	14 Dec.,	1804 –	
John McLean	6 Jan.,	1817 –	1837
Richard Bullock	4 May,	1837 –	
Allan McDonell	28 Apr.,	1838 –	
Thomas H. Corbett	17 Oct.,	1842 –	(1849)

Treasurers

Thomas Markland	June,	1796 –	(1837)
John Marks	19 July,	1839 –	1840
David John Smith		1840 –	1846
William Ferguson		1846 –	(1849)

182

District Court Judges

Thomas Fisher	9 July,	1794 –		
Timothy Thompson	16 Sept.,	1797 –		
Alexander Fraser	1 Jan.,	1800 –		(1825)
John Ferguson	16 Nov.,	1802 –		(1826)
Jonas Jones	31 Dec.,	1825 –	23 Mar.,	1837
John Solomon Cartwright	14 Jan.,	1834 –	15 Jan.,	1845+
John Richardson Forsyth	20 Mar.,	1839 –		
James Nickalls	3 Apr.,	1839 –		
Stafford F. Kirkpatrick	24 Feb.,	1844 –		(1849)

District Court Clerks

Alexander Pringle	10 Sept.,	1815 –	(1849)

Surrogate Court Judges

Hazleton Spencer		1793 –	
Alexander Fraser	6 June,	1796 –	(1825)
Jonas Jones	31 Dec.,	1825^G–	
Thomas Markland	22 June,	1830 –	1840+
George A. Cummings	19 Feb.,	1840 –	(1849)

Surrogate Court Registrars

James Rogers		1794 –	
Poole England	6 June,	1796 –	
George Macaulay		(1823) –	(1825)
Alexander Pringle			
Isaac Fraser	8 Sept.,	1828 –	(1848)

Inspectors of Licences

John Cumming	Apr.,	1803 –	(1827)
James Sampson	Mar.,	1829 –	(1836)

Schoolmasters

William Merrill			–	30 Jan., 1816
Rev. John Wilson, CE	26 May,	1817 –		(1824)
George Baxter	4 Jan.,	1836 –		1838?
Rev. Wm. M. Herchmer	13 Jan.,	1838 –		
Rev. Rogers	July,	1840 –		
S. Lightburne				(1848)

Wardens

John B. Marks	23 Dec., 1841 -	(1848)
David Roblin	1850 -	1857

Clerks of the District Council

Francis Manning Hill	1 Mar., 1842 -	
Samuel McGowan	9 June, 1842 -	(1846)
George H. Detlor	(1848) -	(1849)

13. Newcastle District 1802

i. Legislation

1798 38 George III, c.5, s.25 (Proclaimed 1 Jan., 1800). Provided that when counties of Northumberland and Durham reached a population of 1000, and had six organized townships, they could be separated from the Home District by proclamation and created into a separate district called Newcastle.

1802 Proclamation 23 June, Newcastle created into a district.

1802 42 George III, c.2 (7 July). Provides that jail and court house shall be erected at Newcastle.

1805 45 George III, c.5. (2 Mar.). Jail and Court House to be built at place selected by magistrates in either of the townships of Haldimand or Hamilton, rather than in Newcastle.

1831 1 Wm. IV, c.6 (16 Mar.). As jail and court house need to be replaced magistrates have contracted for building at Amherst and act provides for financing up to £6,000. (Amherst renamed Hamilton and then became Cobourg in 1819).

1834 4 Wm. IV, c.15 (6 Mar.). Certain townships not previously part of counties attached to counties: Ennismore, Harvey, Douro, Dummer, Belmont, Burleigh and Methuen to Northumberland; Verulam, Fenelon and Eldon to Durham.

1836 6 Wm. IV, c.23 (7 Mar.). Site of old court house and jail can be sold.

1838 7 Wm. IV, c.115 (20 Apr.). Northern territory becomes District of Colborne with Peterborough as district town.

1849 12 Vic., c.78 (30 May). Abolished. United Counties of Northumberland and Durham succeed.

ii. Officials

Clerks of the Peace

David McGregor Rogers	16 July, 1802 -	
Thomas Ward	15 Mar., 1808 -	(1849)

Sheriffs

John Peters	16 July, 1803 -	
John Spencer	23 Mar., 1810 -	1827
Henry Ruttan	24 Oct., 1827 -	(1849)

Treasurers

John Peters	(1806)-	1814
Zaccheus Burnham	(1814)-	(1849)

District Court Judges

Timothy Thompson	16 July,	1802 -		
Richard Cockerell	24 Apr.,	1810 -		
David McGregor Rogers	16 May,	1815 -	13 July,	1824+
Thomas Ward	1 Aug.,	1824 -		(1827)
William Falkner	18 Feb.,	1828 -		(1840)
Zaccheus Burnham	16 July,	1839 -		
George M. Boswell	25 May,	1845 -	1 Nov.,	1882

District Court Clerks

Elias Jones	15 Mar.,	1808 -	1836+
Henry Covert	8 Apr.,	1836 -	(1846)
Richard D. Chatterton		(1847)-	(1849)

Surrogate Court Judges

Timothy Thompson	16 July,	1802 -		
David McGregor Rogers		(1818)-	13 July,	1824+
Thomas Ward	16 Aug.,	1824 -		(1849)

Surrogate Court Registrars

David McGregor Rogers	16 July,	1802 -		
Thomas Ward	15 Mar.,	1808 -	16 Aug.,	1824
Marcus F. Whitehead	25 Aug.,	1824 -		(1849)

Inspectors of Licences

Thomas Ward			1816
Elias Jones	8 Dec.,	1816 -	(1831)
H. W. Jones	23 July,	1836 -	

Schoolmasters

Vacant		(1818)-	
Rev. Wm. Macaulay		(1821)-	(1824)
David Ovans	July,	1825 -	(1832)
John Tripp	7 Dec.,	1832 -	
W. Crofton	1 July,	1835 -	(1836)
R. Hudspeth			(1848)

Wardens

Walter Boswell	23 Dec.,	1841 -
John Steele	13 Aug.,	1845 -
George S. Boulton	5 Nov.,	1845 -
Henry S. Reid (Read)		(1848) -	1850

Clerks of the District Court

Morgan Jellett	9 Mar.,	1824 -	(1849)

14. Niagara District 1800

i. Legislation

1798 38 George III, c.5 s.27-32 (Proclaimed 1 Jan., 1800). Separated the four Ridings of Lincoln and Haldimand from the Home District and created them into the District of Niagara. By Section 28 the name of the town and township of Newark changed to Niagara.

1801 41 George III, c.6. s.2 (9 July). District town Niagara.

1816 56 George III, c.19 (22 Mar.). Parts of 1st Riding of Lincoln and Haldimand separated and joined with parts of the Home District to form the Gore District.

1827 7 George IV, c.13 (30 Jan.). As district town of London District moved from Vittoria to London, townships of Rainham and Walpole are transferred from Norfolk to Haldimand as Niagara a more convenient court location.

1843 7 Vic. c.40 (9 Dec.). Defines boundary between Niagara and Gore to be the boundary line between Townships Oneida and Seneca in Niagara and Tuscarora and Onondaga in Gore.

1847 10 and 11 Vic. c.55 (28 July). Quarter Sessions and district courts can be held in new court house built by the Board of Police.

1849 12 Vic. c.78 (30 May). Abolished. United Counties of Lincoln, Haldimand and Welland succeed.

1849 12 Vic. c.98 (25 Apr.). Divides Township Cayuga into two townships.

ii. Officials
Clerks of the Peace

Ralfe Clench	1 Jan.,	1800 -	19 Jan.,	1828+
Thomas Buller(Commission in error?)	3 Apr.,	1814 -		
Charles Richardson	21 Feb.,	1828 -	15 Mar.,	1848+
Joseph Woodruff		1848 -		(1849)

Sheriffs

James Clark	1 Jan.,	1800 -		1803
Thomas Merritt	5 Oct.,	1803 -		1820
Richard Leonard	20 Jan.,	1820 -	Oct.,	1833+
Alexander Hamilton	5 Nov.,	1833 -	Feb.,	1839+
Kenneth Cameron	20 Mar.,	1839 -		
William Kingsmill	23 July,	1840 -		(1849)

Treasurers

John Symington	(1806)-	(1812)
Thomas McCormick	(1816)-	(1827)
William Clark	(1829)-	(1837)
Malcolm Laing (Lang or Long)	(1839)-	
Daniel McDougall	(1840)-	(1849)

District Court Judges

William Dickson	1 Jan.,	1800 -		
Samuel Street	7 Jan.,	1807 -		
Joseph Edwards	16 May,	1815 -		
Ralfe Clench	11 Nov.,	1815 -	19 Jan.,	1828+
George Ridout (Dismissed)	3 Apr.,	1828 -	16 July,	1836
Thomas Butler	17 Apr.,	1832 -		
Robert Easton Burns	16 July,	1836 -		(1839)
Edward Clarke Campbell	23 Dec.,	1841 -		(1849)

District Court Clerks

Joseph Brant Clench		(1818)-		(1821)
Johnson Clench	24 Nov.,	1828 -	15 Sept.,	1863

Surrogate Court Judges

Dr. Robert Kerr	1 Jan.,	1800 -		1824
Robert Nichol	11 Mar.,	1824 -	3 May,	1824+
Alexander Hamilton	16 May,	1824 -		1833
James Secord	25 Sept.,	1833 -	23 July,	1835
Warren Claus	25 July,	1835 -		(1849)

Surrogate Court Registrars

Allan Macnab (McNabb)		(1794)-	(1796)
Ralfe Clench		(1815)- 19 Jan.,	1828+
Charles B. Secord	1 Feb.,	1828 -	(1849)

Inspectors of Licences

Isaac Swayze	1 Mar.,	1803 -	(1827)
John Claus		(1831)-	
John Jordan	15 May,	1835 -	1839+
W. D. Miller	10 Oct.	1839^G-	

Schoolmasters

Richard Cockrel

Rev. John Burns, P.		(1818)-		(1824)
Rev. Thomas Green, P.		1824)-	14 Oct.,	1829
James L. Ralston	Oct.,	1829-		(1831)
John Whitelaw M.D.	1 July,	1833-		(1848)

Wardens

David Thorburn	23 Dec.,	1841 -		1849

Clerks of the District Council

Erastus B. Raymond	1 Mar.,	1842 -		
Charles Richardson	8 Nov.,	1845 -	15 Mar.,	1848+
J. G. Stevenson		1848 -		1849

15. Ottawa District 1816

i. Legislation

1816 56 George III c.2 (22 Mar., 1816). Counties of Prescott and Russell separated from the Eastern District and henceforth to form the District of Ottawa. Operation of district to begin immediately. Justices to decide district town (L'Orignal chosen).

1838 1 Vic., c.25 (6 Mar.). Two townships of County Russell transferred to new district of Dalhousie.

1843 7 Vic., c.39 (9 Dec). Township Hawkesbury divided into Townships of East and West Hawkesbury.

1847 10 and 11 Vic., c.52 (9 July). Township Plantagenet divided into Townships of North and South Plantagenet.

1849 12 Vic., c.78 (30 May). Abolished. United counties of Prescott and Russell succeed.

ii. Officials

Clerks of the Peace

Joseph Fortune (Dismissed)	4 Apr.,	1816 -		1821
Richard P. Hotham	1 May,	1821^G-	10 Oct.,	1840+
Donald McDonald	17 Dec.,	1841 -		(1849)

Sheriffs

Thomas Mears	25 Mar.,	1816 -	16 Sept.,	1822+
Alexander Macdonell	6 Dec.,	1822 -	16 Feb.,	(1835)
Charles P. Treadwell	26 May,	1835 -		(1849)

Treasurers

Thomas Mears	(1821)-	16 Sept.,	1822+
Donald McDonald (Roy)	(1824)-		(1834)
Thomas H. Johnson	(1836)-		(1849)

District Court Judges

John Macdonell	25 Mar.,	1836 –	(1825)
George Hamilton	25 Mar.,	1816 –	(1831)
George Stephen Jarvis	21 Dec.,	1825 –	(1839)
Charles Adamson Low	9 Feb.,	1839 –	
George Macdonell	17 Dec.,	1841 –	
Peter Freel	15 Oct.,	1842 –	1863

District Court Clerks

Peter F. LeRoy	4 Apr.,	1816^G–		(1831)
Charles P. Treadwell (Gazetted in error?)	4 Feb.,	1826^G–		
Richard P. Hotham	1 Aug.,	1835 –	10 Oct.,	1840+
George D. Reed	17 Dec.,	1841 –		
Chandos Hoskyns	26 Oct.,	1842 –		
J. W. Marston		(1848)–		(1849)

Surrogate Court Judges

David Potter (or Pattie)	4 Apr.,	1816 –	(1849)

Surrogate Court Registrars

Joseph Fortune (Dismissed)	4 Apr.,	1816 –		1821
Richard P. Hotham	1 May,	1821^G–	10 Oct.,	1840+
George D. Reed	17 Dec.,	1841 –		
Chandos Hoskyns	26 Oct.,	1842 –		
J. W. Marston		(1848)–		(1849)

Inspectors of Licences

Thomas Mears	4 Apr.,	1816 –	(1831)
Donald McDonald	Mar.,	1834 –	(1836)

Schoolmasters

Vacant		(1818)–	(1821)
Rev. John McLaurin P.		(1824)–	(1828)
			1833+
Rev. Colin Gregory	1 June,	1833–	(1848)

Wardens

Charles Adamson Low	23 Dec.,	1841 –	
Archibald Petrie	2 July,	1845 –	
Chauncey Johnson		(1847)–	(1849)

Clerks of the District Council

Donald McDonald	1 Mar., 1842 -	(1846)
Peter O'Brien	(1848) -	(1849)

16. Prince Edward District 1834

i. Legislation

Pre-District Legislation for Township Division

1797 37 George III c.7 (3 July). Authorizes creation of new township out of south parts of Marysburgh and Sophiasburgh. (Becomes Hallowell Township).

1823 4 George IV c.38 (19 Mar.). Ameliasburg Township divided into Ameliasburg in north and Hillier in south.

District Legislation

1831 1 Wm. IV c.6 (16 Mar.). Governor can separate Prince Edward County from Midland District and proclaim it a separate district as soon as jail and court house facilities available. Picton to be district town.

1832 2 Wm. IV c.17 (28 Jan). Provides for purchase of site of district buildings.

1833 3 Wm. IV c.23 (13 Feb.). Resolves certain claims of Midland District on Prince Edward.

1834 Proclamation of 6 Feb. creates district.

1840 3 Vic. c.39 (10 Feb.). Township Hallowell divided into Hallowell in north and Athol in south.

1849 12 Vic. c.78 (30 May). Abolished. County of Prince Edward succeeds.

1849 12 Vic. c.100 (25 Apr.). Changes boundary line between Hallowell and Sophiasburg.

1869 33 Vic. c.63 (24 Dec.). Marysburgh Township divided into North and South Marysburgh.

ii. Officials

Clerks of the Peace

David L. Fairfield	21 Feb., 1834 -	(1839)
Phillip Low		(1849)

Sheriffs

Richard Bulloch	12 Feb., 1834 -	1837
Owen McMahon	7 Aug., 1837 -	(1849)

Treasurers

David Smith	1834 -	(1849)

District Court Judges

Donald Bethune	15 Mar., 1834 -	1837
James Cotter	27 Sept., 1837 -	

Archibald Gilkinson	18 Dec., 1841 -	(1846)
David L. Fairfield	29 Apr., 1847 - 8 Aug., 1871	

District Court Clerks

Thomas Nash	22 Mar., 1834 -	
Cecil Mortimer	4 Sept., 1837^G-	(1849)

Surrogate Court Judges

Simon Washburn	15 Mar., 1834 -	(1849)

Surrogate Court Registrars

Paul F. McCuaig	21 May, 1834 -	(1839)
John McCuaig	7 Apr., 1840 -	
H. W. Peterson	5 Aug., 1840^G-	(1846)
Samuel Merill	7 July, 1841^G-	(1846)

Inspectors of Licences

Adam Hubbs	10 June, 1834 -	(1836)

Schoolmasters

Moses Marcus	20 June, 1834 -	(1836)
John Deacon	20 Sept., 1839 -	
W. Cockell		(1848)
Samuel Merill	7 July, 1841^G-	

Wardens

John P. Roblin	23 Dec., 1841 -	
Jacob Howell	29 Sept., 1842 -	
D. B. Stevenson	(1848)-	
John Howell		1850

Clerks of the District Council

Thomas Moore	1 Mar., 1842 -	
R. J. Chapman	(1848)-	(1849)

17. Simcoe District 1843

i. Legislation

1821 2 Geo. IV c.3 (14 Apr.). Section 7 created the county of Simcoe out of several townships, and Section 8 provided that the governor could separate the county from the Home District by proclamation when he saw fit.

1837 7 Wm. IV c.32 (4 Mar.). Simcoe can be proclaimed separate district when court house and jail built at Barrie. Section 2 provided that certain townships were to be transferred from the county of Simcoe to the counties of Waterloo and York.

1838 7 Wm. IV c.116 (20 Apr). Townships of Proton, Luther, Melancthon, and Amaranth transferred from county of Simcoe to new District of Wellington.

1838 1 Vic. c.39 (6 Mar.). Authorized loan of £4,000 to build the court house and jail at Barrie.

1841 4 and 5 Vic. c.78 (18 Sept.). Authorized the borrowing of an additional £3,000 for the same purpose.

1843 Proclamation of 11 Jan. Simcoe declared a separate district.

1849 12 Vic. c.78 (30 May). District abolished effective next 1 Jan. County of Simcoe succeeds.

ii. Officials

Clerks of the Peace

William B. McVity	27 Jan., 1843 -	1877

Sheriffs

Benjamin Walter Smith	24 Feb., 1843 -	1875+

Treasurers

Sidney M. Sanford	Apr., 1838 -	July, 1841
Samuel Richardson	July, 1841 -	2 Mar., 1843+
James Adam	18 Apr., 1843 -	1844?+
Edmund Lally	22 Feb., 1845 -	Mar., 1861

District Court Judges

Sir James Robert Gowan	16 Jan., 1843 -	21 Sept. 1883

District Court Clerks

Jonathan Lane	24 Jan., 1843 -	1870

Surrogate Court Judges

James Robert Gowan	16 Jan., 1843 -	(1849)

Surrogate Court Registers

Jonathan Lane	24 Jan., 1843 -	1870

Inspectors of Licences

Unknown

Schoolmasters

Vacant	(1827)	
Frederick Gore		(1848)

Wardens

Jacob AEmelius Irving	8 Jan., 1843 -	
James Dallas	27 Mar., 1844 -	1845
William Armson	1846 -	1852

Clerks of the District Council

John McWatt	1843 - Jan., 1852

18. Talbot District 1837

i. Legislation

1837 7 Wm. IV c.33 (4 Mar.). County of Norfolk to become the Talbot District when jail and court house completed. Simcoe to be the district town. Loan of £5,000 authorized.

1837 Proclamation of 30 December creates district.

1838 1 Vic. c.36 (6 Mar.). Authorized additional tax, and sale of site of old court house at Vittoria, to raise funds for new court house.

1849 12 Vic. c.78 (30 May). Abolished. County of Norfolk succeeds.

ii. Officials

Clerks of the Peace

John Stuart	27 Mar., 1838 -	
William Mercer Wilson	15 Dec., 1838 -	(1846)

Sheriffs

Henry van Allen Rapelje	22 Mar. 1838 -	(1849)

Treasurers

Henry Webster	(1839)-	(1848)
Henry Grott		(1849)

District Court Judges

John Peter Carey	8 June, 1838 -	
Edward Gilman	11 May, 1841 -	
William Salmon	26 May, 1845 -	1868

District Court Clerks

John Stuart	27 Mar., 1838 -	
William Mercer Wilson	15 Dec., 1838 -	(1849)

Surrogate Court Judges

John Peter Carey	12 Dec., 1838 -	
Rowland Williams	6 July, 1839 -	
Edward Gilman	11 May, 1841 -	
William Salmon	22 Oct., 1845 -	1849

Surrogate Court Registrars

William Mercer Wilson	1 July, 1841 -	(1849)

Inspectors of Licences

E. P. Ryerse	1 Nov., 1839^G-	

Schoolmasters

Rev. George Salmon	Sept., 1838?-	(1848)

Wardens

Israel Wood Powell	23 Dec., 1841 –	1846
Dr. John B. Crouse	1847 –	1850
Laurence H. Hunt	1851 –	1855

Clerks of the District Council

Frederick Thomas Wilkes	1 Mar., 1842 –	
John H. Davies	19 May, 1843 –	(1846)
Michael H. Foley	(1848)–	

19. Victoria District 1839

i. Legislation

1837 7 Wm. IV c.31 (4 May.). As soon as jail and court house erected governor can declare county of Hastings a separate district (ex. Midland), Belleville district town. Loan of £6,000 authorized. Governor to choose name of district as he sees fit.

1839 Proclamation of 15 October creates district of Victoria.

1840 3 Vic. c.42 (10 Feb.). Extends time to pay debt.

1849 12 Vic. c.78 (30 May). Abolished. County of Hastings succeeds.

ii. Officials

Clerks of the Peace

Edward Murney	10 Oct., 1839 –	
W. W. Fitzgibbon	26 Nov., 1842 –	(1849)

Sheriffs

John Wedderburn Dunbar Moodie	19 Nov., 1839 –	(1849)

Treasurers

Philip Hans	(1841)–	(1847)
N. G. Reynolds	(1848)–	(1849)

District Court Judges

Benjamin Dougall	21 Oct., 1839 –	
William Smart	17 Oct., 1843 –	(1849)

District Court Clerks

William H. Ponton	18 Oct., 1839 –	(1849)

Surrogate Court Judges

John Brooks Crowe	21 Oct., 1839 –	(1849)

Surrogate Court Registers

William Bowen	26 Feb., 1840 –	(1849)

Inspectors of Licences

Anthony Marshall	9 Mar., 1840[G] –	

Schoolmasters

Alex Burdon	Aug., 1840 –	(1848)

Wardens

William Hutton	23 Dec., 1841 –	(1846)
George Benjamin	(1848) –	

Clerks of the District Council

P. O'Reilly	(1846)	
William W. Fitzgibbon	(1848) –	(1849)

20. Wellington District 1840

i. Legislation

1838 7 Wm. IV c.116 (20 Apr.). Parts of Halton (Gore District), Simcoe (Home District) and Huron (London District) to be separate district, district town Guelph, name Wellington, as soon as jail and court house erected. Loan of £6,000 authorized. Section 28 new district to comprise the new County of Waterloo.

1840 Proclamation of 18 June creates district.

1849 12 Vic. c.78 (30 May). Abolished. County of Waterloo succeeds.

ii. Officials

Clerks of the Peace

Thomas Saunders	25 July, 1840 –	(1849)

Sheriffs

George John Grange	15 Aug., 1840 –	(1849)

Treasurers

William Hewat	(1841) –	(1849)

District Court Judges

Adam Johnston Ferguson	23 July, 1840 –	
William Dummer Powell	12 Apr., 1847 –	(1849)

District Court Clerks

William Dummer Powell	25 July, 1840 –	1840
Robert Alling	13 Aug., 1840 –	(1846)
John Smith	1848 –	(1849)

Surrogate Court Judges

Adam Johnston Ferguson	23 July, 1840 –	(1846)
William Dummer Powell	12 Apr., 1847 –	(1849)

Surrogate Court Registrars

William Dummer Powell	25 July, 1840 -	
Thomas R. Brock	(1847)-	(1849)

Inspectors of Licences

James Hodgert   13 Aug., 1840^G

Schoolmasters

E. M. Stewart   (1848)

Wardens

Arthur Dingwall Fordyce	23 Dec., 1841 -	(1846)
James Wright	(1848)-	

Clerks of the District Council

Richard F. Budd   20 Apr., 1842 -   (1848)

21. Western District [Hesse] 1788

i. Legislation

1788 Proclamation of 24 July Lord Dorchester divided modern southern Ontario into four districts. Hesse was the area west of a line running due north from the tip of Long Point on Lake Erie.

1792 32 George III c.8. s.5 (15 Oct.). Name of district changed from Hesse to Western.

1798 38 George III c.5. s.38-40. (Proclaimed 1 Jan., 1800) separated parts of district, and joined them to parts of Home District, to create London District by Sections 33-37. Western District henceforth to consist of counties of Kent and Essex and any territory not assigned to another district.

1801 41 Geo. c.6 s.2 (9 July). District town Sandwich.

1835 4 Wm. IV c.55 (Proclaimed 5 May). Creates County of Huron (in London district) out of new townships and adds others to Middlesex and Kent.

1839 2 Vic. c.32 (11 May). Magistrates can borrow £1,000 to pay debts and improve jail at Sandwich.

1847 **10 & 11 Vic.**c.39 (9 July). County of Kent except Township W. Tilbury to be District of Kent as soon as facilities built at Chatham.

1849 12 Vic. c.78 (30 May). Abolished. United counties of Essex and Kent succeed.

1849 12 Vic. c.79 s.1 (30 May). Changed to United Counties of Essex, Kent and Lambton.

ii. Officials

Clerks of the Peace

Walter Roe	9 Sept., 1794 -	7 Aug., 1801+
William Hands	29 Aug., 1801 -	5 Sept.,1802
James Allan	5 June, 1802 -	(1810)
George Thomas Frederick Ireland	(1817)-	1823+

Charles Askin	31 July, 1823 -	(1835)
William R. Wood (Deputy)	20 Oct., 1835 -	
Charles Baby	9 Mar., 1836 -	(1872)

Sheriffs

Gregor McGregor	1789 -	1790
Rev. Richard Pollard	16 July, 1792 -	
William Hands	7 June, 1802 -	10 Jan., 1833
Ebenezer Reynolds	10 Sept., 1833 -	22 Mar., 1837
Robert Lachlan	7 Aug., 1837 -	1839
John B. Laughton (Acting)	Apr., 1839 -	
Raymond Baby	1 Aug., 1839 -	1840+
George Wade Foott	23 Oct., 1840 -	1848
John Waddell	16 Jan., 1849 -	(1849)

Treasurers

William Hands	(1806)-	19 Feb., 1836+
Felix Hands	12 Apr., 1836 -	by July, 1837+
Jean Baptiste Baby	1837 -	(1849)

District Court Judges

Thomas Harffy	4 July, 1794 -	
Prideaux Selby	1 Jan., 1800 -	
Dr. Robert Richardson	12 June, 1807 -	(1827)
William Berczy (Resigned to avoid dismissal)	5 Apr., 1826 -	Feb., 1833
Charles Eliot	30 Nov., 1832 -	(1841)
Alexander Chewett	26 May, 1845 -	(1851)

District Court Clerks

George Thomas Frederick Ireland	(1818)-	1823+
Charles Askin	31 July, 1823^G-	(1839)
John Cowan	(1842)-	
William R. Wood	(1847)-	(1848)
John McEwan		(1869)

Surrogate Court Judges

Jacques Baby	1793 -	
Walter Roe	20 Aug., 1796 -	7 Aug., 1801+
Jacques Baby	1 Jan., 1800 -	
Rev. Richard Pollard	29 Aug., 1801 -	6 Nov., 1824+

Table I
Evolution of Districts in Upper Canada
1788-1849

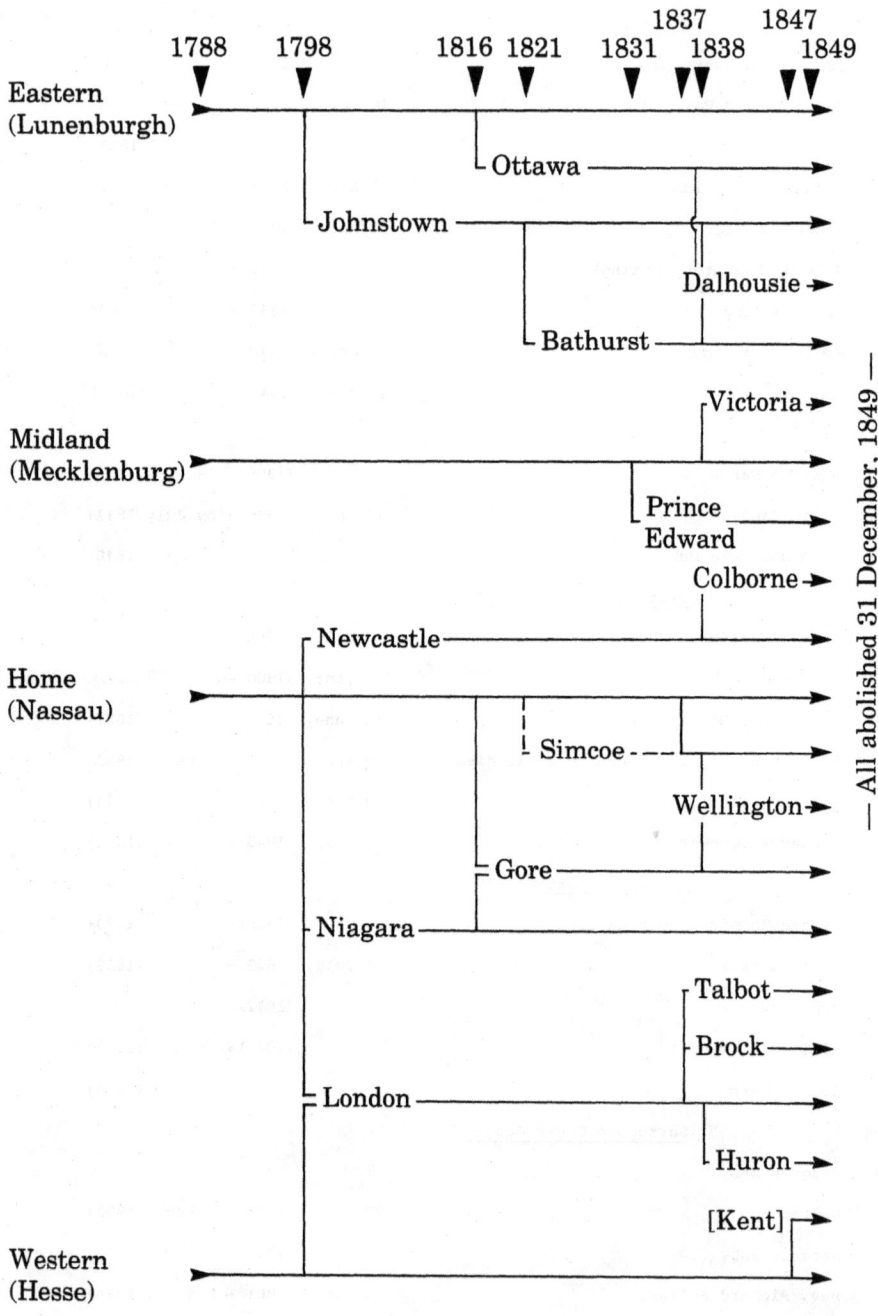

William Hands	20 Aug., 1824	-19 Feb., 1836+
John Alexander Wilkinson	9 Mar., 1836 -	(1851)

Surrogate Court Registrars

Thomas Reynolds		
Rev. Richard Polland	1794 -	29 Aug., 1801
William Hands	29 Aug., 1801 -	20 Aug., 1824
James Askin	14 Feb., 1825 -	(1851)

Inspectors of Licences

at Sandwich

Samuel Culbertson	(1803)-	1806
William Hands	13 Sept., 1806 -	1836+
William Gaspe Hall	3 Apr., 1836^G-	1848
W. A. McCrae	1848 -	(1849)

at Drummond

T. G. Anderson	(1821)-	(1827)

Schoolmasters

William Merrill	30 Jan., 1816 -	(1821)
David Robertson	(1823)-	
Rev. William Johnson, P/CE	1 Jan., 1828 -	(1836)
A. C. Salter		(1848)

Wardens

John Dolsen	29 Dec., 1841 -	1846
William Thompson (pro tem)	6 Oct., 1846 -	
George Bullock	Feb., 1847 -	1849

Clerks of the District Court

John Cowan	1 Mar., 1842 -	(1848)

D. Towns and Cities

a. Introduction

For some years after 1791 the municipal centres of the province were fully under the control of the Magistrates of the Quarter Sessions of their districts and had no more privileges or rights than a rural township. They did not even necessarily have separate township meetings; York Town and Township meeting jointly up until nearly the incorporation of the former as The City of Toronto in 1834. St. John, New Brunswick had been incorporated in 1785 and Simcoe had some idea of setting up municipal corporations, but the Home Secretary, the Duke of Portland, who was in charge of colonies turned down the scheme.

As the population of the province grew, urban nucleii began to form. It became obvious that special arrangements would have to be made for municipal government at the main centres. Had it merely been a case of granting the magistrates special powers for certain purposes municipal government would not have presented too great a problem; but the York oligarchy—the Family Compact—was soon faced with the problem of what element of democracy should be permitted. This question became particularly acute in the years after the War of 1812.

Not surprisingly, Kingston, as the largest town, was the first to receive any special privilege, the Magistrates of the Midland District being permitted to establish a market by an act of 1801 (41 George III, c.3.). In the years that followed there were suggestions that the town be incorporated, a plan originally proposed by Legislative Councillor and leading merchant Richard Cartwright, but these were blocked in 1812. The next advance in municipal government did not come until 1816, when the local magistrates were given special policing powers in Kingston, (56 George III, c.33); a system that was extended to York, Amherstburg and Sandwich (now in Windsor) in 1817 (57 George III, c.2), and Niagara in 1819 (59 George III, c.5).

As the 1820's progressed there were increasing demands for elected Boards of Police with some administrative powers in the larger centres. In late 1828, when the reformers were in power, bills passed the Legislative Assembly for elected governments for Kingston and Belleville, but these were thrown out by the Legislative Council. Finally, in 1832 Brockville was given an elected Board of Police with powers equivalent to the magistrates (2 Wm. IV, c.17). This was soon followed by the incorporation of York/Toronto as the first city in the province in 1834 (4 Wm. IV, c.23), and similar bills followed for the other towns in the colony. In the case of York, at least, the grant of local government was attributable to the fact that the system of government by the magistrates had virtually collapsed, not through any desire to spread democratic institutions.

By the end of the Upper Canadian period most towns of any size had been incorporated, but, though the legislation was gradually showing more sophistication in its wording, no overall enabling act had been adopted. The same system was continued under the union of Upper and Lower Canada until 1847, when a limited general scheme for the incorporation of small towns came into force (10 and 11 Vic., c.42). In 1849 local government was finally formalized under the Baldwin Act. (see b. below).

b. General Legislation Relating to Towns and Cities

```
1847 10 and 11 Vic., c.42 (28 July).  Provides limited corporate powers for
     all towns and villages in Upper Canada where there are thirty inhabited
     houses.  In each such town trustees are to be elected on the first Monday
     in October with power to regulate fire protection, gunpowder, filth, and
     similar matters.

1849 12 Vic., c.81 (30 May) (see also under districts).  The Baldwin Act.
     Provided for a new system of municipal government in the province to
     replace that swept away by the three preceding statutes.  The system of
```

municipal government was revised and regularized and municipalities divided into six categories of which the last three were: incorporated villages, towns and cities. Appended to the act were three schedules listing the municipalities in each category. These, with the dates of incorporation added, were as follows:

Schedule A: Villages   (all new)

1. Chippawa
2. Galt
3. Oshawa
4. Paris
5. Richmond (County of Carleton)
6. Thorold

Schedule B: Towns

1. Belleville   (1834)
2. Brantford   (1847)
3. Brockville   (1832)
4. Bytown   (1847)
5. Cobourg   (1837)
6. Cornwall   (1834)
7. Dundas   (1847)
8. Goderich   (New)
9. London   (1840)
10. Niagara   (1845)
11. Peterborough (New)
12. Picton   (1837)
13. Port Hope   (1834)
14. Prescott   (1834)
15. St. Catharines (1845)

Schedule C: Cities

1. Hamilton   (1833 town - 1846 city)
2. Kingston   (1838 town - 1846 city)
3. Toronto   (1834 city)

1850 13 & 14 Vic., c.64 (10 Aug.). Amends Municipal Corporations Act of 1849 to correct errors and adds Schedule D which was omitted by accident.

Schedule D: Towns with Municipalities only, or without any Municipal organization.

First Division

1. Amherstburgh
2. Chatham
3. Guelph
4. Perth
5. Simcoe
6. Woodstock

Second Division

1. Barrie
2. L'Orignal
3. Queenston
4. Sandwich

Announcements of the creation of villages in the Gazette:
- Port Sarnia (Sarnia)   7 Apr., 1836[G]
- Frankford (Scott's Mill, Hastings County)   27 June, 1837[G]

c. Towns and Cities with Legislation and Officials

In the following tables the dates of the most important acts are underlined.

1. Amherstburgh

i. Legislation

1817 57 Geo. III c.2 (7 Apr.). Magistrates of district given additional policing powers and administrative authority in Amherstburgh (and York and Sandwich).

1831 1 Wm. IV c.3 (16 Mar.). Authorizes the establishment of a market.

1851 (1 Jan.), Incorporated as a town by proclamation.

2. Belleville

i. Legislation

1834 4 Wm. IV c.24 (6 Mar). Found inadequate and replaced by 6 Wm. IV c.14.

1836 6 Wm. IV c.14 (20 Apr.). Establishes limits, divides town into two wards, provides for elected Board of Police and for borrowing of £1000 for market.

ii. Officials

Presidents of the Board of Police

Billa Flint Jr.	1836
H. W. Yager	1837
Billa Flint Jr.	1838-9
Charles O. Benson	1840
A. O. Petrie	1841
F. McAnnany	1842-7
James Whiteford	1848-9

Clerks

George Benjamin	1836-47
Robert M. Roy	1848
M. Sawyer	1849-59

Treasurers

Zenas Dafoe	1836-40
Jacob Bonter	1841-3
James Whiteford	1844-7
M. Sawyer	1848-59

3. Brantford

i. Legislation

1847 10 & 11 Vic. c.49 (28 July). Establishes government by mayor and elected Town Council, defines limits, divides the town into seven wards, and authorises the borrowing of £1000 for a town hall and market.

ii. Officials.

Mayors

  William Muirhead 1847 (Sept. 9)

  Dr. Digby 1848-9

  P. C. VanBrocklin 1850

Clerks

  J. R. McDonald 1847-50

Treasurers

  W. Walker 1847

  E. McKay 1848-51

4. Brockville

i. Legislation

1832 2 Wm. IV c.17 (28 Jan.). Divides town into wards, and sets up elected Board of Police.

1833 3 Wm. IV. c.40 (13 Feb.). Authorizes the establishment of a market.

1836 6 Wm. IV c.13 (20 Apr.). Authorizes the establishment of a market in the west ward.

1847 10 & 11 Vic. c.44 (28 July). Revises assessment laws.

ii. Officials

Mayor (President of the Board of Police)

  Daniel Jones 1832 (5 Apr.)

  Jonas Jones 1833

  Daniel Jones 1834

  ? 1835

  George Malloch 1836

  Charles Jones 1837

  David Jones 1838

  Ephraim Dunham 1839

  George Sherwood 1840

  Thomas D. Campbell 1841

  D.B.O. Ford 1842

  William Buell 1843-44

  Thomas Webster 1845

  George Crawford 1846-47

  Ormond Jones 1848

John Crawford	1849
Robert Pedan	1850

Clerk

William M. Hynes	1832 (5 Apr.).
Albert McLean	1833
Alfred Hall	1834
Richard F. Steele	1835
William F. Meudell	1836
R. F. Steele	1837-41
William Hayes	1841 (26 Apr.)
?	1842
J. O'Hare	1843-53
Worship B. McLean	1845-53

Treasurer

George Crawford	1832
?	1833
Samuel Pennock	1834
?	1835
F. L. Lothrop	1836
E. J. Hubbell	1837
?	1838
Thomas D. Campbell	1839
?	1839-47
Cashier Commercial Bank	1848

5. Bytown (Ottawa Jan. 1, 1855)

i. Legislation

1847 10 & 11 Vic. c.43 (28 July). Fixes limits, divides town into three ridings, establishes town council of six members, two from each ward, who elect a chairman from among their numbers, and authorizes borrowing £3000 for market house.

1849 (12 Oct.), Queen Victoria disallows bill on request of military which did not want to lose control of planning. (Bytown finally becomes the city of Ottawa in 1855).

ii. Officials

Mayors

John Scott	1847
John Bower Lewis	1848

Robert Hervey	1849
John Scott	1850

Clerks

John Aikin	1847-49
Francis Scott	1850-54

Treasurers

Francois Masse	1850

6. Cobourg

i. Legislation

1837 7 Wm. IV c.42 (4 Mar.). Defines boundaries, divides town into four wards, and provides for an elected Board of Police. The town is authorized to borrow £1000 for a market.

1846 9 Vic. c.71 (9 June). Amends incorporation to allow borrowing of £6000 for town hall and market, as well as other changes.

ii. Officials

Mayors (up to 1846 assumed office in June, from 1847 on in January)

Ebenezer Perry	1837-38
George Ham	1838-39
W. S. Conger	1839-40
D. E. Boulton	1840-42
William Weller	1842-44
Asa A. Burnham	1844-45
D. E. Boulton	1845-46 (December)
Asa A. Burnham	1847-49 (January-December)
William Weller	1850-51

Clerks

Kenneth MacKenizie	1838-June 1839
George Hargraft	1839 (June-December)
David Brodie	1840-51

Treasurers

Robert Henry	1837
James Tremble	1838-December 1839

7. Cornwall

i. Legislation

1818 59 Geo. III c.4 (27 Nov.). Authorizes the establishment of a market.

1834 4 Wm. IV c.25 (6 Mar.). Provides for a government by an elected Police Board, defines the town limits, divides it into two wards, and authorizes the borrowing of £1000 for a market.

1846 9 Vic. c.72 (9 June). Board of Police abolished and a town council established in its place; town redivided into three wards.

ii. Officials

Presidents of the Board of Police

Archibald McLean	1834
George S. Jarvis	1835-6
Robert Cline	1837-6
George S. Jarvis	1840
J. S. Macdonald	1841
Robert Cline	1842
George McDonell	1843
Roderick McDonald	1844
George McDonell	1845
Alexander McLean	1846

Mayors

George McDonell	1847
Chas. Rattray	1848
William Mattice	1849-51

Clerks

John Peckman	1834
D. W. B. McAulay	1835
J. S. Macdonald	1836
George M. Chrysler	1837
J. F. Pringle	1838
John Peckman	1839-40
James Loney	1841
John Blackwood	1842
Archibald J. McDonell	1843
Charles Poole	1844-57

Treasurers

James Pringle	1834-36
William M. Park	1837-49

8. Dundas

i. Legislation

1847 10 & 11 Vic. c.45 (28 July). Defines limits, divides town into four wards each electing one member to the council. These co-opted a fifth member and then elected a president from among their number. Also provides for the borrowing of £2000 for market and town hall.

1848 11 Vic. c.12 (23 Mar.). Amends above.

ii. Officials

Presidents of the Board of Police

J. Patterson	1848
J. B. Ewart	1849
James Coleman	1850-52

Clerks

John L. Smith	1848-9
W. Chisholm	1849-63

9. Hamilton

i. Legislation

1833 3 Wm IV c.16 (13 Feb.). Defines limits, divides town into four wards, provides for the election of officials, and for the borrowing of £1000 to erect a market.

1839 2 Vic. c.45 (11 May). Authorizes second market in a more convenient and central location.

1846 9 Vic. c.73 (9 June). Hamilton erected into a city with a mayor and Common Council. Limits redefined, and area divided into five wards.

ii. Officials

Presidents of the Board of Police

Thomas Taylor	1833
John Law	1834
Andrew McIlroy	1835-6
James L. Willison	1837
Miles O'Reilly	1838
W. J. Gilbert	1839
Thomas Duggan	1840
Richard Oliver Duggan	1841
George S. Tiffany	1842-3
Robert I. Hamilton	1844
Richard I. Beasley	1845
Daniel MacNab	1846

Mayors of the City

Colin C. Ferrie	1847 (January)
George S. Tiffany	1848
W. L. Diston	1849
John Fisher	1850

Clerks

Stephen Randal	1833
Joseph Davis	1834
Charles Durand	1835-6
George C. Street	1837-6
Charles Magill	1839
L. Downing	1840-6
C. S. Stokoe	1847-50

Treasurers (complete information unavailable)

David Beasley	1833
Henry Beasley	1844
John Brown	1847-50

10. Kingston

i. Legislation

1801 41 Geo. III c.3 (9 July). Authorizes the establishment of a market.

1816 Bill 279. To set up Kingston Board of Police - defeated.

1816 56 Geo. III c.33 (22 Mar.). Magistrates given policing powers.

1824 4 Geo. IV c.30 (19 Jan.). Magistrates given policing authority.

1826 7 Geo. IV c.12 (30 Jan.). Magistrates given the power to define town limits and regulate other matters.

1838 1 Vic. c.27 (6 Mar.). Kingston incorporated as a town and divided into four wards each electing one alderman and one common councilman, one-fourth of whom shall retire each year. Mayor to be elected by the Council annually.

1839 2 Vic. c.36 (1 May). Validates the first election.

1839 2 Vic. c.37 (18 May). Amends 1 Vic. c.27.

1846 9 Vic. c.75 (19 May). Incorporates the town of Kingston as a city and divides it into five wards.

1847 10 & 11 Vic. c.46 (28 July). Clarification of harbour limits regarding Wolfe Island.

ii. Officials

Town Mayors

Thomas Kirkpatrick	1838 (Apr. 2)
Henry Cassidy	1839 (+ Sept.)

James Sampson	1839-40
John Counter	1841-3
James Sampson	1844
Thomas W. Sampson	1844
Thomas W. Robinson	1844-5
Robert McLean	1846

City Mayors

John Counter	1846
Thomas Kirkpatrick	1847
William Ford Jr.	1848
Francis Manning Hill	1849, 1851
John Counter	1850, 1852-3, 1855

Clerks

William Dawe	1838-41
Francis M. Hill	1841-5
M. Flanagan	1845-97

Chamberlain or Treasurer

Wm. R. Sanders	1838-41
J. J. Burrowes	1841-5
Wm. Anglin	1845-66

11. London

i. Legislation

1840 3 Vic. c.31 (10 Feb.). Establishes an elected Board of Police, defines limits, and divides town into four wards.

1847 10 & 11 Vic. c.48 (28 July). Substitutes mayor and town council for Board of Police, with two members for each ward and mayor elected separately.

ii. Officials

Presidents of the Board of Police

George J. Goodhue	1840
James Givins	1841
Edward Matthews	1842-3
James Farley	1844
John Balkwill	1845
T. W. Shepherd	1846
Dr. Hiram D. Lee	1847

Mayors

Simeon Morrill	1848
Thomas C. Dixon	1849
Simeon Morrill	1850-1

Clerks

Alexander Robertson	1840
D. J. Hughes	1841
W. K. Cornish	1842-3
George Railton	1844
Thomas Scatcherd	1845-6
Henry Hamilton	1847
Alfred Carter	1848
James Farley	1849-54

Treasurers

W. W. Street	1840-52

12. Merrickville

i. Proclamation

1834 Proclamation of 18 Apr. Authorizes the establishment of a market. (Merrickville not incorporated before 1850).

13. Napanee

i. Proclamation

1834 Proclamation of 18 Apr. Authorizes the establishment of a market. (Napanee not incorporated before 1850).

14. Niagara-On-The-Lake (Newark)

i. Legislation

1816 56 Geo. III c.14 (22 May). Town limits extended.

1817 57 Geo. III c.4 (7 Apr.). authorizes the establishment of a market.

1819 59 Geo. III c.5 (12 July). District magistrates given policing powers for four years.

1819 59 Geo. III c.11 (12 July). Amends 57 Geo. III c.4 and authorizes magistrates to choose location.

1823 4 Geo. IV c.34 (19 Mar.). Magistrates policing power extended indefinitely.

1839 2 Vic. c.46 (11 May). Trustees of market authorized to borrow £1500 to erect building.

1845 8 Vic. c.62 (29 Mar.). Incorporates town with Board of Police, defines limits, divides town into five wards, and makes provision for £3000 to be borrowed for market and town hall.

1866 29-30 Vic. c.70. County seat moved to St. Catharines.

ii. Officials

Presidents of the Board of Police

Richard Miller	1845 (May 6)
Alexander C. Hamilton	1846
John Simpson	1847-8, 1852-6
Alexander Davidson	1849-50

(became first mayor in January 1850)

Clerks

Isaac H. Johnson	1845-56+

Treasurers

Uncertain: Thomas McCormick is shown by Carnochan as treasurer in 1845, and Scobie's Almanac gives him again in 1850, but shows I. H. Johnson as treasurer in 1848. Town Clerk's office believe that Johnson may have held both posts in the early years.

15. Perth

i. Legislation

1822 2 Geo. IV c.15 (17 Jan.). Authorizes the establishment of a market. (Perth not incorporated before 1850).

16. Picton

i. Legislation

1837 7 Wm. IV c.44 (4 Mar.). Unites Hallowell and Picton and incorporates them as the Town of Picton, defines the town limits, divides it into three wards, and provides for an elected Board of Police.

ii. Officials

It would appear that there is no complete listing extant of the early officials, and the Town Clerk's Office advises that it does not have any information. Picton's Hundred Years 1837-1937, shows the first officials in 1837 as:

Calvin Pier - President of the Board of Police

Thomas Rorke - Clerk

David Smith - Treasurer

Scobie's Almanacs show:

1848 - Alexander Macalister, President, Lempriere Murray, Clerk-Treasurer

1850 - Philip Low, Mayor, Lempriere Murray, Clerk, no treasurer listed.

211

17. Port Hope

i. Legislation

1834 4 Wm. IV c.26 (6 Mar.). Defines boundaries, divides town into four wards, and provides for the election of a Board of Police and for the borrowing of £1000 to build a market.

ii. Officials

Presidents of the Board of Police

Marcus F. Whitehead	1834-7
John Brown	1838
James Smith	1839
Charles Hughes	1840-1
William Henderson	1842
John D. Smith	1843
William Furby	1844
James Smith	1845-7
Nesbitt Kirchhoffer	1848
Robert Armour	1849

Mayors

John T. Williams	1850

Clerks

Robert Syers	1834-41
Morgan Jellett	1842-4
George C. Ward	1845-6
Benjamin Bird	1847
Francis Evatt	1848-52

Treasurers

John Crawford	1834-5
James Smith	1836-7
W. Mitchell	1838
Morgan Jellett	1839-42
John Wright	1843-7
Charles Hughes	1848-50

18. Prescott

i. Legislation

1834 4 Wm. IV c.27 (6 Mar.). Defines boundaries, divides town into two wards, provides for an elected Board of Police, and authorizes the borrowing of £1000 to establish a market.

1847 10 & 11 Vic. c.47 (28 July). Revises assessment laws.

1850 (1 Jan.) erected into a town under Schedule B of 1849, c.81.

ii. Officials (all assumed office in April except as noted).

Presidents of the Board of Police

Alexander McMillan	1834 (16 April)
Thomas Fraser	1835
Samuel Crane	1836
Thomas Tom	1837
Alexander McMillan	1838
John Ramage	1839
Alfred Hooker	1840
Reid Burritt	1841
George Scott	1842
Hamilton D. Jessup	1843-5
H. B. Wells	1846
Reid Burritt	1847
Robert Headlam	1849 (4 Jan.)

Mayors

Bartholomew White	21 Jan. 1850 - 31 Dec. 1855

Clerks

Robert Headlam	1834-5
James O'Brien	1836
Daniel McLeod	1837
John Wilson	1838
James Higgins	1839
James Buckley	1840
William Grant	1841
Francis Belfoy	1842
Samuel W. Moss	1843
Roger McCarthy	1844-6
Daniel McCarthy	1847-9

Treasurers

Robert Headlam	1834 (25 June) - 1835
Thomas Tom	1836
Donald Murray	1837

Robert Campbell	1838
William Hillyard	1839
Alfred Hooker	1840
James Higgins	1841
C. H. Peck	1842
Patrick Mooney	1843
James Higgins	1844
Peter Moran	1845
Charles Vallance	1846
Peter Moran	1847
Charles Vallance	1846
Peter Moran	1847
Alex Smith	1848 (22 May)
J. Ferguson	1849 (11 Jan.)

19. Sandwich (now in Windsor)

i. Legislation

1817 57 Geo. III c.2 (7 Apr.). Magistrates of district given special policing and administrative powers in Sandwich, Amherstburg and York.

1857 20 Vic. c.94 (10 June). Sandwich incorporated as a town.

20. St. Catharines

i. Legislation

1845 8 Vic. c.63 (29 Mar.). Defines limits, divides town into four wards, establishes a Board of Police, and provides for the borrowing of £2000 for a market.

ii. Officials

Presidents of the Board of Police

Alphens Spencer St. John	1845 (May)
E. S. Adams	1846-9

Clerks

William E. Whitlaw	1845-6
Charles Hughes	1846-7
C. M. Arnold	1847-50

Treasurer (office established on re-incorporation 1850).

Henry Mittleburger	1850

21. Woodstock

i. Legislation

1841 4 & 5 Vic. c.70 (27 Aug.). Extends the limits of the town. (Woodstock not incorporated before 1850).

22. York/Toronto

i. Legislation

1814 54 Geo. III c.15 (14 Mar.). Authorizes the establishment of a market.

1817 57 Geo. II c.2 (7 Apr.). Magistrates given policing authority in York, Sandwich and Amherstburgh.

1831 1 Wm., IV c.10 (16 Mar.). Vests market square in Trustees (the church and town wardens).

1834 4 Wm. IV. c.23 (6 Mar.). Extends the limits of the town of York and incorporates it as the City of Toronto.

1837 7 Wm. IV c.39 (4 Mar.). Amends 4 Wm. IV c.23.

1837 7 Wm IV c.41 (4 Mar.). Authorizes two additional markets.

1840 3 Vic. c.47 (10 Feb.). Amends 4 Wm. IV c.23.

1846 9 Vic. c.70 (9 June). Amends incorporation to add a court of Request and makes other changes 2 Vic. c.44 (1839).

ii. Town of York Officials

Records for the town meetings are not complete, some are lost and there were changes in the system of reporting in 1824. Theoretically, there were to be two wardens in each town or township, one elected and one appointed by the Church of England, but this was not consistent. There was often no second warden and D'Arcy Boulton in 1807 was the only one apparently appointed by the church except for John Dennison in 1811, who was both elected by the meeting and appointed by the church.

Year		Town Wardens	Town Clerk
1797	Thomas Barry	Samuel Heron	Thomas Barry
1798	Archibald Cameron	Archibald Thomson	"
1799	Samuel Heron	"	Edward Hayward
1800	E. Payson	Andrew Thomson	"
1801	Duncan Cameron	Jacob Herchmer	Ely Playter
1802	John Beikie	Joseph Willcocks	"
1803	William Allan	Jacob Herchmer	William Bond
1804	Alexander Wood	-	Ely Playter
1805	Joseph Hunt	-	"
1806	Robert Henderson	-	"

1807	William Allan	D'Arcy Boulton	"
1808	"	-	"
1809	"	-	"
1810	"	-	Hugh Heward
1811	John Dennison	same	Ezekiel Benson
1812	Alexander Legge	-	"
1813	Thomas Ridout	-	"
1814	Jordan Post Sr.	-	"
1815	?	?	?
1816	Jesse Ketchum	Jonathan Cawthra	William Barber
1817	Thomas Stoyle	Collin Drummond	"
1818	Jordan Post	-	"
1819	- Anderson	Collin Drummond	Morris Lawrence
1821	Collin Drummond	-	William Barber
1822	Jesse Ketchum	-	John Smith
1823	Jordan Post	-	John Lea
1824 or 5			"

1825 -1833 no surviving records
1834   William Lyon Mackenzie

iii. Toronto Officials (assumed office 1st Monday in February)

Mayors

William Lyon Mackenzie	1834 (3 Apr.)
Robert Baldwin Sullivan	1835
Dr. Thomas D. Morrison	1836
George Gurnett	1837
John Powell	1838-40
George Monro	1841
Hon. Henry Sherwood	1842-44
William Henry Boulton	1845-47
George Gurnett	1847-50

Clerks

James Hervey Price	8 Apr. 1834 - 12 Nov. 1834
John Elliott, acting	8 Jan. 1835 - 20 Feb. 1835
Charles Daly	20 Feb. 1835 - 1864+

Chamberlains (Treasurers)

Matthew Walton	19 May, 1834 - 14 Aug. 1834+
Andrew T. McCord	15 Sept.1834 - 1874+

Part VI
Special Government Departments and Commissions

A. The Customs Department

a. Introduction

The Customs Department of Upper Canada was exclusively concerned with trade with the United States. Goods entering via Lower Canada passed through customs at Quebec or Montreal, and Upper Canada's portion of the duties was regulated by a special series of agreements which were a subject of long-standing discord between the two provinces. Lists of the arbitrators appointed to handle this phase of customs duties will be found under the Special Commissions (VI.D.d. below).

Trade between the United States and Upper Canada was first regulated by a temporary act in 1797 (37 Geo. III c.16). In 1801 this was followed by a further act which established customs duties and designated eleven ports of entry (41 Geo. III c.5). It received Royal Assent on 9 July and on 6 August the first collectors of customs were appointed. Further ports were created under acts passed in 1802 (42 Geo. III c.4); 1807 (47 Geo. III c.4); 1816 (56 Geo. IV c.8); and 1819 (59 Geo. III c.22). In 1822 an Imperial act simplified the process by providing that the Lieutenant-Governor could designate or abolish ports of entry by proclamation; this was the method used for the rest of the Upper Canadian period.

The system was at first little affected by the Union of 1841, new ports continuing to be created and old ones abolished as the trade of the province required. The lucrative collectorships were often held by members of the leading families, who could appoint a deputy to do the work, and there seems to have been a certain tendency to hereditary succession. By 1850, however, a more integrated system was developing and officials were being regularly transferred from one port to another instead of being left as little monarchs of their own domain. The service was becoming more professional and advancement by seniority was the norm. At the same time, however, the old Family Compact appointees appear to have been left at their places until removed by death or retirement.

b. Ports of Entry and Collectors of Customs

In the following table the underlined date following the name of the port, where given, is the date at which it was declared a port of entry. The names of the county and township follow the name of the port in brackets. Old names are given in brackets.

Amherstburgh   9 July, 1801

    (Essex - Malden)

John Wilson (Dismissed)	2 June,	1817^G -	1831
Francis Caldwell	15 Apr.,	1831 - 5 June,	1851

Antrim - see Port Antrim

Bath (Ernestown)   5 June, 1817

    (Lennox and Addington - Ernestown)

    Bath was proclaimed a port of entry in 1817 as Ernestown, abolished 20 Mar., 1824, and again proclaimed, this time under the name Bath, on 3 Jan., 1829.

Roderick McKay	2 June,	1817^G -	
James Rankin	10 Jan.,	1820 -	
Colin McKenzie	27 Apr.,	1829 -	(1850)
John Cameron		- 5 Apr.,	1851

Belleville (River Moira)   10 June, 1816

    (Hastings - Thurlow)

Simon McNabb	27 Sept.,	1816^G -	1821+
Robert Smith	20 July,	1821^G -	(1832)
Henry Baldwin	25 June,	1833 -	(1848)
William B. Gwynn		- 16 May,	1849
S. S. Finden	17 May,	1849 -	(1852)

Bond Head Harbour (later Newcastle)   24 Sept., 1840

    (Durham - Clarke)

    Joined with Port Darlington when originally established in 1840, but separated by 1846.

Edward Clarke	(1846) -	(1852)

Bowmanville - see Port Darlington.

Brighton - see Presq'Ile.

Brockville   10 June, 1816

    (Leeds - Elizabethtown)

Levius Peters Sherwood		(1818) -	(1825)
William Jones		(1827) -	(1831)
W. H. Denaut		-	1832
Richard D. Fraser	Feb.,	1832 -	(1841)
W. F. Meudell	21 Jan.,	1843 -	(1850)
W. B. Simpson		(1851) -	(1852)

Burlington Bay (Called Port of Hamilton)   20 Dec., 1816

    (Wentworth - Barton/Flamborough West)

Burlington Bay also listed as the outlet of Burlington Bay, disappears from the lists by the early 1840's, when Hamilton replaced it. On 27 Mar., 1828 the collectorship was extended to include the Burlington Canal.

John Chisholm	14 Mar.,	1817^G -	(1841)

Charlotteville - see Turkey Point.

Chatham   19 Nov., 1835

    (Kent - Raleigh)

William Cosgrave		1835 -	(1852)

Chippawa   29 Jan., 1803

    (Welland - Willoughby)

Originally on the north bank of the Chippawa River in the Township of Stamford.

Robert Kirkpatrick		(1818) -		1835
James Secord	23 July,	1835 -	22 Feb.,	1841+
Oliver Tiffany Macklem	29 Apr.,	1842 -	15 May,	1851

Cobourg   27 Mar., 1829

    (Northumberland - Hampton)

Dougald Campbell		(1829) -	(1832)
Allan McLean		(1833) -	1835
Robert Brown	11 July,	1835 -	(1837)
Sheppard McCormick	22 Jan.,	1839 -	
William H. Kittson		1839 -	(1852)

Cornwall   9 July, 1801

    (Stormont - Cornwall)

Joseph Anderson	6 Aug.,	1801 -	
John Chrysler		(1818) -	1833
William J. Chrysler	13 Aug.,	1834 -	1836
George S. Jarvis	20 July,	1836^B -	(1841)
Guy Carleton Wood	25 Aug.,	1842 -	(1852)

Dickinson's Landing   6 Apr., 1846?

    (Stormont - Osnabruck)

H. Macgregor	6 Apr.,	1846 -	16 May,	1847
R. K. Bullock	17 May,	1847 -	5 July,	1848
John Verner	6 July,	1848 -		(1852)

Drummond Island   5 June, 1817

   As the result of the 1822 Boundary Commission, Drummond Island was transferred to the U.S.A. It is the most westerly of the Manitoulin chain.

Dr. David Mitchell	2 June,	1817[G] -
Thomas Gumersal Anderson	10 Jan.,	1820 -14 Nov.,1828?
Ceded to the United States	14 Nov.,	1828 -

Dunnville   9 Aug., 1841

   (Haldimand - Moulton)

   Originally joined with Port Colborne.

Walter B. Sheehan	(1842) -	(1852)

Ernestown - see Bath.

Fort Erie Passage   9 July, 1801

   (Welland - Bertie)

John Warren	6 Aug.,	1801 -		1815+
John Warren Jr.	16 May,	1815 -	5 Sept.,	1832+
George Hardison	10 Oct.,	1832[G] -		1834
James Kerby	12 Sept.,	1834 -	20 June,	1852

Gananoque   14 Feb., 1803

   (Leeds - Leeds)

William M. Stone	4 May,	1803 -		
Vacant		(1818)		
Joel Stone		(1821) -		1832
Ephraim Webster	22 May,	1832[B] -	18 May,	1851

Goderich (Mouth of the River Maitland)   14 May, 1829

   (Huron - Goderich)

John Brewster		1829 -		(1832)
John Galt	11 Nov.,	1834 -	15 Nov.,	1851

Grafton   6 July, 1848

   (Northumberland - Haldimand)

S. S. Walsh	6 July,	1848 -		(1849)

Hallowell (now in Picton)   10 Jan., 1821[G]

   (Prince Edward - Hallowell)

Andrew Deacon (Dismissed)	9 Jan.,	1821 -	6 Apr.,	1836
Edward Beeston	6 Apr.,	1836 -		
William Rorke	9 Feb.,	1839[B] -	21 May,	1846
J. B. Roblin	22 May,	1846 -		(1852)

Hamilton - See also Burlington

    (Wentworth - Barton)

John Davidson	14 Jan.,	1843	-	(1852)

Johnstown   9 July, 1801 -

    (Grenville - Edwardsburgh)

Levius Peters Sherwood	6 Aug.,	1801	-	(1818)
William Jones		(1829)	-	1831
W. H. Denaut		1831	-	
John Webster	22 June,	1833	-	(1837)

Abolished 11 April., 1837

Kettle Creek Harbour - see Port Stanley

Kingston   9 July, 1801

    (Frontenac - Kingston).

Joseph Anderson	6 Aug.,	1801	-	
Christopher A. Hagerman		(1818)	-	1828
Thomas Kirkpatrick	24 June,	1828^G	-	1845
John Macaulay		1845	-	26 June, 1846
G. A. Maillieu (Acting)	27 June,	1846	-	1847
James Hopkirk		1847	-	(1852)

Maitland - see Port Maitland

Maria-Town   2 Apr., 1839^G

    (Dundas - Williamsburgh)

Alexander Macdonell	28 Apr.,	1839^B	-	(1852)

Milford - see Port Milford

Newcastle   9 July, 1801

    (Durham - Clarke)

Timothy Thompson	6 Aug.,	1801	-	
Alexander Clark			-	1817
James Richardson	2 June,	1817^G	-	1826
William M. Bullock	9 Mar.,	1826^G	-	(1833)
Bernard McMahon	7 May,	1834	-	(1841)
Charles Short	20 Aug.,	1842^B	-	17 Feb., 1849+
Joseph Bertram	6 Mar.,	1849	-	5 Apr., 1851

Niagara (on-the-Lake)   9 July, 1801

    (Lincoln - Niagara)

Colin McNabb (Dismissed)	6 Aug., 1801 -	
John Symington	(1807)-	(1818)
Thomas McCormick	11 Sept., 1820 -	(1852)

<u>Oakville</u>   5 July, 1834

    (Halton - Trafalgar)

William Chisholm	10 Aug., 1834 -	(1841)
R. K. Chisholm	30 Aug., 1842 -	(1852)

<u>Owen Sound</u>

    (Grey - Owen Sound)

Richard Carney	(1846)-	5 Apr.,	1851

<u>Penetanguishene</u>   14 May, 1829

    (Simcoe - Tiny).

Thomas Gumersal Anderson	14 May, 1829^G -	1839
William Simpson	6 Nov., 1839^G -	(1852)

<u>Picton</u> - see Hallowell

<u>Port Antrim</u>   28 Dec., 1841

    (Kent - Howard)

James Coll	6 Sept., 1842 -	

<u>Port Burwell</u>   30 May, 1834

    (Elgin - Bayham)

John Burwell	13 Aug., 1834 -	1840
James Peel Bellairs	20 May, 1840^B -	(1852)

<u>Port Colborne</u>   11 June, 1834

    (Welland - Humberstone).

W. B. Sheehan	13 June, 1834 -	(1841)
James Black	4 July, 1844 -	
Thomas Parke	(1846)-	(1852)

<u>Port Credit</u>   4 June, 1839

    (Peel - Toronto)

James William Taylor	6 July, 1839^B -	(1841)
William Adamson (acting)	(1846)-	(1848)
James R. Yeilding	23 Feb., 1848 -	(1852)

<u>Port Dalhousie</u>   2 Dec., 1829

    (Lincoln - Grantham)

Edward Oates		15 Aug., 1827+

William Hamilton Merritt	2 Dec.,	1829^G -	(1834)
George Smith?		(1832) -	
John Clark	23 Feb.,	1835^B -	(1852)

Port Darlington and Bond Head Harbour   31 Oct., 1840

    (Durham - Darlington)

    Bond Head separated by 1846, Port Darlington later Bowmanville.

Henry Solomon Reid	28 Nov.,	1840^B -	(1852)

Port Dover   10 June, 1816

    (Norfolk - Woodhouse)

Robert Nichol		(1818) -			(1821)
George J. Ryerse	3 Jan.,	1821^G -			(1843)
J. Hemphill (acting)		(1846) -	5 May,	1846	
Henry Forbes (acting)	6 May,	1846 -	5 Aug.,	1846	
John Haycock	6 Aug.,	1846 -			
Henry Forbes (acting)	22 Nov.,	1847 -			(1848)
F. H. Haycock					(1852)

Port Hope (Smith's Creek)   21 June, 1819^G

    (Durham - Hope)

Marius F. Whitehead	6 Nov.,	1819^G -	1830
Richard Bullock	28 May,	1830^G -	(1833)
William Kingsmill	7 Apr.,	1834 -	1840
Marcus F. Whitehead	26 July,	1840 -	(1852)

Port Maitland   6 June, 1831

    (Grenville - Augusta)

Alexander McQueen	21 Nov.,	1833 -		(1841)
John Verner (acting)		(1846) -	5 July,	1847
Dunham Jones	6 July,	1847 -		(1852)

Port Milford.   16 July, 1847?

    (Prince Edward - South Marysburgh).

John Verner	6 July,	1847 -	5 July,	1848
R. K. Bullock	6 July,	1848 -		(1852)

Port Robinson - attached to Chippawa 9 Aug., 1841.

Port Sarnia - see Sarnia.

Port Stanley   18 Feb., 1834

    (Elgin - Yarmouth)

    Formerly Kettle Creek Harbour.

John Bostwick		20 July, 1831 -		1843
Richard Smith		23 May, 1843 -		(1852)

Port Talbot   18 Mar., 1819^G

    Ceased to make returns 1842 - Port Stanley succeeds?

    (Elgin - Dunwich)

Mahlon Burwell		10 Jan., 1820 -		(1841)

Prescott   5 June, 1817

    Grenville - Augusta)

Alexander McMillan		21 June, 1817^G -		(1821)
Alpheus Jones		14 Apr., 1823 -		(1839)

Presq'Isle (Brighton)

    (Northumberland - Brighton)

Charles Short		20 Aug., 1842 -		
John Short		1846 -		

Queenston   9 July, 1801

    (Lincoln - Niagara)

Thomas Dickson		(1818) -		1825+
Robert Grant		27 Apr., 1825 -	16 May,	1838+
Gilbert McMicken		1 Aug., 1838 -		(1852)

River Moira - see Belleville.

Riviere-Aux-Raisins   10 June, 1816

    (Glengarry - Charlottenburgh)

John Cameron (The Rich)		18 July, 1832^G -	27 Aug.,	1829+
John Cameron (The Wise)		21 Dec., 1829^G -	22 Jan.,	1847
William Robinson		23 Jan., 1847 -		(1852)

Rond Eau (Rondeau)   1844

    (Kent - Harwich)

    Subsidiary to Chatham 1866

Thomas Cronyn		(1846) -		(1849)

Sandwich   9 July, 1801

    (Essex - Sandwich West)

    Office transferred to Windsor 1854

John Askin Jr.		6 Aug., 1801 -		(1803)
William Duff		22 June, 1807 -		
William Hands		6 Mar., 1809 -	19 Feb.,	1836+

Felix Hands	24 Mar.,	1836^G -	by July,	1837+
William Anderton	25 July,	1837 -		1841
John Frazer Elliot	26 Jan.,	1841^B -		(1852)

St. Joseph's and St. Mary's   18 May, 1807

    (Head of Lake Huron)

Joseph Chiniquy	8 May,	1807 -
John Ersking Jr.	11 July,	1809^G -
John Askin	22 July,	1809^G -

Sarnia (Port Sarnia)   23 July, 1840

    (Lambton - Sarnia)

    Pre-1840 subsidiary to Sandwich with a deputy collector

Richard Emeric Vidal	29 Aug.,	1840^B -		(1852)

Sault Ste. Marie

    (District of Algoma)

George Wilson	20 Aug.,	1843 -	5 Apr.,	1848
Joseph Wilson	6 Apr.,	1848 -		(1852)

Smith's Creek - see Port Hope

Toronto (York)   9 July, 1801

    (York - York)

William Allan	6 Aug.,	1801 -	1 Oct.,	1828
George Savage	1 Oct.,	1828^G -	9 Sept.,	1835+
Thomas Carfrae Jr.	21 Sept.,	1835 -	1 June,	1841+
Anthony Manahan	18 June,	1841^G -		
William M. Kelly	6 Apr.,	1842 -		
Robert Stanton	7 Aug.,	1843 -	20 Nov.,	1849
W. F. Meudell		-		(1856)

Trent Port (Trenton)   4 Feb., 1837

    (Hasting - Sidney)

Charles Short	20 Aug.,	1842^B -

Turkey Point (Charlotteville)   9 July, 1801

    (Norfolk - Charlotteville)

Richard Vanderberg (Deputy)		1801 -	
Joseph Ryerson		1803 -	
George Ryerson		-	1821
James Mitchell	17 Feb.,	1821^G -	1838

Donald Fraser		18 July, 1838[B] -	
Donald Fisher (same man?)		15 Nov., 1838 -	(1839)
George J. Reade		(1846) -	(1849)

Wallaceburg   6 Apr., 1846?

    (Kent - Chatham)

John Bell		6 Apr., 1846 -	(1862)

Wellington   1 May, 1846?

    (Prince Edward - Hiller)

Thomas Worthington		1 May, 1846 -	(1852)

Whitby - see Windsor

Windsor (Big Bay)   12 May, 1831 (now Whitby, for modern Windsor see Sandwich)

    (Ontario - Whitby)

F. R. Tincombe		6 Sept., 1831[G] -	19 July, 1833+
Henry Boys, M.D.		10 Aug., 1833 -	(1839)
William Dow Jr.		30 July, 1840[G] -	(1841)
William Warren		10 Oct., 1842 -	(1852)

B. The Emigrant Office

a. Superintendents of Emigrants or alternatively Chief Emigrant Agent for U.C.

Anthony B. Hawke	June, 1832 -	**1864**

b. Clerks

Robert Beekman

W. J. McKay

c. Agents at Toronto

Dr. Bradley	4 June, 1841 -	

d. Agent at Quebec

Alexander Carlisle Buchanan	1828 -	1836

    There were also various minor officials appointed for specific townships on a temporary basis.

C. The Post Office

a. Introduction

Until 1851 the post offices in British North America were branches of the British Post Office. There were thus two sets of officials, British in London and local. The Canadas were administered from Quebec City.

In England the office of Postmaster General was a patronage appointment which was held as a joint commission from 1691 to 1823. It was basically a subordinate department, but was increasingly held by peers, who from 1765 became privy councillors on appointment. Technically the Postmaster General supervised the posts of the Empire, but there were few actual duties. In the eighteenth century the stipend was a very comfortable £2,900 per annum.

The senior official of the post office in England was the Secretary, an office which dated from 1694. Unlike the Postmaster General the Secretary usually remained in office for years. He basically made the decisions and summoned the Postmaster General to the meetings of the Board to accept his suggestions or ratify his decisions. He was usually the one who made major appointments.

In Scotland, Ireland and the colonies authority for administration was delegated to Deputy Postmasters General. The local postmasters were chosen from among the resident merchants or political leaders for the office was a lucrative one. In British North America there was a joint local Deputy Postmaster General from 1753, what is now Canada coming under the jurisdiction of the northern Deputy Postmaster General in Philadelphia. After the Revolution the postmaster at Quebec was gradually given extended power and from 1784 was Deputy Postmaster General for Canada (Quebec), with at first some authority over the Maritimes.

The following tables include all these officials beginning with those in office at the time of the Conquest. The post offices are shown with the district in which they were located by the final distribution of the districts in the 1840s and their dates of opening, or the earliest date at which they were known to be operating. The individual postmasters are also given for all the major centres and for all the district towns as far as they can be established. A fire at the General Post Office at Quebec on 29 November, 1841 destroyed many of the records prior to 5 April, 1841.

b. Post Office Officials in Britain

1. Postmasters General

		From	To
Thomas Coke, Earl of Leicester		1733	1759
Sir Everard Faukener		1745	1758
William Ponsonby, Earl of Bessborough	(1)	1759	1762
Robert Trevor, Baron Trevor (later Viscount Hampden)		1765	1766
John Percival, Earl of Egmont		1762	1763

Name		Start	End
Thomas Villiers, Earl of Clarendon	(1)	1763	1765
	(2)	1768+	
Thomas Robinson, Baron Grantham		1765	1766
Wills Hill, Marquis of Downshire		1766	1768
Sir Francis Dashwood, Baron Le Depensier		1766	1781+
John, Earl of Sandwich		1768	1770
Henry Frederick Thynne, Baron Carteret		1770	1789
William, Viscount Barrington		1782	
Charles, Earl of Tankerville	(1)	1782	1783
	(2)	1784	1786
Thomas, Baron Foley		1783	
Thomas De Grey, Baron Walsingham		1787	1794
John, Earl of Westmorland		1789	1790
Philip, Earl of Chesterfield		1790	1798
George Townshend, Earl of Leicester and Marquis Townshend		1794	1799
William Eden, Baron Auckland		1798	1804
George Granville Leveson-Gower, Baron Gower, later Duke of Sutherland		1799	1801
Lord Charles Spencer		1801	1806
James Graham, Duke of Montrose		1804	1806
Earl of Carysfort		1806	1807
Richard, Marquis of Buckingham		1806	1807
John Montagu, Earl of Sandwich		1807	1814+
Thomas Pelham, Earl of Chichester		1807	1826+
Richard Trench, Earl of Clancarty		1814	1816
James Cecil, Earl (later Marquis) of Salisbury		1816	1823+
Lord Frederick Montague		1826	1827
William Montagu, Duke of Manchester		1827	1830
Charles Lennox, Duke of Richmond		1830	1834
Francis Nathaniel Pierpont-Burton, Marquis of Coningham	(1)	1834	
	(2)	1835	
Lord Maryborough		1834	1835
Thomas William Anson, Earl of Lichfield		1835	1841
William Lowther, Viscount Lowther, 1841 later Earl of Lonsdale		1846	

2. Secretaries of the Post Office

	From	To
George Shevlrocke	1742	1760+
Henry Potts	1760	1764
Anthony Todd	1764	1798+
Sir Francis Freeling (joint secretary)	1797	1798
	1798	1836
William Leader Maberly	1836	1854

c. Post Office Officials for British North America

1. Deputy Postmasters General for British North America

	From	To
Benjamin Franklin, Philadelphia (joint)	1753	1774
William Hunter, Williamsburg (joint)	1753	1761
John Foxcroft (joint)	1761	1774?
Office Vacant	1774	

2. Deputy Postmasters General for Canada

	From	To
Hugh Finlay (Surveyor)	1772	1784
(deputy postmaster general)	7 July, 1784	Oct., 1799
George Heriot	1799	1816
Daniel Sutherland	Apr., 1816	1827
Thomas Allen Stayner	1827	6 Apr., 1851

d. Post Offices in Upper Canada

Location	District	Opened
Adelaide	London	6 July, 1839
Adolphustown	Prince Edward	1822
Albion	Home	6 Oct., 1832
Aldboro	London	1829
Alexandria	Eastern	1825
Allen's Mills	Prince Edward	6 Aug., 1836
Ameliasburg	"	6 Oct., 1832
Amherstburg	Western	1815
Amiens	London	6 Feb., 1837
Ancaster	Gore	1825

Asphodel	Colborne	6 Jan., 1836
Augusta (see Prescott)		
Aylmer	London	6 Oct. 1836
Ayr	Gore	6 May, 1840
Barrie	Home	6 Oct., 1835
Bath	Midland	1819
Bay of Quinte (see Belleville)		
Bayham	London	1829
Beachville	"	6 July, 1836
Beamsville	Niagara	6 Oct., 1832
Beaverton	Home	6 Jan., 1836
Belleville (formerly Bay of Quinte)	Midland	1816
Beverley	Johnstown	1828
Bloomfield	Prince Edward	6 July, 1836
Bond Head	Home	6 Aug., 1837
Bradford	"	5 July, 1840
Brantford	Gore	1825
Brighton	Newcastle	6 July, 1831
Brock	Home	6 Aug., 1836
Brockville (formerly Elizabethtown)	Johnstown	1811
Brougham	Home	6 Aug., 1836
Burford	London	1819
Burritt's Rapids	Johnstown	6 Oct., 1839
Bytown	Dalhousie	6 Apr., 1829
Caledon	Home	6 Oct., 1839
Caledonia	Ottawa	6 May, 1837
Camden East (also Camden)	Midland	6 Oct., 1832
Camden West (see Whitehall)		
Canboro	Niagara	6 Apr., 1836
Carleton Place	Bathurst	6 Oct., 1830
Castleford	"	6 Jan., 1832
Cavan	Newcastle	6 Jan., 1830
Chinguacousy	Home	6 Oct., 1832

Chippawa	Niagara	Oldest record 23 July, 1801
Churchville	Home	6 Oct., 1830
Clarke	Newcastle	6 Apr., 1835
Clearville (formerly Orford)	Western	6 Oct., 1831
Cobourg (formerly Hamilton)	Newcastle	1819
Colborne (formerly Cramahe)	"	1820
Colchester	Western	6 Oct., 1831
Coldwater	Home	6 Oct., 1835
Consecon	Prince Edward	6 Jan., 1836
Cooksville (formerly Toronto)	Home	1829
Cornwall	Eastern	1789
Cramahe (see Colborne)		
Credit	Home	6 Oct., 1831
Darlington	Newcastle	1824
Dawn Mills	Western	1834
Delaware	London	1820
Demorestville	Prince Edward	5 Apr., 1829
Drummondville	Niagara	6 Apr., 1830
Dundas	Gore	1814
Dunnville	Niagara	6 July, 1830
Edwardsburg	Johnstown	6 Apr., 1837
Ekfrid	London	6 Feb., 1837
Eldon	Colborne	6 Nov., 1837
Elizabethtown (see Brockville)		
Elora	Gore	6 Oct., 1839
Embro	London	6 July, 1836
Emily	Colborne	6 Aug., 1836
Eramosa	Gore	6 Oct., 1839
Erieus	Western	6 Oct., 1831
Erin	Gore	6 Oct., 1839
Errol	Western	6 Feb., 1837
Esquesing	Gore	6 Oct., 1832
Etobiocoke	Home	6 Apr., 1832

Farmersville	Johnstown	6 July, 1836
Fenelon Falls	Newcastle	6 July, 1838
Fergus	Gore	6 Apr., 1836
Fitzroy Harbour	Dalhousie	6 Jan., 1832
Flos	Home	6 Aug., 1837
Fort Erie	Niagara	Oldest record 23 July, 1801
Fort Wellington (see Prescott)		
Frankford	Midland	6 July, 1838
Franktown	Bathurst	6 Oct., 1832
Fredericksburg	Midland	1826
Galt	Gore	1825
Gananoque	Johnstown	1817
Georgina	Home	6 Oct., 1831
Goderich	London	6 Oct., 1835
Gosfield	Western	6 Oct., 1831
Grimsby	Niagara	1816
Guelph	Gore	1827
Haldimand	Newcastle	6 Apr., 1832
Hallowell (see Picton)		
Hamilton	Gore	1825
Hamilton (see Cobourg)		
Hawkesbury	Ottawa	1819
Hillier	Prince Edward	1825
Holland Landing	Home	6 Oct., 1831
Howard	Western	6 Oct., 1831
Huntley	Dalhousie	6 Apr., 1837
Jordan	Niagara	6 Apr., 1840
Katesville	London	6 Feb., 1837
Kemptville	Johnstown	6 Apr., 1831
Keswick	Home	1835
Kilmarnock	Johnstown	6 Aug., 1829
Kingston	Midland	1780
Kitley	Johnstown	6 Jan., 1832
Lanark	Bathurst	1823
Lancaster	Eastern	1816

Lindsay	Colborne	6 Aug., 1836
Lloydtown	Home	6 Oct., 1831
Lochiel	Eastern	1822
London	London	1825
Long Point (see Vittoria)		
L'Orignal	Ottawa	6 Apr., 1829
Loughboro'	Midland	6 July, 1836
McGillivray	London	6 Oct., 1836
McKillop	"	6 Oct., 1836
McNab	Bathurst	6 May, 1839
Madoc	Midland	6 July, 1836
Maitland	Johnstown	5 July, 1828
March	Dalhousie	1824
Markham	Home	6 Jan., 1829
Mariposa	Colborne	6 Aug., 1836
Marmora (formerly Marmora Iron Works)	Midland	1821
Marmora Iron Works (see Marmora)		
Marshville	Niagara	6 Apr., 1836
Martintown	Eastern	1824
Matilda	Eastern	1789
Merrickville	Johnstown	6 July, 1829
Mersea	Western	6 Oct., 1835
Middleton	London	6 July, 1831
Milford	Prince Edward	6 Oct., 1832
Mill Creek	Midland	1838
Milton	Gore	6 Apr., 1836
Mohawk	"	6 Apr., 1836
Mono Mills	Home	6 Oct., 1839
Moore	Western	6 Feb., 1837
Mosa	London	6 Apr., 1832
Moulinette	Eastern	6 Oct., 1835
Murray	Newcastle	1820
Nanticoke	Niagara	6 Aug., 1839
Napanee (formerly Napanee Mills)	Midland	1820

Napanee Mills
  (see Napanee)

Nassagaweya	Gore	6 Jan., 1840
Nelson	"	1822
Newborough	Johnstown	6 Jan., 1836
Newmarket	Home	1822
Niagara (on-the-Lake)	Niagara	1789
North Augusta	Johnstown	5 July, 1840
North Port	Prince Edward	6 Aug., 1836
Norval	Gore	6 Oct., 1836
Norwich	London	1829
Oakville	Gore	6 Oct., 1835
Oakland	London	6 Apr., 1840

Orford (see Clearville)

Orillia	Home	6 Oct., 1835
Oro	Home	6 Oct., 1835
Osgoode	Dalhousie	6 July, 1838
Osnabruck	Eastern	1803
Otonabee	Colborne	6 Apr., 1832
Otterville	London	6 Aug., 1837
Oxford	"	1822

Oznabruck (- See Osnabruck)
Oznaburg (- See Osnabruck)

Pa(c)kenham	Bathurst	6 Apr., 1832
Palermo	Gore	6 Apr., 1837
Paris	"	6 Jan., 1832
Penetanguishene	Home	1829
Percy	Newcastle	6 Jan., 1836
Perth (upon-Tay)	Bathurst	1816
Peterboro'	Colborne	1829
Pickering	Home	1828
Picton (formerly Hallowell)	Prince Edward	1820
Plantagenet	Ottawa	6 July, 1838
Point Abino	Niagara	6 July, 1838
Port Burwell	London	1829
Port Colborne	Niagara	6 Apr., 1836

Port Dalhousie	"	6 July, 1831
Port Dover	London	6 July, 1831
Port Hope (formerly Toronto)	Newcastle	1817
Port Robinson	Niagara	1835
Port Sarnia	Western	6 Feb., 1837
Port Stanley	London	1829
Port Talbot	London	1820
Port Trent (also River Trent)	Newcastle	1826
Prescott (formerly Augusta, and Fort Wellington)	Johnstown	1789
Preston	Gore	6 Feb., 1837
Princeton	London	6 May, 1836
Queenston	Niagara	Oldest record 23 July, 1801
Raleigh	Western	1816
Ramsay	Bathurst	6 Apr., 1837
Rawdon	Midland	6 Apr., 1832
Richmond	Dalhousie	1820
Richmond Hill	Home	6 Jan., 1836
River Trent (see Port Trent)		
Romney	Western	6 Oct., 1831
St. Andrews	Eastern	6 Apr., 1830
St. Catherines (also St. Catharines)	Niagara	1817
St. George	Gore	6 Oct., 1835
St. Johns	Niagara	6 Oct., 1831
St. Thomas	London	1825
Sandwich	Western	1801
Scarboro'	Home	6 Apr., 1832
Seneca	Niagara	1838
Seymour East	Colborne	6 Apr., 1837
Seymour West	"	1827
Shannonville	Midland	6 July, 1833
Sheffield	Gore	6 Apr., 1837
Simcoe	London	6 July, 1829
Smith's Falls	Johnstown	6 July, 1830
Smithville	Niagara	5 July, 1831

Place	District	Date
South Gower	Johnstown	6 Oct., 1836
Stanley's Mills	Home	6 Oct., 1832
Stoney Creek	Niagara	6 Apr., 1831
Stratford	London	6 Oct., 1835
Streetsville	Home	1828
Thamesville	Western	1832
Thornhill	Home	1828
Thorold	Niagara	1826
Toronto (City) (formerly York)	Home	1797
Toronto (see Cooksville)		
Toronto (see Port Hope)		
Trafalgar	Gore	1824
Tryconnell	London	6 Feb., 1837
Uxbridge	Home	6 Aug., 1836
Vankleek Hill	Ottawa	6 July, 1831
Vaughan	Home	6 Nov., 1837
Vienna	London	6 Apr., 1836
Vittoria (formerly Long Point)	"	1816
Wallaceburg	Western	6 Feb., 1837
Walpole	Niagara	6 Apr., 1836
Walsingham	London	6 July, 1831
Warwick	Western	6 Feb., 1837
Waterloo	Gore	6 Oct., 1831
Wellington	Prince Edward	6 Apr., 1830
Wellington Square	Gore	1826
West Flamboro'	Gore	6 Apr., 1840
Westmeath	Bathurst	6 May, 1837
Westminster	London	6 Jan., 1840
Whitby	Home	1825
Whitehall (formerly Camden West)	Western	1830
Williamsburg East	Eastern	6 Oct., 1835
Williamsburg West	"	6 July, 1830
Williamstown	Eastern	6 Apr., 1833
Wilmot	Gore	6 May, 1837

Wilton	Midland	6 Oct., 1832	
Woodstock	London	6 Oct., 1835	
Woolwich	Gore	6 May, 1837	
Yonge	Johnstown	6 Jan., 1833	
York (see Toronto (City))			
York Mills	Home	6 Jan., 1836	
Zone Mills	Western	6 Jan., 1840	

e. Postmasters in the Major Centres

Amherstburg

William Hands	1817	-
John Wilson	1831	- 1835
John Stayner	1836	-
William Kevill	1837	-
James Kevill	6 Apr., 1838	- (1841)

Barrie

Sydney M. Sandford	6 Oct., 1834	- (1841)

Belleville (Bay of Quinte)

Simon McNab	1817	- 1820
Thomas Parker	1821	- 1837
Donald Cameron	6 Apr., 1839	- (1841)

Brockville (Elizabethtown)

Charles Jones	1811	- 1820
Henry Jones	1821	- (1841)

Bytown

M. Connell	1830	- 1834
George William Baker	5 Oct., 1834	- (1841)

Cobourg (Hamilton)

James George Bethune	1821	- 1834
Frederick Henry Hall	13 Nov., 1834	- 1840
Thomas Scott	(1841)	-

Cornwall

Samuel Anderson	1789	- 1806
W. B. Wilkinson	1807	-
Unknown	1808	- 1811

J. C. Wood	1812	- 1816
Guy C. Wood	1817	- (1841)

Fort Erie

Jonathan Sills	1803	
James Kerby	1827	- 1828
William Smith	1829	- 1831
R. Thompson	1832	-
G. Mackenzie	1833	- 1836
James Kerby	6 July, 1836	- (1841)

Goderich

E. Griffin	1835	- 1837
Thomas Kydd	6 Apr., 1840	- (1841)

Guelph

John Reid	1829	
T. B. Husband	1830	
A. McVenn	1831	
T. B. Husband	1832	- 1834
Mary Hume	1835	- 1837
Robert Corbet	6 July, 1837	- (1841)

Hamilton

W. B. Sheldon	1826	- 1827
A. R. Smith	1828	
J. M. Cameron	1829	
J. McA. Cameron	1830	- 1831
Edmund Ritchie	6 Oct., 1831	- (1841)

Kingston

Peter Clarke	1780	- 1804
Jermyn Patrick	1804	- 1807
Thomas Deacon	1808	- 1814
John Macaulay	1815	- 1837
Robert Deacon	29 Nov., 1837	- (1841)

London

Laurence Laurason	1826	- 1828
Major Schofield	1829	
Ira Schofield	1830	

George Jervis Goodhue	6 Apr., 1830	- (1841)

L'Orignal

Olmstead Gates	1831	- 1834
Thomas Hall Johnston	6 Apr., 1834	- (1841)

Newcastle

D. M. Rogers	1814	- 1820

Niagara (on-the-Lake)

Joseph Edwards	1789	- 1811
John Crooks	1812	- 1834
R. Clench	1835	- 1837
Alexander Davidson	6 Jan., 1837	- (1841)

Perth (upon-Tay)

Daniel Deverne	1817	- 1820
Josias Taylor	1821	- 1837
Francis Allan	3 June, 1837	- (1841)

Peterborough

T. V. Tupper (or Tucker)	1830	- 1833
J. B. Ferguson	1834	- 1835
J. Ferguson	1836	- 1837
Ephraim Sandford	6 Jan., 1838	- (1841)

Picton

Ebenezer Washburn	1821	- 1825
M. Patterson	1826	- 1828
J. S. Hierman	1829	
J. S. Heermans	1830	
William Rorke	6 Jan., 1831	- (1841)

Queenston

Thomas Dickson	1802	- 1814
Thomas McCormick	1818	- 1820
Alexander Hamilton	1821	- 1837
John Stayner	6 Apr., 1839	- (1841)

St. Catherines

William Hamilton Merritt	1821	- (1841)

Sandwich

R. Pollard	1803	
William Hands	1803	- 1836

John Gentile	1837	
Edward Holland	6 Feb., 1840	- (1841)
Simcoe		
Duncan Campbell	6 July, 1829	- (1841)
Woodstock		
Thomas Spunner Shortt	6 Oct., 1835	- 1840
H. G. Barwick	(1841)	
York (Toronto)		
D. McLean	1803	- 1807
William Allan	1808	- 1828
J. S. Howard	1829	- 1837
Charles Berczy	2 Apr., 1838	-
		- (1841)

D. Special Commissions
a. Introduction

During the Upper Canadian period there were innumerable commissions set up for special purposes, many of them of a legal nature. Details may be found in the "General Index of Commissions" (PAC:RG68). The following are merely a few of the more important ones.

b. Commissions Arising from the War of 1812
1. Special Commission for the Trial of High Treason in Upper Canada 11 Apr., 1814

Thomas Scott	William Dummer Powell
William Campbell	John Small
Richard Hall	Thomas Dickson
Samuel Hatt	

(There were also local commissions for the same purpose).

2. Commissioners to Receive Claims for War Losses 21 Dec., 1815[G]

William Dummer Powell	
John Strachan	William Kemble
Lt. Col. Battersby	Secretary to the Commission
George Crookshank	

240

3. Commissioners for Investigating Claims for War Losses 26 May, 1822ᴳ

Joseph Wells	William Allan
Lt. Col. Foster	Alexander Wood
Peter Robinson	

c. Commissions Arising from the Rebellion of 1837

1. Special Commission to examine Persons arrested for High Treason 11 Dec., 1837

R. S. Jameson	Alexander Wood
R. B. Sullivan	John G. Spragge
William Allan	

2. Board to distribute Money to the Wounded 27 May, 1839ᴳ

Alexander Wood	Thomas G. Ridout
Col. F. A. M. Fraser	George Monro
Robert Stanton	

d. Civil Commissions

1. Commission to lay an Address at the foot of the Throne. 22 Jan., 1822 (re: Union Bill)

J. B. Robinson
(This is Robinson's commission to oppose the Union Bill for Upper and Lower Canada which was then before the British Parliament and seek a new customs arrangement with Lower Canada).

2. Arbritrators of Customs

Upper Canada

J. D. Baby	------	1822
G. H. Markland	16 Sept.,	1828
John Macaulay	13 Oct.,	1836

Lower Canada

John Hale	13 Jan., 1823
James Irvine	19 July, 1824
John Richardson	28 June, 1825
Toussaint Pottier	2 June, 1832

3. Provincial Board of Education 26 May, 1822^G

John Strachan   Rev. H. Addison

Joseph Wells   J. B. Robinson

G. H. Markland   Thomas Ridout

4. Commission to revise the Statutes 25 July, 1840

J. B. Robinson   W. H. Draper

J. B. Macaulay   J. H. Cameron

E. Surveyors

a. Introduction

Provincial Land Surveyors for parts of what became Upper Canada were appointed as early as the mid-1780s. These men reported to the provincial department in Upper Canada, as soon as it separated from Quebec, and operated under its authority. Although they were often assigned specific areas of concentration the surveyors could work in widely separate areas of the province as townships were only surveyed, a few concessions at a time, as they were needed for settlement. They also frequently were sent to check each other's work in different areas, as lack of adequate training, assistants and equipment, coupled with the often wilderness terrain made accurate surveying very difficult.

The following list shows the surveyors appointed up until 1850 together with their dates of assuming office. Many continued surveying for years. For data on the dates of survey of individual townships see end of list.

b. Provincial Land Surveyors

Names	Date of Appointment	
Aitken, Alexander	....	1785
Allchin, Thomas	29th September	1837
Ambrose, Charles	22nd July	1844
Anderson, James		
Antill, John Collins	17th November......	1793
Austin, George Frederick	5th August	1847
Ball, George A...............	7th May	1834
Ball, Jesse P.	3rd April	1833
Barris, Josiah	....	1795
Bartley, Onesiphorus	24th January	1840
Beaupre, Pierre	22nd June	1791
Beckwith, Adolphus John	....	....
Bedard, J. B.	13th June	1790
Bell, Robert	16th June	1843
Benson, Samuel Manson	4th November	1819
Birdsall, Richard	....	1819
Black, Hugh	7th April	1820
Black, James jr.	9th May	1849
Blakely, John	23rd July	1830

Blyth, Thomas A.	20th April	1836
Booth, John	....	1816
Booth, Norman	2nd September	1846
Bostwick, John	21st May	1819
Bouchette, Joseph	25th February	1791
Bower, Thomas T.	27th September	1826
Boyce, George	22nd April	1835
Bridgland, James William	6th May	1844
Bristol, Richard	24th April	1818
Brough, Allan P.	28th October	1844
Brown, David R.	10th October	1850
Browne, John O.	18th November	1848
Browne, William	....	....
Bruce, George	7th January	1833
Bruce, John S.	14th November	1835
Burch, John	....	....
Burke, William	....	....
Burrows, Thomas	6th October	1831
Burt, John	30th September	1823
Burwell, Lewis	24th October	1818
Burwell, Mahlon	....	1809
Caddy, Edward C.	18th December	1846
Caldwell, Thomas	20th November	1816
Callaghan, Patrick	....	1833
Campbell, Alexander	20th September	1830
Campbell, William	25th January	1823
Carroll, Peter	14th October	1828
Carroll, William	8th September	1842
Castle, Henry J.	5th December	1832
Cattanack, Angus	11 April	1820
Chapman, Amos	....	....
Chewett, James G.	6th March	1819
Chewett, William	....	1774
Clapp, Gilbert S.	16th March	1835
Cleaver, James	21st June	1824
Clements, Edgar	31st October	1832
Clendinen, James K.	6th June	1845
Cockrell, Richard	....	....
Coffin, Nathaniel	July	1790
Collins, John	8th September	1764
Conger, John O.	30th April	1844
Conger, Wilson, ...	7th February	1811
Cromwell, Joseph M. O.	1st October	1846
Currie, Robert	....	1822
Cusack, Rheddy	....	1827
Daniell, John D.	15th January	1844
Deane, Michael	26th May	1848
Deane, William H.	31st May	1847
DeCew, Edmund	11th July	1836
Demers, Jean B.	24th March	1792
Dennehy, Thomas J.	3rd October	1836
Dennis, John S.	4th January	1842
Dennison, John	20th March	1823
Depensier, Theodore	27th February	1789
Devens, Marie des de Glondon.	11 May	1789
Devine, John	31st March	1820
Devine, Thomas	11th June	1846
Dezery, Amable	9th May	1792
Dies, Mathew	....	....
Donnelly, Philip S.	19th January	1849
Driscoll, Alfred	16th July	1850
Egan, Michael R.	8th August	1821
Elmore, Publius V.	2nd June	1821
Emerson, John	31st October	1833
Everitt, Daniel	27th February	1811
Ewing, Henry	28th October	1820

Name	Date	Year
Fairfield, W. J.	17th June	1822
Falls, Hugh	1st December	1841
Farquharson, John	28th May	1830
Fell, Charles, K.	10th March	1831
Fell, James W.	14th November	1835
Fell, Zenas	21st October	1830
Fleming, Sandford A.	28th April	1849
Fletcher, Edward T.	28th April	1842
Fortune, Joseph	4th May	1796
Fortune, William	....	1788
Fraser, Charles	5th August	1847
Fraser, Thomas	4th August	1825
Fraser, William	5th August	1847
Frey, Philip	....	....
Galbraith, John	4th November	1819
Galbraith, William	30th September	1842
Gibbard, William	29th May	1844
Gibbs, Thomas F.	....	....
Gibson, David	27th December	1825
Gill, Valentine	17th March	1824
Goesman, John	9th March	1821
Grant, John	8th June	1848
Grant, Lewis	....	....
Graves, William	6th October	1809
Greely, Aaron	18th November	1797
Guy, Louis	....	....
Hall, James	27th October	1825
Hambly, William	....	1795
Hamilton, James	27th November	1835
Hamilton, Robert	16th February	1848
Hanchette, Hiram	24th July	1820
Hanchette, William	....	....
Hanvey, Daniel	9th July	1832
Harley, William	31st December	1832
Harper, John S.	2nd June	1842
Harris, John	13th April	1819
Haslett, John J.	6th June	1843
Hawkins, William	31st October	1832
Hazen, Daniel	....	1788
Hood, Andrew	17th December	1836
Howard, John G.	25th January	1836
Hudson, John H.	18th February	1819
Hughes, Christopher	24th May	1822
Huston, John	28th October	1820
Iredell, Abraham	....	....
Ivory, Patrick	25 November	1842
Jessup, ------	....	....
Jones, Augustus	....	1791
Jones, E. Robert	9th July	1850
Jones, Francis	7th July	1840
Jones, Robert	....	....
Keating, John William	20th January	1832
Keefer, Thomas C.	14th August	1840
Kelly, Thomas	21st January	1831
Kennedy, Charles	19th May	1819
Kerr, Francis	11 April	1844
Kerr, Robert W.	1st April	1836
Kertland, Ed. Henry	23rd April	1849
Kilborn, Joseph	26th March	1813
Kilborn, William H.	2nd June	1821
Kirk, Joseph	16th February	1843
Kirkpatrick, James	16th April	1823
Kotte, Lewis	....	....

Name	Date	Year
Landon, Asa	5th June	1819
Lawe, George		
Lawe, William Parren	1st August	1797
Legendre, Francois	16th May	1792
Liddy, George P.	4th November	1844
Lind, Joshua	27th June	1831
Lount, Gabriel	1st May	1819
Lount, George	6th April	1820
Lynn, Robert	28th January	1835
Lyons, James	7th July	1847
Malcolm, Eliakim	21st July	1821
Marcoullier, Pierre	28th July	1788
Marlett, Adrian		
Maxwell, John	23rd January	1849
McCallum, James, jr.	30th March	1849
McCarthy, Jeremiah		
McClary, William	1st July	1843
McDermott, Michael	16th December	1843
McDonald, Allan		1796
McDonald, John	26th April	1823
McDonald, John S.	16th August	1822
McDonald, Neill	29th August	1825
McDonald, William	14th March	1820
McDonell, Duncan		1808
McDonell, Hugh		1788
McDonell, James		1796
McDonell, John R.	3rd October	1845
McDonell, Robert		
McGillis, John	14th October	1825
McIntosh, Alexander	12th August	1825
McLaren, Peter	6th January	1848
McLean, Neal	20th January	1835
McLean, Robert	12th February	1811
McLennan, Roderick	20th June	1846
McLeod, John	1st May	1833
McMahon, Hugh		1836
McMillan, William	29th March	1836
McNab, Archibald	29th April	1846
McNaughton, John	2nd June	1821
McNiff, Patrick		1784
McPhillips, George	6th June	1848
Merriman, Isaiah	16th August	1822
Miller, Andrew	16th May	1822
Miller, Chisholm	29th July	1847
Misner, Jacob	8th December	1827
Moore, James	2nd March	1835
Morris, John	9th June	1847
Mount, Roswell	17th February	1820
Nelson, John	20th January	1835
Newman, John	28th September	1842
Nickalls, James	3rd September	1817
O'Hara, Felix		
O'Mara, John	18th February	1833
Park, Shubal	4th April	1812
Parr, Richard	19th July	1843
Passmore, Frederick F.	1st October	1846
Pauling, Jesse		
Peachy, -----		
Pennock, John	28th July	1821
Pennoyer, Jesse	20th October	1788
Perrault, Louis	30th June	1789
Perry, Aylesworth B.	3rd March	1842
Peterson, Joseph S.	8th June	1842
Pollock, James	6th August	1845
Preston, Reuben	10th November	1819

Name	Date	Year
Quinn, Owen	30th August	1822
Rankin, Arthur	6th April	1836
Rankin, Charles	27th December	1820
Rankin, James	5th March	1789
Rath, William	13th September	1848
Rees, Richard	26th May	1835
Reid, John	3rd March	1837
Richardson, Samuel	10th March	1821
Richey, James	13th March	1843
Richey, Josias	22nd November	1819
Rider, John	....	....
Ridout, Edmund J.	2nd May	1836
Ridout, Samuel	18th January	1806
Robertson, John	8th December	1836
Robinson, William	....	1846
Roche, John K.	1st December	1841
Rogers, Jonathan	....	1808
Rombough, W. R.	14th November	1848
Roney, John J.	24th December	1844
Root, Azariah	....	1796
Ross, Robert	4th September	1833
Rubidge, Frederick P.	31st January	1831
Rubidge, Tom S.	9th February	1849
Ryan, John	10th October	1848
Ryckman, Samuel	....	1800
Rykert, George	9th November	1821
Ryle, Mathew	2nd June	1841
Salter, Albert P.	2nd September	1844
Salter, Phiboleth D.	10th March	1846
Sanders, George	25th July	1837
Savigny, H. P.	6th June	1848
Schofield, Milton, C.	28th September	1843
Scott, John	24th February	1832
Shaw, Claudius	....	....
Sherwood, Reuben	....	....
Shier, John	25th April	1844
Shurtliff, Lemuel	9th February	1834
Sinclair, Donald	9th July	1850
Sinclair, Duncan	20th June	1845
Slater, James Dyson	29th May	1849
Smiley, William	8th April	1836
Smith, Christopher	....	1823
Smith, Henry	....	....
Smith, John jr	5th April	1825
Smith, Samuel	24th October	1820
Smith, Thomas	5th March	1799
Smith, William	27th June	1848
Smyth, John	20th July	1834
Snow, John Allen	11th September	1847
Sparke, John F.	6th July	1843
Springer, Benjamin	26th February	1830
Stegmann, John	18th October	1790
Sterrett, James B.	10th June	1826
Strange, Henry	30th November	1838
Swallwell, Anthony	5th July	1823
Tidey, John A.	2nd January	1832
Tiffany, George S.	8th August	1825
Tinling, -----	....	....
Tracey, William	2nd November	1836
Treadwell, P. F.	....	....
Tuffe, -----	....	....
Tully, John	28th November	1845
Turgeon, Charles	16th May	1792
Vidal, Alexander	8th June	1842
Vondenvelden, William	....	....

Walker, William	14th November	1835
Walsh, Robert	5th June	1841
Walsh, Thomas W.	25th April	1842
Watkins, Seth	....	1795
Watson, Simon Z.	2nd May	1810
Welch, Thomas	....	....
Wells, Alphonso	19th April	1842
West, James	27th September	1825
White, Henry	10th October	1842
White, John Ed.	8th December	1819
Whiting, Charles	....	1796
Wilkinson, Alexander	31st October	1843
Wilkinson, John A.	6th May	1835
Wilmot, Samuel S.	6th November	1804
Wonham, William George	19th November	1847
Wright, Richard	14th November	1823
Young, Humphrey	11 November	1840

c. Dates of Township Surveys, 1784-1859

For an introduction and index to the field note books of the Ontario land surveyors, showing the various township surveys with dates and surveyors, see Louis Gentilcore and Kate Donkin *Land Surveys of Southern Ontario, Cartographica Monograph*. No. 8, (Department of Geography, York University, 1973).

F. Agents for the Affairs of Upper Canada in England

Unlike many West Indies colonies Upper Canada never had a regular agent to represent its interests in England. Just after 1800 there were two royal appointments in England. After the War of 1812 an Upper Canadian grant was made under 56 Geo. III c. 35 (22 Mar., 1816) and Lieutenant-Governor Gore's secretary appointed. After the appointee's death the grant was terminated by 2 Geo. IV c. 10 (17 Jan., 1822).

Agents

Robert Moss	- 1801+
Edward Fisher	Oct.-Nov?, 1801 - 1805+
....	
William Halton	4 Apr., 1816^G - 1821+

Part VII
Supplementary Information

A. Corporation Legislation

a. Introduction

The incorporation of companies in Upper Canada only began about 1820 and was never a well regulated process. The incorporation of companies was always done by a special statute, not under any general statute which provided criteria for the incorporation of companies of a specific type. Thus the terms granted could vary widely.

Most companies were not incorporated, and it would be impossible to attempt to list such organizations, but later statutes could be passed which referred to or partially controlled an unincorporated company. To further add to the confusion many statutes provided that incorporation had to take place within certain time limits. Even if the act of incorporation had expired it could be revived later, sometimes with the company name changed.

As well as the companies that were incorporated in the province, a few companies were chartered in Great Britain to do business in British North America specifically (Section i below) and other corporations, such as the East India Company, had rights in certain types of trade. Universities could also have a British charter. Finally, Quebec-incorporated companies, such as the Bank of Montreal, would carry on business in Upper Canada at times.

b. Banks and Financial Institutions

1819 59 Geo. III, c.15 (12 July)   Bank of Kingston, Incorporated
- Forfeited by non-user.

1819 59 Geo. III, c.24 (21 Apr., 1821) Bank of Upper Canada, Incorporated (Reserved Act)
- Amended 2 Geo. IV, c.7; 4 Geo. IV, c.11; 2 Wm. IV, c.10.

1823 4 Geo. IV, c.22 (19 Mar.) Bank of Upper Canada (pretended).
- Estate vested in Commissioners.
- Also: 9 Geo. IV, c. 11.
- Repealed: 10 Geo. IV, c.7.
- Disposal of real estate: 6 Wm. IV, c.22.

1832 2 Wm. IV, c.11 (28 Jan.) Commercial Bank, Midland District, Incorporated.
- Amended: 3 Wm. IV, c.42; 5 Wm. IV, c.45.

1833 3 Wm. IV, c.18 (13 Feb.) British America Fire and Life Assurance Company, Incorporated.
- Amended: 6 Wm. IV, c.20.

1833 3 Wm. IV, c.19 (13 Feb.) St. Lawrence Inland Marine Insurance Company, Incorporated.

1835 5 Wm. IV, c.46 (16 Apr.) Gore Bank, Incorporated.
- Amended: 2 Vic., c.41.

1836 6 Wm. IV, c.18 (20 Apr.) Mutual Insurance Companies.

1837 7 Wm. IV, c.34 (4 Mar.) Bank of British North America, authorized to sue.

1837 7 Wm. IV, c.35 (4 Mar.) Bank of Montreal authorized to sue.

1838 1 Vic., c.23 (6 Mar.) Agricultural Bank, bills and notes of in bankruptcy. (partnership - not incorporated).

c. Canals

1823 4 Geo. IV, c.8 (19 Mar.) Burlington Bay Canal, Construction.
- Also: 4 Geo. IV, c.16; 8 Geo. IV, c.19;
11 Geo. IV, c.12; 11 Geo. IV, c.27;
1 Wm. IV, c.20; 2 Wm. IV, c.26;
3 Wm. IV, c.36; 7 Wm. IV, c.91.

1824 4 Geo. IV, c.17 (19 Jan.) Welland Canal Company, Incorporated
- Amended: 6 Geo. IV, c.2; 7 Geo. IV, c.19 and 20; 8 Geo. IV, c.2; 8 Geo. IV, c. 17; 11 Geo. IV, c. 11;
1 Wm. IV, c. 17; 3 Wm. IV, c.54;
4 Wm. IV, c.39; 5 Wm. IV, c.24;
6 Wm. IV, c.34; 7 Wm. IV, c.92;
7 Wm. IV and 1 Vic., c.4;
1 Vic., c.28.

1826 7 Geo . IV, c.18 (30 Jan.) Desjardins Canal Company, Incorporated.
- Amended: 2 Wm. IV, c.24; 5 Wm. Iv, c.34;
7 Wm. IV, c.65.

1827 8 Geo. IV, c.1 (17 Feb.) Rideau Canal, Construction authorized.
- Amended: 9 Geo. IV, c.16; 6 Wm. IV, c.16; 2 Vic., c.19.

1827 8 Geo. IV, c.12 (17 Feb.) Cataraqui Bridge Company, Incorporated.
- Amended: 10 Geo. IV, c.16.

1829 10 Geo. IV, c.9 (20 Mar.) Niagara Canal Company Incorporated.
- Amended: 2 Wm. IV, c.12; 4 Wm. IV, c.22.

1834 4 Wm. IV, c.30 (6 Mar.) Port Hope and Rice Lake Canal Company, Incorporated.
- Expired by non-user.

1834 4 Wm. IV, c.31 (6 Mar.) Richmond Canal Company, Incorporated.
- Expired by non-user.

1837 7 Wm. IV, c.46 (4 Mar.) Fort Erie Canal Company, Incorporated.

d. Educational and Institutional (See also section i below)

1797 37 Geo. III, c.13 (3 July) Practice of Law: Law Society.
- amended: 47 Geo. III, c.5; 2 Geo. IV, c.5.

1815 55 Geo. III, c.18 (14 Mar.) Midland District School Society, Incorporated.
- Amended 7 Wm. IV, c.113.

1816 56 Geo. III, c.24 (1 Apr.) Legislative Assembly Library, grant.

1829   10 Geo. IV, c.17 (20 Mar.) Dundas Free Church, Incorporated.

1830   11 Geo. IV, c.13 (6 Mar.) Grantham Academy, Trustees Incorporated.
       - Loan: 7 Wm. IV, c.84.

1830   11 Geo. IV, c.31 (6 Mar.) York Hospital, aid.
       - also: 1 Wm. IV, c. 23; 2 Wm. IV, c.29;
       3 Wm. IV, c. 52; 7 Wm. IV, c.97;
       2 Vic., c.64.

1830   11 Geo. IV, c.32 (6 Mar.) Kingston Female Benevolent Society, aid.
       - Aid: 4 Wm. IV, c.46.

1832   2 Wm. IV, c.28 (28 Jan.) Kingston Hospital, grant for construction.
       - Aid: 7 Wm. IV, c.98.

1833   3 Wm. IV, c.31 (13 Feb.) York (Toronto) Harbour, grant.
       - Also: 7 Wm. IV, c.64.

1834   4 Wm. IV, c.33 (6 Mar.) Bath School Society, Incorporated.

1835   5 Wm. IV, c.38 (16 Apr.) Mechanics' Institute, Toronto, grant.

1835   5 Wm. IV, c.40 (16 Apr.) Mechanics' Institute, Kingston, grant.

1837   7 Wm. IV, c.16 (4 Mar.) King's College, (Royal) charter amended.
       (See section i below).

1837   7 Wm. IV, c.56 (4 Mar.) Regiopolis College, Kingston, Incorporated.

1837   7 Wm. IV, c.99 (4 Mar.) Provincial Library, grant.

1839   2 Vic., c. 11 (11 May) Provincial Lunatic Asylum, construction.

1839   2 Vic., c.38 (11 May) Upper Canada College of Physicians and Surgeons, Incorporated.
       - Disallowed.

1839   2 Vic., c.63 (11 May) Toronto House of Industry, grant.
       - Also: 3 Vic., c.67.

1840   3 Vic., c.35 (10 Feb.) Kingston University, Incorporated.
       - Disallowed.
       - Temporary accommodation: 3 Vic., c.36.

e. Harbours and Bridges

1827   8 Geo. IV, c.18 (17 Feb.) Kettle Creek Harbour, Construction.
       - Also: 1 Wm. IV, c.25; 2 Vic., c.54.

1828   9 Geo. IV, c.12 (25 Mar.) Burlington Bay Harbour, Valuation of labour and materials.

1828   9 Geo. IV, c.19 (25 Mar.) Oakville or Sixteen Mile Creek (Harbour), Construction.
       - Also: 1 Wm. IV, c.24; 3 Vic., c.50.

1829   10 Geo. IV, c.11 (20 Mar.) Cobourg Harbour Company, Incorporated.
       - Also: 2 Wm. IV, c.22; 5 Wm. IV, c.43; 2 Vic., c.42.

1829   10 Geo. IV, c.12 (20 Mar.) Port Hope Harbour and Wharf Company, Incorporated.
       - Loan: 2 Wm. IV, c.23.
       - Amended: 6 Wm. IV, c. 17; 3 Vic., c.52.

1831   1 Wm. IV, c.12 (16 Mar.) Niagara Harbour and Dock Company, Incorporated.

1832   2 Wm. IV, c.14 (28 Jan.) Port Dover Harbour Company, Incorporated.
        - Amended: 5 Wm. IV, c.23.
        - Loan: 7 Wm. IV, c.86.

1832   2 Wm. IV, c.15 (28 Jan.) Port Burwell Harbour Company, Incorporated.
        - Loan: 7 Wm., IV, c.72.

1833   3 Wm. IV, c.22 (13 Feb.) Louth Harbour Joint Stock Company, Incorporated.
        - Loan: 7 Wm. IV, c. 67.

1834   4 Wm. IV, c.32 (6 Mar.) Credit Harbour Company, Incorporated.
        - Loan: 7 Wm. IV, c.70.

1835   5 Wm. IV, c.14 (16 Apr.) Stoney Creek Harbour Company, Incorporated.

1835   5 Wm. IV, c.16 (16 Apr.) Grimsby Breakwater, Pier and Harbour Company, Incorporated.

1836   6 Wm. IV, c.10 (20 Apr.) Cayuga Bridge Company, Incorporated.

1836   6 Wm. IV, c.12 (20 Apr.) Niagara River Suspension Bridge Company, Incorporated.
        - Expired by non-user.

1837   7 Wm. IV, c.47 (4 Mar.) Grafton Harbour Company, Incorporated.

1837   7 Wm. IV, c.48 (4 Mar.) Colborne Harbour Company, Incorporated.

1837   7 Wm. IV, c.49 (4 Mar.) Port Darlington Harbour Company, Incorporated.
        - Amended: 3 Vic., c.37.

1837   7 Wm. IV, c.50 (4 Mar.) Goderich Harbour, erection of by Canada Company.

1837   7 Wm. IV, c.71 (4 Mar.) Whitby Harbour, improvement.

1838   1 Vic., c.32 (6 Mar.) Waterloo Bridge Company, Incorporated.
        - Amended: 2 Vic., c.40.

1838   1 Vic., c.31 (6 Mar.) Bond Head Harbour Company, Incorporated.

1839   2 Vic. c.39 (11 May) Bayfield Harbour Company, Incorporated.

1840   3 Vic., c.33 (10 Feb.) Bronte Harbour Company, Incorporated.

1840   3 Vic., c.34 (10 Feb.) York Bridge Company, Incorporated.

f. Manufacturing

1831   1 Wm. IV, c.11 (16 Mar.) Marmora Foundry Company, Incorporated.

1833   3 Wm. IV, c.20 (13 Feb.) Saint Catherines Salt Company, Incorporated.

1835   5 Wm. IV, c.15 (16 Apr.) Saltfleet Salt Company, Incorporated.

1835   5 Wm. IV, c.18 (16 Apr.) Cayuga Glass Manufacturing Company, Incorporated.

1836   6 Wm. IV, c.9 (20 Apr.) Toronto Gas Light Company, Incorporated.
        - Expired by non-user.

1836   6 Wm. IV, c.11 (20 Apr.) Hamilton Water Works Company, Incorporated.
        - Expired by non-user.

1837   7 Wm. IV, c.54 (4 Mar.) Lyndhurst Mining and Manufacturing Company, Incorporated.

1837   7 Wm. IV, c.55 (4 Mar.) Caledonia Mineral Springs Company, Incorporated.

1840   3 Vic., c.32 (10 Feb.) Oakville Hydraulic Company, Incorporated.

g. Navigation

1831   1 Wm. IV, c.10 (16 Mar.) Tay Navigation Company, Incorporated.
        - Loans: 4 Wm. IV, c.42, 7 Wm. IV, c.75.

1832   2 Wm. IV, c.13 (28 Jan.) Grand River Navigation Company, Incorporated.
        - Amended: 3 Wm. IV, c.21.
        - Loan: 7 Wm. IV, c.73.

1836   6 Wm. IV, c.8 (20 Apr.) Gananoque and Wiltsie Navigation Company, Incorporated.
        - Loan: 7 Wm. IV, c.69.

1837   7 Wm. IV, c.51 (4 Mar.) Beverly Navigation Company, Incorporated.

1838   1 Vic. c.29 (6 Mar.) Grantham Navigation Company, Incorporated.

h. Railroads

Except for the Erie and Ontario, which succeeded in building a horse drawn railroad from Queenston to Chippawa, all the Upper Canadian railroad ventures were brought to a halt by the depression that began in 1837. When times improved after 1844-45 several were revived including lines that became the Great Western and the Northern Railroads.

1834   4 Wm. IV, c.29 (6 Mar.) Cobourg Railroad Company, Incorporated.
        - Amended: 6 Wm. IV, c.19.
        - Loan: 7 Wm. IV, c.74.
        (becomes Cobourg and Rice Lake Plank-Road and Ferry Co.).

1834   4 Wm. IV, c. 29 (6 Mar.) London and Gore Railroad Company, Incorporated.
        - Amended: 7 Wm. IV, c.61, 62 and 63. (becomes Great Western Railroad).

1835   5 Wm. IV, c.17 (16 Apr.) Hamilton and Port Dover Railroad Company, Incorporated.
        Expired.

1835   5 Wm. IV, c.19 (16 Apr.) Erie and Ontario Railroad Company, Incorporated.
        - Amended: 3 Vic., c.49.
        - Loan: 7 Wm. IV, c.68.

1836   6 Wm. IV, c.5 (20 Apr.) City of Toronto and Lake Huron Railroad Company, Incorporated.
        - Aid: 7 Wm. IV, c.60 and c.63.
        (becomes The Northern Railroad).

1836   6 Wm. IV, c.6 (20 Apr.) Niagara and Detroit Railroad Company, Incorporated.
        - Expired by non-user.

1836   6 Wm. IV, c.7 (20 Apr.) Burlington Bay and Lake Huron Railroad Company, Incorporated.
        - Expired by non-user.

1837   7 Wm. IV, c.52 (4 Mar.) London and Devonport Railroad Company, Incorporated.

1838   1 Vic., c.30 (6 Mar.) Kingston Marine Railway Company, Incorporated.

1838   1 Vic., c.33 (6 Mar.) Windsor Railway or Macadamized Road Company, Incorporated.

i. British Statutes and Charters

1600
- The East India Company
- Royal Charter from Elizabeth I (had monopoly on tea sales in British North America including Upper Canada).

1670
- Hudson's Bay Company
- Royal Charter of Charles II (administered parts of Northern Ontario and had judicial connections with Upper Canada).

1825
- Canada Company
- incorporated by act of Parliament in June, 1825, Royal Charter, Aug., 1826 to purchase and develop lands.
- (Purchased the Crown Reserves of 1,384,413 acres and a special grant of 1,100,000 acres in the Huron County area).

1827
- King's College (University of Toronto, receives Royal Charter, 15 March.

1836
- Bank of British North America.
  (Amalgamated with Bank of Montreal, 1918).

1836
- Upper Canada Academy (Victoria College), receives Royal Charter, 12 October.

B. Corporate Officers

a. Introduction

This list only attempts to include the information on some of the leading companies and organizations where most of the names are available. Some of the organizations included were not among those incorporated but were of importance in the colony.

Lists of directors are not included both because of the space that would be involved, and because of the fragmentary nature of the information available.

1. The "Pretended" Bank of Upper Canada

<u>Started</u> - 1819   <u>Dissolved</u>   - 1823

<u>Office</u> - Kingston

     i. <u>Presidents</u>

Benjamin Whitney   - 1823

     ii. <u>Cashiers</u>

Smith Bartlett   - 1823

2. Bank of Upper Canada, York/Toronto

<u>Incorporated</u> - 1821   <u>Bankrupt</u>   - 1866

<u>Office</u> - York/Toronto

i. Presidents

William Allan	1822 - 1825
George Crookshank	1825 - 1826
William Allan	1826 - 1835
William Proudfoot	1835 - 1860

ii. Vice-Presidents

Probably did not exist in the early years.

John Spread Baldwin	1837 - 1843+
Dr. Christopher Widmer	1843 - 1849
James Grant Chewett	**1849 - 1856**

iii. Cashiers (General Managers)

Thomas Gibbs Ridout	1822 - 1861

3. Bank of British North America

Founded - 1836 by British charter with directors in London, England and local committees of directors in British North America cities. Taken over by Bank of Montreal, 1918.

Office - Montreal

Representative of Court of Directors in America

Robert Carter	1836 - (1837)

4. British America Fire and Life Assurance Company

Incorporated - 1833, began operating 1835 (now Royal Insurance Company)

Office - York/Toronto

i. Governors

William Proudfoot	1834 - 1836
William Allan	1836 - 1853

ii. Deputy-Governors

John Spread Baldwin	1834 - 1843+

iii. Managing Directors

Thomas William Birchall	1834 - 1872

5. Canada Company

Incorporated - 1826 by British Charter.

Offices - London, England, Goderich, York/Toronto

i. Governors

Charles Bosanquet	1826 - 1838
Charles Franks	1838 - 1863

ii. Deputy-Governors

William Williams	1826 - 1830
Edward Ellis	1830 - 1831
Charles Franks	1831 - 1838
James Mackillop	1838 - 1865

iii. Commissioners in Canada

John Galt	1826 - 1829
William Allan (York/Toronto)	1829 - 1839
Thomas Mercer Jones (Goderich)	1829 - 1853
Frederick Widder (Toronto)	1839 - 1864

6. Commercial Bank of the Midland District

Incorporated - 1832

Taken over by Bank of Montreal, 1868

Office - Kingston

i. Presidents

John Solomon Cartwright	1832 - 1845+

ii. Vice-Presidents

John Strange	(1837) -	(1841)

iii. Cashiers (General Managers)

Francis A. Harper	1832 -	(1838)

7. Farmer's Joint Stock Banking Company

Established - 4 Sept., 1835

Office - Toronto

i. Presidents

John Elmsley	1835 - Oct., 1837
Francis Hincks	(1843)

ii. Cashiers or Managers

Hilary Dupuy	1835 -	Mar., 1837
Walter Rose	Mar., 1837 -	1838
W. B. Phipps		(1843)

8. Gore Bank

Incorporated - 1835 - opened, 1836

Taken over by Bank of Commerce 1870

Office - Hamilton

i. **Presidents**

James Matthew White   1836 - 1839

Colin Campbell Ferrie   1839 - 1856

ii. **Cashiers**

Andrew Stephen   1836 - 1856

9. Home District Savings Bank

<u>Founded</u> - 5 June, 1830, for savings of mechanics, tradesmen, servants, labourers, etc.

<u>Office</u> - York/Toronto at Office of the Treasurer of the Home District initially.

<u>Direction</u> - Run by a board of directors whose members took turns in running the office. Alexander Wood and later William Proudfoot were among the most active.

10. People's Bank (or Bank of the People)

<u>Founded</u> - 2 Nov., 1835

Sold to Bank of Montreal 1840

<u>Office</u> - Toronto

i. **Presidents**

Dr. John Rolph   1835 - 1837

James Lesslie   (1838)

ii. **Cashiers**

James Lesslie   1835 -

Dr. Thomas D. Morrison   - 1837

Frances Hincks   1837 - June, 1838

11. Toronto Board of Trade

<u>Founded</u> - c.1834/5, <u>Reestablished</u> - 1844

<u>Office</u> - Toronto

i. **Presidents**

William Allan   (1835)-(1837)

ii. **Secretary**

J. W. Brent   (1835)-(1837)

12. Welland Canal Company

<u>Incorporated</u> - 1824   **Nationalized** - 1843

<u>Office</u> - St. Catharines

i. **Presidents**

George Keefer   1824 -

John Henry Dunn   - 1832

William Hamilton Merritt   1832 -

John Simcoe Macaulay   (1839)-

   ii. Agents (General Managers)

William Hamilton Merritt   1824 -

   iii. Secretaries

John Blank   1824 - (1831)

George Prescott   (1839)-

   iv. Treasurers

James Gordon   1824 -

Captain Ogden Creighton   (Nov., 1835)-

C. Disasters

The following table attempts to list the major natural disasters that afflicted Upper Canada; but any complete table of disasters would be very difficult to construct as so many were of a local nature. Some nautical disasters that occurred on The Great Lakes before Upper Canada was established have been added.

1721 - 2 July, Shipwreck, 15 miles from Barcelona, N.Y., frigate La Jean Florin lost with cargo reportedly $500,000 in gold and silver.

1764 - 17 June, Shipwreck, Wolf Island split near Kingston, Le Blanc Heurs lost with reportedly $100,000 in gold and silver.

1783 - 23 Nov., Shipwreck, three miles from Oswego, N.Y., sloop Ontario disappeared, 190 lives lost and gold and silver reported aboard.

1788 - Great famine, province generally, resulting from poor harvest in 1787. Often called the "Scarse Year".

1792 - Tornado - S.W. part of Thorold Twp., Niagara Peninsula, cleared route that later became "Hurricane Road" from Fonthill to Port Robinson.

1795 or 1798 - Tornado, Mississauga land near the River Credit. Samuel Wilmot's survey plan of 1806 shows the windfall as being ¼ mile wide.

1796 - Tornado, Northern parts of Caistor, Gainsboro and Pelham townships were swept by a tornado clearing ¼ mile wide strip of Timber.

1804 - 8 Oct., Shipwreck, schooner Speedy, off Presqu'ile Point, Lake Ontario, foundered with some 20 passengers and crew.

1818 - 18 Sept., Shipwreck, two miles off Long Point, Lake Erie, schooner, Young Phoenix foundered.

1820 - Shipwreck, off Long Point, Canadian schooner Owen foundered.

1827 - Shipwreck, off Long Point, Lake Erie, schooner America.

1827 - Shipwreck, off Long Point, Lake Erie, schooner Ann value $15,000.

1827 - 5 Nov., Shipwreck off Long Point, Lake Erie, schooner Young Farmer.

1829 - May, Tornado, Guelph. Eramosa road was blocked by trees, fences were destroyed, several houses lost their roofs, a barn raised and the floor of a log house was carried through its roof.

1830 - 15 Nov., Shipwreck, Lake St. Clair, schooner Emily seven lives lost.

1832 - 16 June - late Sept., epidemic, entire province, first outbreak of cholera starting at Prescott and spreading westwards. Strachan estimated 1000 cases in York/Toronto alone with 400 dead. Minimum mortality at some dozen locations, 550.

1832 - 16 Nov. - Great Fire, Hamilton, business centre - damage estimate £13,000 (i.e. $50,000 in 1832).

1833 - 9 Oct., Shipwreck, off Long Point, Lake Erie, steamer. George Washington stranded, 50 lives lost.

1834 - Mid-July - mid-Sept., epidemic, entire province, second outbreak of cholera.

1834 - 29 July, collapse, Toronto, part of gallery around market courtyard falls during political meeting. Five killed and many injured.

1837 - late August, tornado, after a day of 98° heat, swept across the upper Katchawanook Lake to Lakefield flattening several acres of woods.

1837 - 29 Dec., Shipwreck, Loyalist forces burned the Caroline which was used as a supply ship for American patriots.

1838 - 30 May, Shipwreck, an Upper Canadian steamboat, Sir Robert Peel was burned by American desperados in the Thousand Islands.

D. Ecclesiastical

a. Anglican Church (Church of England)

1. Archbishops of Canterbury

John Moore	31 Mar.,	1783	-	18 Jan., 1805+
Charles Manners Sutton	1 Feb.,	1805	-	21 July, 1828+
William Howley	6 Aug.,	1828	-	11 Feb., 1848+

2. Bishops presiding over Upper Canada

i. Upper Canada part of Diocese of Nova Scotia, 1791 - 1793

Charles Inglis	1 Oct.,	1787	-	18 Feb., 1816+

ii. Upper Canada part of Diocese of Quebec, 1793 - 1839

Jacob Mountain	1 Nov.,	1793	-	18 June, 1825+
Charles James Stewart	4 June,	1826	-	13 July, 1837+
George Jehosaphat Mountain	14 July,	1837	-	6 Jan., 1863+

iii. Upper Canada becomes the Diocese of Toronto, 1839

John Strachan	9 Nov.,	1839	-	1 Nov., 1867+

3. Archdeacons

i. Archdeaconry of Upper Canada, 1821 - 28 June, 1827

George Okill Stuart	1821	-	28 June, 1827

ii. Archdeaconry of Kingston, 1827 - (Eastern Upper Canada)

George Okill Stuart	28 June,	1827	-	25 Mar., 1862

iii. Archdeaconry of York, 1827 - (Western Upper Canada).

John Strachan	28 June,	1827	-	1846
Alexander Neil Bethune		1846	-	25 Jan., 1867

b. Baptists
Major Events [Provisional]

1802 - Thurlow Baptist Association formed by the three Baptist churches of the Bay of Quinte region.

- met in 1803, 1804, 1805, 1806, 1808, 1809.

- re-organized in 1819 and called the Haldimand Association after it had been disrupted by the War of 1812.

- separated from its parent, the American Shaftsbury Association.

1819 - Churches east of Kingston withdrew to form the Johnstown Association.

1810 - Clinton Conference was informally established.

1816 - formally established
- separated from its parent, the American Shaftsbury Association

---

1836 - Ottawa Association formed and including the Montreal church (Lower Canada)

1820s - became known as the Eastern Association.

1830 - Eastern Association split western members forming the Western Association

1837 - Long Point Association devolved from the Western Association

1843 - 19 June, Canada Baptist Union formed in Paris.

- included all the Baptists of Canada East and Canada West.

1848 - St. George, Canada West. Regular Baptist Union was formed which included most of the close-communion churches in Canada West.

c. Roman Catholic Church
Bishops

i. Upper Canada as Part of the Diocese of Quebec, 1791 - 1826

Jean Francois Hubert	12 June,	1788	-	1 Sept., 1797+
Pierre Denault	4 Sept.,	1797	-	17 Jan., 1806+
Joseph Octave Plessis	27 Jan.,	1806	-	4 Dec., 1825+
Bernard Claude Panet	12 Dec.,	1825	-	14 Feb., 1833+

ii. Diocese of Regiopolis (Kingston)

Alexander Macdonell

Vicar Apostolic and Bishop of Regina	12 Jan.,	1819	-	14 Feb.,	1826
Bishop of Kingston	14 Feb.,	1826	-	14 Jan.,	1840+
Remigius Gaulin	14 Jan.,	1840	-	8 May,	1857+

iii. Diocese of Western Upper Canada (Toronto)

Michael Power (settled at Toronto 1842)	1841	-	1 Oct.,	1847+
See vacant	1847	-		1850

iv. Ecclesiastical Province of Quebec

Formed 12 July, 1844 encompassing the Dioceses of Quebec, Montreal, Kingston and Toronto. Bishop of Quebec becomes archbishop.

d. Methodist Church
1. Major Events

1791 For first two decades Upper Canadian Methodist missionaries are associated largely with various conferences of the Methodist Episcopal Church in the United States.

1812 Formation of the Genesee Conference of the American Methodist Episcopal Church which included Upper Canada.

1814 British Wesleyan Methodists formed in Upper Canada.

1820 British Wesleyan Methodists and American Episcopal Methodists divide Canada; former take Lower Canada, latter Upper Canada.

1824 Upper Canada becomes a separate conference in the American Episcopal Methodist Church.

1828 Agreement on the separation of the Episcopal church in Canada from that in the United States.

1828 Canadian Wesleyan Methodists secede from the Canadian Methodist Episcopal Church.

1829 Oct. Methodist Episcopal Church in Canada organized.

1831 Bible Christian Church of Canada formed.

1833 Oct. Union of episcopal Methodist Church in Canada with the British Wesleyan Methodist Church to form the Wesleyan Methodist Church. New Episcopal Methodist Church established by secessionist ministers.

1840 Break-up of Wesleyan Methodist Church union.

1843 Canadian Conference of the Wesleyan Methodist New Connection Church.

1847 Re-establishment of Wesleyan Methodist Church Union.

2. Conferences in Canada
i. Episcopal Methodist Conferences

Wesleyan Methodists 1833, re-established 1834.

Date	Place	Presiding Officer	Secretary
1824	Hallowell	Bishops George and Hedding	William Case
1825	Saltfleet	Bishop Hedding	"

Table II
The Union of Methodism

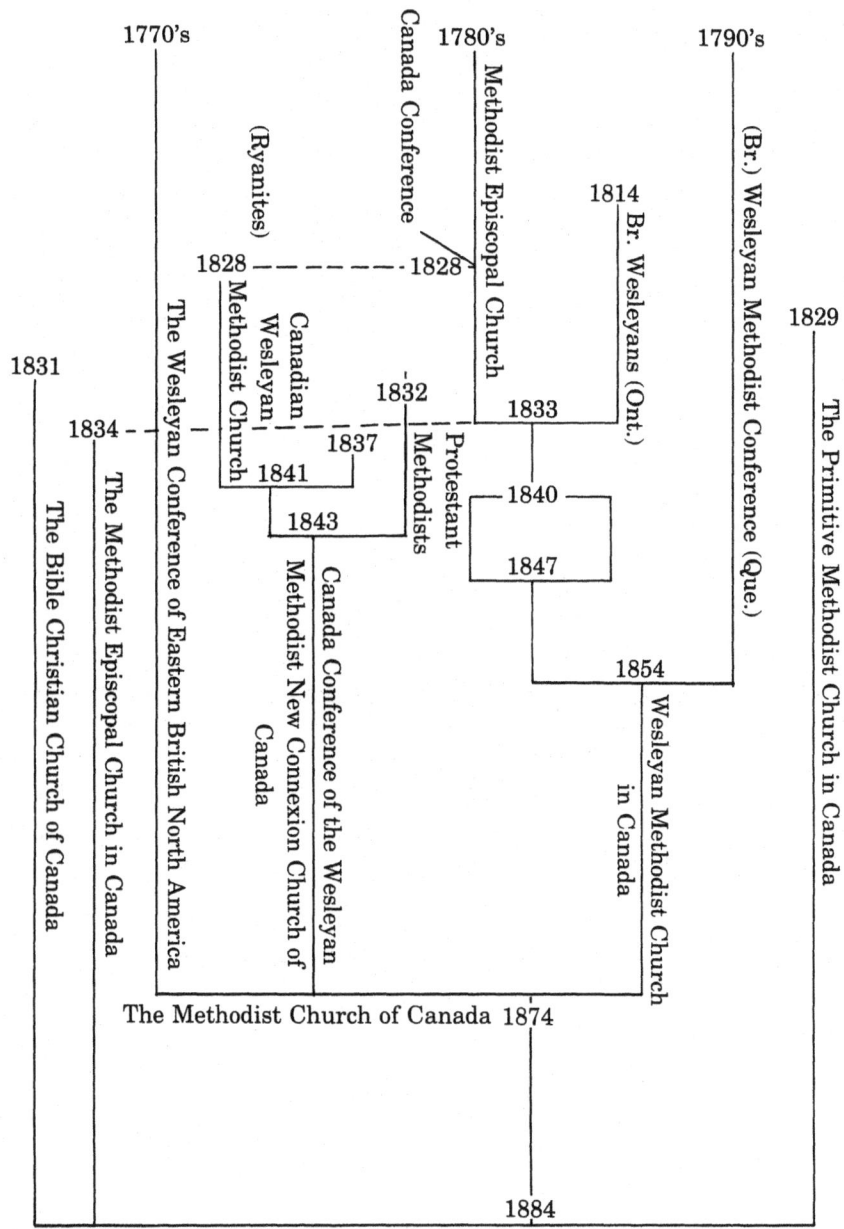

© United Church Archives, 1978
Neil Semple

1826	Hamilton Township.	Bishop George	"
1827	Hamilton (Town)	Bishop Hedding	"
1828	Ernestown	"	James Richardson
1829	Ancaster	William Case Gen. Supt. pro tem.	"
1830	Kingston & Belleville	"	"
1831	York (Town)	"	"
1832	Hallowell	"	"

ii. Wesleyan Conferences 1832-41

1833	York (Town)	George Marsden, President	Egerton Ryerson
1834	Kingston	Edmund Grindrod	James Richardson
1835	Hamilton	William Lord	Egerton Ryerson
1836	Belleville	William Lord	William Case
1837	Toronto	William M. Harvard	Egerton Ryerson
1838	Kingston	"	"
1839	Hamilton	Joseph Stinson	"
1840	Belleville	"	"
1840	Toronto	Thomas Whitehead	John C. Davidson
1841	"	William Ryerson	Anson Green

iii. Canadian Wesleyan Methodists New Connection Conferences
(Also known as Ryanites)

1829 - 1834 - no surviving records.

1835	Grantham	James Jackson	A. K. McKenzie
1836	Hamilton & Hillier	Michael Aikman	William Jackson
1837	Cavan	Moses Blackstock	H. R. Smith
1838	Grantham	"	James Jackson
1839	Ancaster	Robert Earl	K. Creighton
1840	Cavan	Michael Aikman	"
1841	Hamilton	James Jackson	Michael Aikman

3. Editors of *Christian Guardian*

Egerton Ryerson	1829	1832
James Richardson	1832	1833
Egerton Ryerson	1833	1835
Ephraim Evans	1835	1838
Egerton Ryerson	1838	1840
Jonathan Scott	1840	1844

4. Stewards of the Book Room

Editor of the Christian Guardian	1829	1835
Matthew Lang	1835	1837
John Ryerson	1837	1841
Alexander McNab	1841	1843

e. Presbyterian Church
Major Events

1818 Organization of the Presbytery of Canada in Montreal. (Independent of Scotland).

1819 Presbytery divided into three presbyteries in Upper Canada and one in Lower Canada.

1820 3 Feb. United Synod of Canada established at Cornwall as body supervising the four presbyteries.

1825 Synod dissolved. Most members in Upper Canada join to form the United Presbytery of Upper Canada.

1831 8 June. Organization of the Presbyterian Church of Canada in connection with the Church of Scotland. (separate body).

1831 17 June. United Presbytery of Upper Canada reorganized as the United Synod of Upper Canada, with two presbyteries centred at Brockville and York.

1833 May. Organization of the Niagara Presbytery by members of the American Presbyterian Church.

1834 General Assembly of the Church of Scotland passes Veto Act designed to counteract the problems of patronage appointments.

1834 25 Sept. Missionary Presbytery of the Canadas in Connection with the United Secession Church of Scotland organized.

1836 Presbytery of Stamford in connection with the Associate Reformed Church of the United States organized.

1840 Union between United Synod (16 ministers) and Presbyterians in connection with the Church of Scotland (60 ministers).

1843 Disruption of the Church of Scotland over patronage appointments.

1844 Disruption of the Presbyterian Church of Canada in connection with the Church of Scotland.

1844 Free Church Synod organized with 23 ministers. 68 ministers remain with Church of Scotland Synod.

1844 College in Connection with Presbyterian Church in Canada opened (Knox College name taken 1846).

1847 15 July. Missionary Synod of Canada assumes name of the Synod of the United Presbyterian Church of Canada in connection with the United Presbyterian Church of Scotland.

f. Quakers
Major Events

1799 - 1 Oct. Pelham Monthly Meeting was established reporting directly to Philadelphia. Yearly Meetings held.

1810 - Jan. First Session of Canada Half Year's Meeting.

1812 - David Willson and several members of the Yonge Street Preparative Meeting were dropped from the Quaker organization. Their sect was based around Sharon and became known as the "Children of Peace" or "Davidites".

1829 - Canada Half Year's Meeting split into two groups known as the Hicksite and Orthodox.

1832 - Establishment of Pelham Half Year's Meeting.

1834 - Organization of Yearly Meeting for Hicksite group.

E. Imperial Honours

Granted to Upper Canadians, or Imperial officials for military or governmental services in Upper Canada.

a. Titles

Charles Poulett Thomson, created Baron Sydenham of Kent in England and Toronto in Canada.	1840

b. Baronetcies

Sir Roger Hale Sheaffe	1813
Sir David William Smith	1821
Sir Francis Bond Head	1837

c. Knighthoods

Sir Isaac Brock	1813
Sir Gordon Drummond	1815
Sir Frederick Philipse Robinson	1815
Sir Francis, Baron de Rottenburg	1818
Sir John Harvey	1824
Sir William Campbell	1829
Sir David Jones	1835
Sir Richard Bonnycastle	1838
Sir Allan Napier MacNab	1838

F. Population Statistics

a. Introduction

Accurate population figures for the province and its major centres are difficult to establish. For the province itself the census of Canada up to and including 1790 did not cover the western regions which became Upper Canada, so there are no census figures until 1824. Thus the early figures are estimated.

From 1824 until 1841 there are annual censuses for the province which do provide gross totals and breakdowns under administrative areas, sex and numbers by sex under and over 16. These are given here for every three years; further details can be obtained from the *Census of Canada, 1871. Vol. IV*, which provides the retrospective figures for most earlier censuses.

The first major census of the Province of Canada (Upper and Lower) was in 1842; there was a follow-up in 1848 and then a quite thorough census, the beginnings of our modern censuses, in 1851/2. The totals for these are provided also.

For urban population statistics the data are even more unsatisfactory. The census shows York/Toronto as a separate unit from 1824 to 1841; but the other major centres are not separated. The census of 1842 does not give separate urban figures, even for Toronto. In 1848, however, the three cities—Toronto, Kingston and Hamilton—and the two major towns—Bytown/Ottawa and London—are shown, and the same is the case in 1851/2.

To fill in the gaps one has to fall back on the local assessment figures, where they survive, as in the case of York to 1824 and such estimates by local authorities, almanacs or travellers as are available. These are often none too reliable and are not always available for every year.

The Public Archives of Canada, Returns for Population and Assessment, 1800-1862 (RG5, B26, available on microfilms numbers H-1174-76, with Finding Aid 1296 at the beginning of H-1174) provide further material.

In the table at the end of the book a star (*) indicates that the figure is actually for the year before or after the date shown. It should be noted that the figures for the same political unit and year can differ from one type of record to another.

G. War and Revolution

a. The Engagements of the War of 1812 (Affecting The Upper Canadian Sector)

1812

5 June, The schooner, Lord Nelson, was captured by the Americans.

14 June, Two additional British schooners, the Ontario and the Niagara were captured.

18 June, President James Madison declared war on Breat Britain.

29 June, Eight American schooners were captured off the foot of the Thousand Islands. Two, the Sophia and Island Packet, were burned.

2 July, The schooner, Cuyahoga was captured by the British at Malden.

11 July, British ship, Prince Regent, was hit by cannon fire which killed 14 men.

12 July, Americans captured Sandwich without resistance.

13 July, Colonel McArthur travelled up the Thames River capturing goods and ammunition.

16-18 July, Americans repulsed at Riviere Aux Canards.

17 July, Mackinaw (Michilimackinac) surrendered to British.

5 Aug., Americans defeated at Brownstown by Tecumseh losing 17 men in the skirmish.

7 Aug., Gen. Hull ordered Americans to retreat from Sandwich.

9 Aug., British defeated at Maguaga. U.S. Lieutenant Colonel Miller lost 18 men killed while the British lost six men and 40 Indians killed.

10 Aug., Twelve American boats captured by the British as they attempted to relieve the forces of Lieutenant-Colonel Miller at Maguaga.

16 Aug., Detroit captured by Brock.

16 Sept., Americans repulsed at Presqu'Isle.

20 Sept., Captain Forsyth and 95 Americans attacked Gananoque and burned the store-house.

4 Oct., British repulsed at Ogdensburg. Where 750 British encountered 1,200 Americans.

9 Oct., British vessels captured off Black Rock.

13 Oct., Americans defeated at Queenston. American loss: 90 killed, 100 wounded, and between 800 and 900 made prisoners. British loss: 130 killed, wounded and prisoners at Queenston. General Sir Isaac Brock among those killed.

23 Oct., British defeated at St. Regis.

25 Oct., The ship, United States captured the British, Macedonian. British loss: 36 killed, 68 wounded. American loss: 5 killed, 6 wounded.

10 Nov., Kingston bombarded by Americans.

20 Nov., Americans repulsed at Odelltown.

21 Nov., British and Americans exchanged fire along the Niagara frontier.

23 Nov., Americans repulsed at Salmon River.

28 Nov., 220 American soldiers repulsed near Fort Erie.

1813

18 Jan., British repulsed at Frenchtown.

22 Jan., Americans defeated at Frenchtown. 100 Americans were killed.

23 Jan., 197 Americans killed after Indians plundered Frenchtown.

6 Feb., Brockville raided by Americans.

22 Feb., Ogdensburg taken by British after 800 militia and volunteers crossed from Prescott. Two schooners and two gunboats were burned.

27 Apr., York/Toronto taken by Americans (first capture). American loss: 85 killed and wounded. British loss: 60 killed, 89 wounded.

5 May, 800 Americans defeated before Fort Meigs where they attacked British batteries. Only 150 escaped from the Indians and the British.

8 May, Americans abandon York.

27 May, Fort Erie was evacuated and burnt by the British.

27 May, Fort George taken by Americans. American loss: 40 killed, 100 wounded. British loss: 41 killed, 350 wounded, missing and prisoners.

28-29 May, 1000 to 1200 British attacked Sackett's Harbour but were not able to secure it.

6 June, Americans defeated at Stoney Creek. American loss: 17 killed, 38 wounded, 99 missing. British loss: 23 killed, 100 wounded, 55 missing.

19 June, American stores captured at Great Sodus.

24 June, 570 Americans surrendered to 450 Indians and 50 British at Beaver Dam. Laura Secord made her walk to warn the British.

5 July, Americans made prisoners at Fort Shlosser.

11 July, British force of about 250 regulars and militia took Black Rock but could not retain it.

20 July, Americans defeated at Goose Creek.

31 July, 1,400 sailors led by Colonel Murray invaded Plattsburg and destroyed the blockhouse and storehouses.

31 July, Second capture of York/Toronto. Colonel Scott burnt the barracks and storehouses of York. Americans withdrew 2 Aug.

2 Aug., Fort Stephenson assaulted by British. American loss: 1 killed, 7 wounded. British loss: 120 killed or wounded.

10 Sept., British fleet captured on Lake Erie. American loss: 27 killed, 96 injured. British loss: 41 killed, 94 injured.

27 Sept., Americans under General Harrison landed on the shore by Fort Malden which had been burnt by the fleeing British and Indian troops.

28 Sept., British defeated in York Bay.

1 Oct., Americans repulsed at Four Corners.

5 Oct., Five British vessels were captured by the American ship, _Pike_, in the Duck Islands. 264 prisoners were taken.

5 Oct., British defeated on the Thames River near Moravian Town. Tecumseh killed in the battle; but General Proctor escaped. American loss: 15 killed, 20 wounded. British loss: 18 killed, 26 wounded, 600 made prisoners.

26 Oct., Americans defeated at Chateauguay.

11 Nov., Americans defeated at Chrysler's Farm.

10 Dec., Newark (Niagara-on-the-Lake) totally destroyed by fire set by the retreating American forces.

19 Dec., Fort Niagara captured by 1,000 British led by Murray. American loss: 80 killed, 14 wounded 344 made prisoners.

19 Dec., Lewiston destroyed by British.

31 Dec., Black Rock captured by British.

31 Dec., 800 American militia deserted in the face of the Canadian and British force which took possession of Buffalo. Four American vessels were burned. Buffalo burnt in retaliation for Newark (December 10).

1814

4 March, British repulsed at the Battle of the Longwoods.

30 March, Americans repulsed at La Colle Mill. American loss: 13 killed, 128 wounded, 13 missing. British loss: 11 killed, 46 wounded, 4 missing.

6 May, Oswego captured by 1,200 British.

7 May, British left Oswego after burning the barracks and dismantling the fort.

30 May, British defeated at Sandy Creek.

3 July, Fort Erie surrendered to Americans.

5 July, British defeated at Chippewa. American loss: 61 killed, 255 wounded, 19 missing. British loss: 236 killed, 322 wounded, 46 missing.

19 July, Prairie du Chien surrendered to British.

25-26 July, 2,600 Americans defeated at Lundy's Lane by 4,500 British. American loss: 171 killed, 571 wounded, 110 missing. British loss: 84 killed; 559 wounded, 193 missing, 42 prisoners.

3 Aug., Americans repulsed the British from landing at Black Rock.

4 Aug., Americans defeated at Fort Mackinaw.

15 Aug., British repulsed at Fort Erie. American loss: 17 killed, 56 wounded, 11 missing. British loss: 221 killed, 174 wounded, 186 prisoners.

16 Aug., 100 Americans and Indians robbed the residents of Port Talbot.

29 Aug., General Brisbane, occupied Champlain, New York.

6 Sept., British attack Plattsburg without success.

11 Sept., British defeated at Plattsburg. With the exception of the British galleys, the British squadron repulsed by their American counterpart. American loss: 37 killed, 62 wounded. British loss: 35 killed and 47 wounded.

17 Sept., 2,000 Americans assaulted the British batteries around Fort Erie. American loss: 79 killed, 432 wounded or missing. British loss: 115 killed, 176 wounded, 315 missing.

18 Oct., Colonel Murray met American troops at Lyon's Creek before fleeing to Chippewa. British loss: 150 killed, wounded and prisoners. American loss: 12 killed, 54 wounded.

6 Nov., General McArthur's expedition to Burlington was blocked by the Six Nations and militia at Malcolm's Mills on the Grand River.

24 Dec., Treaty of Ghent end of war on basis of status quo ante bellum. Commissions set up to negotiate points of conflict.

1815

15 Feb., News of peace treaty reaches York.

b. The Mackenzie Rebellion at Toronto, 1837

4 Dec. - Rebels Mustering -
Rebels left from Holland Landing, Sharon, Lloydtown and other areas to gather at Montgomery's Inn on Yonge St. north of Toronto. About 200 to 250 loyalists gathered in Toronto during the night.

4 Dec. - Moodie Shot -
Lieutenant - Colonel Robert Moodie shot and killed as he attempted to warn Sir Francis Head about insurgent gathering.

4 Dec. - Anderson Shot -
Mackenzie captured Alderman John Powell who is not searched. He shot rebels' temporary military commander, Anthony Anderson, who was leading him to captivity and rode to warn Governor Head. City already aroused by general confusion of rebel movements.

5 Dec. - Mackenzie's March on Toronto -
After a day's chaotic march southwards to take Toronto Mackenzie's reputed 500 to 600 troops were repulsed from Toronto by a piquet of men. One rebel was shot and killed, possibly by his own men.

5 Dec. - Loyalist Reinforcements -
100 loyalists left Scarboro for Toronto, while MacNab brought 60 to 70 men from Hamilton by boat in evening.

6 Dec. - Rebel Reinforcements -
Fifty to sixty rebels who left Pickering on 5 Dec., reach Toronto.

6 Dec. - Mail Coach -
Mackenzie seized the mail coach possibly attempting to capture loyalist dispatches.

7 Dec., - Don Bridge -
Mackenzie sent Peter Matthews to burn Don Bridge, to divert loyalist forces from an attack on Montgomery's Inn and prevent loyalist reinforcements from the east reaching Toronto. Attempt failed; but some buildings burned and one bystander killed. Matthews later hanged.

7 Dec. - Loyalist Reinforcements -
350 loyalists prepared to go to Toronto from Streetsville and Trafalgar, as did over 100 men from St. Catharines.

7 Dec. - End of Rebellion -
About 1,000 to 1,500 loyalists moved on Montgomery's Inn. May still have been 400 rebels; but only 200 participated in the losing battle while rest hid in Inn. One rebel was killed, and another died in hospital. No loyalists killed. Mackenzie and rebels fled.

9 Dec. - Loyalist Reinforcements -
About 600 loyalists arrived in Toronto from Tecumseh, Essa. Innisfil and West Gwillimbury; 500 came from Bowmanville.

10 Dec. - Loyalist Reinforcements -
Part of a 1,000 man force which had gathered in Northumberland County by the 7th arrived in Toronto, together with other men they had picked up on route, altogether about 1,000 strong. Rest of Northumberland troops, plus men from Peterborough, gather at Port Hope, in total another 1,000 strong. Additional forces gather north of Lake Simcoe and in the Niagara District.

c. The Duncombe Rebellion in Western Upper Canada, 1837

6 Dec. - Influence of Toronto Rebellion -
News of Mackenzie Rebellion at Toronto reached Dr. Charles Duncombe in Burford. He sent letters to prominent reformers and at a meeting at Sodom on the 7th, he spread the report that warrants were out for the arrest of the leading reformers.

6/7 Dec. - Organization -
People began to gather at Oakland Township in response to the rumours of repressive actions taken against the reformers in Toronto.

7 Dec. - Defence by MacNab -
MacNab ordered to London District with 500 militia volunteers. He had already called up the Brantford militia.

7-9 Dec. - Rebels Organize -
Duncombe, Eliakim and James Malcolm hold organizational meetings. Other reformers meet to organize defence in case Tories attack them. Soon preparations were begun for mustering.

7-12 Dec. - Misinformation -
James and Eliakim Malcom spreading rumours that Mackenzie had seized Toronto and that the reformers in Lower Canada were victorious.

9 Dec. - Mackenzie's Defeat -
London and Ingersoll aware that Mackenzie was defeated in Toronto; but news not known at Oakland which is nearer.

10 Dec. - Local Defence -
MacNab learns about the efforts of Charles Duncombe. Woodstock also learned about Duncombe's activities. Tories already organizing defence in Bayham and Malihide Townships on Lake Erie.

11-12 Dec. - Sparta -
Meeting at Sparta on 11th finalized plans for the march to Oakland on the 12th; 50 rebels gathered.

12 Dec. - MacNab marches on Oakland -
MacNab left Hamilton with 300 volunteers.

13 Dec. - Oakland -
Western rebels were continuing to gather at Scotland and Oakland (Malcolm's Mills) and were billeted with the local people. The most reliable references to the size of Duncombe's army suggest a force of between 400 and 500 men.

13 Dec. - Rebels Retreat -
By evening, the rebels learned that MacNab was in Brantford. The insurgent leaders had been planning to attack Simcoe and Hamilton after seizing Brantford, but retreated to Sodom in Norwich Township instead.

14 Dec. - MacNab Takes Scotland Township -
Colonel Allan Napier MacNab with his 300 men from Hamilton, bolstered by 150 recruits from the Brantford area and 100 Indians from the Six Nations Reserve invaded Scotland. Reportedly three rebels were shot and scalped.

14 Dec. - Rebels Disband -
The remainder of Duncombe's army entered Sodom. During the day, it was disbanded. Duncombe had already fled early in the day.

14 Dec. - MacNab Reinforcements -
200 loyalist volunteers marched from London to Scotland to join MacNab's forces plus 1,000 volunteer from Woodhouse and Yarmouth Townships.

15 Dec. - MacNab Marches on Sodom -
MacNab learns about the dispersal of the rebels and heads for Sodom from Oakland. Rebel army had dispersed; but MacNab took 500 prisoners over the next few days.

16 Dec. - Amnesties -
MacNab allowed many rebels to return home provided they would surrender themselves if the lieutenant-governor did not agree with this pardon. This amnesty concurred with Head's Proclamation of 14 December which provided that only the most active rebels were to be arrested.

d. The Aftermath of 1837 and the Patriot Raids, 1838

1837

12 Dec. - Navy Island, Niagara Falls -
Patriots left Buffalo for Tonawanda; then 24 of them crossed over to Whitehaven on Grand Island. On 13 Dec., they reached Navy Island. There were approximately 45 patriots on the island led by Mackenzie and Van Rensselear.

20 Dec. - Navy Island -
Three hundred volunteers arrived from Toronto to assist in the surveillance of Navy Island.

25 Dec. - Navy Island -
Allan MacNab marched from Hamilton with 700 volunteers and 300 Indians as well as cavalry troops from St. Catharines. They were joined by other cavalry forces of Simcoe. The force at Chippawa varied from 1,800 to 3,800 from 13 Dec., 1837 to 14 Jan., 1838.

29 Dec., - Navy Island -
Late at night, or early on the morning of December 30, 35 loyalist rowers reached Fort Schlosser and attacked the Caroline the supply ship for Naval Island, setting fire to it and forcing off its crew of 30.

1838

8 Jan. - Bois Blanc Island, Detroit River -
Patriot "Army of the North-West" occupied Bois Blanc Island near Fort Malden.

9 Jan. - Bois Blanc Island Detroit River -
One of the patriots' ship, the Anne, came under heavy fire and ran aground. The 350 Upper Canadian militiamen took 30 prisoners as well as the ship. Governor Mason of Michigan had patriots evacuated about the 12th ending threat.

14 Jan. - Navy Island -
Evacuated as Caroline had been burnt and the island was under heavy fire.

30 Jan. - Militia Dismissal -
Most of the provincial militia were dismissed, although 1,950 volunteers were enrolled until 1 July.

22 Feb. - Hickory Island -
Occupied by 200 invaders until driven out by loyalist forces on the 23rd.

23 Feb. - Fighting Island, Detroit River -
Duncombe participated in a raid in which 152 men landed at Fighting Island in the Detroit River. On the 25th, Col. John Maitland's 500 men from the 32nd and 83rd regiments forced the rebels back to the American shore where they were dispersed by American troops.

3 Mar. - Pelee Island, Lake Erie -
Maitland and some of the companies of the 32nd and 83rd regiments from Amherstburg drove 400 to 1,000 rebels from Pelee Island across the ice to Ohio and eleven patriots and two militiamen were killed when 95 regulars, 25 militia cavalry and 6 Indians engaged the invaders.

30 May - Thousand Islands -
An Upper Canadian steamboat, Sir Robert Peel, was burned by American desperados at 2 a.m..

2 June - Short Hills, St. John's, Niagara District -
Attack by 40 to 70 men on a troop of 14 Queen's Lancers in an inn at St. John's. Seized weapons and horses and fled from the Six Nations warriors and the Norfolk militia. Several captured.

28 June, Proclamation granting amnesty to political prisoners.

early July -
   Rumours of invasions from the Hunters and other patriotic organizations increased the fears of loyalists that Americans were planning to invade Upper Canada.

Sept. - Cleveland -
   Convention at which Duncombe spoke, held to establish a provisional republican government for Upper Canada.

11 Nov. - Windmill Raid, Prescott -
   The United States, a steamer, and two schooners carried 500 to 600 patriots to Ogdensburg. Some men may have disembarked that day.

12 Nov. - Windmill, Raid -
   The two schooners landed 150-180 men who took up a position in the windmill at Prescott.

12 Nov. - Windmill Raid -
   About 470 loyalists attacked the windmill without success.

16 Nov. - Windmill Battle -
   With the arrival of 300 men from the companies of the 83rd and one of the 93rd from Kingston, the loyalists gained the windmill. Fifteen militia were kill 150 patriots taken prisoner.

4 Dec. - Battle of Windsor -
   A force between 150 and 400 men crossed the Detroit River and landed on the Windsor shore, killing 4 militiamen and burning the steamer Thames. Twenty-five rebels were slain. Colonel John Prince, commander ordered four prisoners shot. Among the captured was Joshua Doan. The loyalist force that engaged the patriots was comprised of about 300 men.

TABLE III: POPULATION FIGURES

YEAR	UPPER CANADA	TORONTO (York)	OTTAWA (Bytown)	KINGSTON	HAMILTON	LONDON
	(1791)	(1793)	(1826)	(1784)	(1816)	(1826)
1784	6,000	--	--	--	--	--
1791	10,000	--	--	376*	--	--
1811	77,000	684	--	1,000	--	--
1824	150,066	1,685	--	2,336	1,000*	--
1827	177,174	1,817	100?	3,210*	--	133
1830	213,156	2,860	--	3,587	--	274
1833	295,863	6,094	1,000	--	1,367*	603
1836	374,099	9,654	1,300*	3,613	2,846	1,246
1839	409.048	12,053	2,073	3,877*	3,116*	1,409
1842	487,053	15,336	3,122*	6,292	4,260	2,616
1848	725,879	23,503	6,275	8,416	9,889	4,668
1851/2	952,004	30,775	7,760	11,697	14,112	7,035

* figure for year before or after

Part VIII
Select Bibliography

A. Introduction

The following brief bibliography is intended only to provide listings of some of the major bibliographies related to Upper Canadian history, plus a few works or articles that deal directly with the matters related to Upper Canadian affairs. The reader is particularly referred to Olga B. Bishop's monumental *Bibliography of Ontario History*. In that work and some of the others cited, the dates in the titles refer to dates of publication *not* to chronological limits for the inclusion of material.

B. Bibliographic Sources

- General

Bishop, Olga B. et. al. *Bibliography of Ontario History, 1867-1976*, 2 vols. Toronto: 1980.

Bishop, Olga B. *Publications of the Province of Upper Canada and of Great Britain Relating to Upper Canada, 1791-1840*. Toronto: 1984.

- Legal History

Maddaugh, Peter D. *A Bibliography of Canadian Legal History*. Toronto: 1972.

- Local History

Aitken, Barbara B. *Local Histories of Ontario Municipalities, 1951-1977: A Bibliography*. Toronto: 1978.

Morley, William F. E. *Canadian Local Histories to 1950: A Bibliography, III: Ontario and the Canadian North*. Toronto: 1978.

C. Special Sources

- Chronologies

Audet, Frances J. *Canadian Historical Dates and Events, 1492-1915*. Ottawa: 1917.

Forward, Debra. *Legislators and Legislatures of Ontario, 1792-1984*, 3 vols. Toronto: 1984.

Powicke, Sir F. Maurice and E. B. Fryde. *Handbook of British Chronology*. London: 1961.

McCord, Fred A. *Handbook of Canadian Dates*. Montreal: 1888.

- Land

Gentilcore, Louis and Kate Donkin. *Land Surveys of Southern Ontario, An Introduction and Index, ... 1784-1854*. *Cartographica*, Monograph No. 8, Toronto, 1973.

Paterson, Gilbert C. *Land Settlement in Upper Canada 1793-1841* (Ontario Archives Report for 1920) Toronto: 1920.

- Local Government

Aitchison, J. H. "The Municipal Corporations Act of 1849", *Canadian Historical Review*, XXX, 1949, pp. 107-22.

Ontario, TEIGA Ministry. *Library Bulletins*, Vol. 16, Nos, 55, 56, 57, 62 and 64 (1978) and Vol. 17, No. 55 (1979).

Spragge, George W. "The Districts of Upper Canada, 1788-1849", *Ontario History*, XXXIX, 1947, pp.91-100.

- Officials

Cote, J. O. and N. Omer. *Political Appointments and Elections in the Province of Canada from 1841 to 1867*, two parts. Ottawa: 1866 and 1918.

Ewart, Alison and Julia Jarvis. "The Personnel of the Family Compact", *Canadian Historical Review*, Mar., 1926, pp. 209-221.

Public Archives of Canada, RG68, "General Index to Commissions." Vol. 1 to 1841.

- Parliament

Bishop, Olga, B. *Publications of the Government of the Province of Canada, 1841-1867*. Ottawa: 1963.

Damphouse, Patricia A. *The Legislative Assembly of the Province of Canada: An Index to Journal Appendices and Sessional Papers, 1841-1866*. London, Ont.: 1974.

Neufeld, David *The House of Assembly of Upper Canada: A Table of Contents and Index to Journal Appendices (Ninth to Thirteenth Parliaments, 1825-1840)*. London, Ont.: 1979.

- Statutes and Proclamations

"Proclamations by Governors and Lieutenant Governors of Quebec and Upper Canada", *Report of the Bureau of Archives for the Province of Ontario, 1906*. Toronto: 1907.

Maxwell, W. Harold and C. R. Brown, *A Complete List of British and Colonial Law Reports* (3rd edition with a check list of Canadian Statutes). Toronto: 1937.

Wicksteed, G. W. *Table of the Provincial Statutes in Upper Canada*. Toronto: 1857.

TABLE III: POPULATION FIGURES

YEAR	UPPER CANADA	TORONTO (York)	OTTAWA (Bytown)	KINGSTON	HAMILTON	LONDON
	(1791)	(1793)	(1826)	(1784)	(1816)	(1826)
1784	6,000	--	--	--	--	--
1791	10,000	--	--	376*	--	--
1811	77,000	684	--	1,000	--	--
1824	150,066	1,685	--	2,336	1,000*	--
1827	177,174	1,817	100?	3,210*	--	133
1830	213,156	2,860	--	3,587	--	274
1833	295,863	6,094	1,000	--	1,367*	603
1836	374,099	9,654	1,300*	3,613	2,846	1,246
1839	409.048	12,053	2,073	3,877*	3,116*	1,409
1842	487,053	15,336	3,122*	6,292	4,260	2,616
1848	725,879	23,503	6,275	8,416	9,889	4,668
1851/2	952,004	30,775	7,760	11,697	14,112	7,035

* figure for year before or after

Subject Index

Addington 93
Adjutants General of the Militia
 Department 42
Agents for the Affairs of Upper
 Canada in England 247
Amherstburgh 202
Anglican Church 258
 Archbishops of Canterbury 258
 Archdeacons 258
 Bishops presiding over Upper
 Canada 258
Attorneys 122
Attorneys General 42
Auditors General of Land Patents 42
Auditors General of Public
 Accounts 43

**Banks and Financial
 Institutions, Legislation** 248
Bank of British North America,
 Officers of 254
Bank of Upper Canada, Officers of 253
Baptists 259
Barristers 127
Bathurst District 162
Battles of the War of 1812 265
Belleville 202
Bibliography 273
Brantford 202
British America Fire and Life
 Assurance Company, Officers of 254
Brock District 164
Brockville 203, 93
Bytown (Ottawa) 204

Canada Company, Officers of 254
Canals, Legislation 249
Capital 37
Carleton 93
Chaplains 113
Chief Superintendents of Indian Affairs
 in Upper Canada 44
Civil Establishment 33
 Clerks 34
Cobourg 205
Colborne District 165
Commercial Bank of the Midland
 District, Officers of 255
Commissioners of Crown Lands 43
Commissions arising from the
 Rebellion of 1837 241
Commissions arising from the
 War of 1812 240
Commissions, Civil 241
Commissions, Special 240
Cornwall 94, 205
Corporate Legislation, British
 Statutes and Charters 253
Counties 149
 Legislation establishing 150

 List of 150
 Lieutenants of 152
 Registrars 154
Court of Chancery 119
 Masters in Chancery 119
 Registrars 119
 Sergeants at Arms 119
 Vice-Chancellors 119
Courts of Common Pleas 116
Court of the King's Bench 117
 Chief Justices 118
 Clerks of the Crown and Pleas 118
 Puisn´e Justices 118
 Reporters 118
Court of Probate 119
 Official Principals 120
 Registrars 120
Crown Lands Office 43
Customs Department 217
 Collectors of 217
 Ports of Entry 217

Dalhousie District 166
Deputy Superintendents of Indian Affairs
 in Upper Canada 44
Disasters 257
District System, Development of 198
Districts, Legislation 160
 List of 161
Doorkeepers 114
Duncombe Rebellion in Western Upper
 Canada - 1837 269
Dundas 207
 Riding 94
 Town 207
Durham 94

Eastern District 116, 167
Ecclesiastical 258
Educational and Institutional,
 Legislation 249
Emigrant Office 226
 Agents at Quebec 226
 Agents at Toronto 226
 Superintendents 226
Essex 95
Executive Council, Alphabetical list 38
 Chronological list 39
 Staff 41

**Farmer's Joint Stock Banking
 Company, Officers of** 255
Frontenac 96

Glengarry 96
Gore District 170
Gore Bank, Officers of 255
Governors in Chief 1791-1841 32
Grenville 97

Haldimand 98
Halton 98
Hamilton 98, 207
Hastings 98
Harbours and Bridges, Legislation 250
Hesse District 117
  see Western District
Home District 117, 172
Home District Savings Bank, Officers of 256
House of Assembly 59
  Alphabetical list 59
  Members by Parliament 74
  Members by Riding 93
  Speakers 113
  Staff 113
Huron 99
Huron District 175

Indian Office 43
Imperial Honours 264
Inspectors General 44
Inspector General's Office 44

Johnstown District 176
Judiciary 115

Kent 99
Kent (Provisional) District 178
King's Printers and Editors of the *Upper Canada Gazette* 44
Kingston 100, 208

Lanark 100
Law Society of Upper Canada, Treasurers 121
Leeds 101
Legal Profession 115, 120
Legislative Council 53
  Alphabetical list 53
  Chronological list 55
  Speakers 57
  Staff 58
Lennox 101
Librarians 114
Lieutenant-Governors of Upper Canada 33
  Civil and Private Secretaries to 33
Lincoln 102
London 105, 209
London District 179
Lunenburgh District 116
  see Eastern District

Mackenzie Rebellion at Toronto, 1837 269
Manufacturing, Legislation 251
Maps, Counties 1792 138
  Counties 1851 140
  Districts 1788 and 1802 138
  Districts 1836 139
  Districts 1841 140
Meckleburg District 117
  see Midland District
Merrichville 210
Methodist Church 260, 261
  Conferences in Canada 260
  Editors of the *Christian Guardian* 262
  Stewards of the Book Room 263
Middlesex 105
Midland District 117, 181
Monarchs 29
Municipal Government 137

Napanee 210
Nassau District 117
  see Home District
Navigation, Legislation 252
Newcastle District 184
Niagara 105
Niagara District 186
Niagara-on-the-Lake 210
Norfolk 106
Northumberland 106
Notaries Public 132

Ontario 107
Ottawa District 188
Oxford 107

Parliaments 48
  Duration 48
  Statistics of Statutes passed 48
Patriot Raids, 1838 271
People's Bank, Officers of 256
Perth 211
Picton 211
Political parties in power, England 29
Population, Statistics 265
  Tables 272
Port Hope 212
Post Office 227
  Deputy Postmasters General for British North America 229
  Deputy Postmasters General for Canada 229
  Officials in Britain 227
  Officials in British North America 229
  Postmasters General 227
Post Offices in Upper Canada 229
Postmasters in the Major Cities 237
Presbyterian Church 263
Prescott 108, 212
"Pretended" Bank of Upper Canada, Officers of 253
Prime Ministers 29
Prince Edward 108
Prince Edward District 190
Provincial Officials 37-47
Provincial Secretaries and Registrars 45
Provincial Secretaries and Registrar's Office 45

277

Quakers 264
Queen's Counsels 136

Railroads, Legislation 252
Rebellion of 1837, Aftermath 271
Receiver General's Office 46
Receivers General of Public Accounts 46
Ridings, legislation establishing 150
Roman Catholic Church 259
    Bishops 259
Russell 109

Sandwich (Windsor) 214
Secretaries of State for the Colonies 29
Secretaries of State for the Home
    Department 30
Secretaries of State for War and the
    Colonies 30
Sergeants at Arms 114
Simcoe 109
Simcoe District 191
Stormont 109
Solicitors 136
Solicitors General 46
St. Catharines 214
Suffolk 110
Superintendents General of Indian Affairs
    in Canada 43
Surveyors 242
    Land Surveyors 242
Surveyor General's Office 47
Surveyors General of the Province of
    Quebec 47
Surveyors General of Upper Canada,
    Deputy 47

Talbot District 193
Toronto Board of Trade, Officers of 256
Towns and Cities, Legislation 200
    Officials 202
Townships, List of 137
Township Surveys, Dates of 247

Under-Secretaries, Parliamentary
31
    Permanent 31

Victoria District 194

War and Revolution 265
Welland Canal Company, Officers of
    256
Wellington District 195
Wentworth 110
Woodstock 215
Western District 117, 196

York (Town) 112
York County 111
York/Toronto 215

www.ingramcontent.com/pod-product-compliance
Lightning Source LLC
Chambersburg PA
CBHW071425150426
43191CB00008B/1050